About the author

Dr Reidar Dale is currently Associate Professor of Development Planning and Management at the Asian Institute of Technology (AIT) in Bangkok, Thailand. For 25 years he has been working in the field of development planning and management in a variety of developing countries – as a planner, manager, researcher, evaluator and university lecturer. For much of this period (1979–87; 1990–94) he worked with the Norwegian Agency for Development Cooperation (NORAD).

He has published widely in his field; his books include *People's Development through People's Institutions* (2002), *Organisations and Development* (2000) and *Evaluation Frameworks for Development Programmes and Projects* (1998).

e-mail: reidar_dale@yahoo.com

development planning

CONCEPTS AND TOOLS
FOR PLANNERS, MANAGERS
AND FACILITATORS

REIDAR DALE

Zed Books
LONDON & NEW YORK

Academic Foundation
NEW DELHI

This edition is published in India in 2006
by
ACADEMIC FOUNDATION
4772-73 / 23 Bharat Ram Road, (23 Ansari Road),
Darya Ganj, New Delhi - 110 002 (India).
Phones : 23245001 / 02 / 03 / 04.
Fax : +91-11-23245005.
E-mail : academic@vsnl.com
www.academicfoundation.com

Originally published in 2004 by Zed Books Ltd.,
7 Cynthia Street, London N1 9JF, UK and
Room 400, 175 Fifth Avenue, New York, NY 10010, USA
www.zrdbooks.co.uk

Development Planning :
Concepts and Tools for Planners, Managers and Facilitators
by
Reidar Dale

ISBN 81-7188-491-1

Printed and bound in India

Contents

Figures, Tables and Boxes

Figures

Tables

Boxes

Acknowledgements

This book was conceived and written over a period of about three years during which I worked as a lecturer at the Asian Institute of Technology (AIT) in Bangkok, Thailand. The more immediate demands of work responsibilities such as course teaching, research and research supervision meant that most of the writing was done during early mornings, evenings and weekends. Naturally, those who experienced this most directly were my closest family – my wife Yee and my son Erlend. They spent more time without me than we liked, but they did so without complaint, and my wife encouraged me to complete the task. My first thanks go to them.

I had the opportunity to discuss the subject and presentation of my book with some highly interested and competent persons, while other professionals contributed more indirectly.

Most of all, I wish to thank Dr Hellmut Eggers, former head of the evaluation division of the Directorate General for Development of the European Commission, for his contribution. Hellmut has shown an extraordinary interest in this book and an unconditional readiness to provide feedback on many chapters, even in several drafts. Both his general encouragement and specific inputs were so valuable that it is difficult to express the gratitude I feel. I am happy to know that he shares my satisfaction in seeing the book published by a highly regarded international publisher of development literature.

My special thanks also go to W. M. Leelasena, a highly competent and respected development planner and manager in Sri Lanka. Besides giving my undertaking much-valued recognition and contributing more specific feedback on a draft manuscript of the book, Leelasena has been a source of professional inspiration for me over many years. Indeed, many of my most interesting, challenging and rewarding development planning and management experiences have been in programmes and projects on which we have collaborated, starting as far back as the late 1970s.

Many others have contributed more indirectly by way of experiences I have gained from working with them. Their ranks include development analysts, planners, managers, facilitators and evaluators with whom I have cooperated in many programmes and projects in many countries, and academic colleagues at my present university.

I also wish to extend my thanks to the many students who have participated in courses I have taught on development planning, both ordinary academic courses and special courses for development practitioners. They have helped sharpen my analysis and have contributed in various ways in enhancing my ability to present my subject as I have in this book.

My last, but definitely not least, special thanks go to staff members at Zed Books. I have been impressed by the way they combine a friendly and welcoming attitude with a high level of professionalism. My deep appreciation and sincere thanks go to editor Robert Molteno, who has responded and interacted with me in an exceptionally helpful manner. I think few book authors have had so much useful professional feedback directly from an editor. Robert has helped in a big way to improve the quality of this piece of writing.

Reidar Dale

Preface

Reidar Dale's comprehensive, lucidly written and easily accessible book on development planning is the kind of literature I have missed during a lifelong career as development analyst, planner and manager. Its most outstanding feature is the way in which it links theoretical constructs about development and development work with practical application, illuminated through numerous highly instructive examples. This makes the book extraordinarily relevant and useful both for students of development sciences and for those involved in the planning and management of development programmes and projects.

The interaction between the conceptual and the practical also enables the author to make instructive use of known planning tools, such as the logical framework and techniques of problem analysis and prioritisation, and greatly helps to clarify and make operational central concepts in current development thinking such as participatory development, institution building and process planning.

Moreover, and highly importantly in my view, the analysis builds on a clear value foundation, namely, that the purpose of any development work is to help improve the quality of life of people, with the main emphasis on those who are most deprived. This also means that any such work must be shown to relate to aspects of people's lives and evaluated accordingly.

This book deserves to become a classic in its field. One may even hope that it will initiate a paradigm shift in development science from abstract theorising to a more direct concern with the lives of disadvantaged people and real-world challenges of development planning and management.

Development Planning – Concepts and Tools for Planners, Managers and Facilitators ought to be compulsory reading in a range of academic courses and other courses on societal development and development work, and it ought to be read and actively used by all of us who are faced with the formidable task of helping to improve the living conditions of some of the huge numbers of deprived people in our world.

W. M. Leelasena
Project Director
Southern Province, Sri Lanka

Foreword

We are living in a world of accelerating complexity. Technological, economic, political, cultural and even religious influences, emanating from anywhere around the globe, may come to be felt in regions far removed, or so it seems, from their places of origin. Such influences may be judged welcome and positive, they may be accepted with indifference or they may be rejected and even bitterly opposed. Our relatively short experience with this all-pervading phenomenon has taught us already that its dynamics cannot be controlled, let alone 'planned', in a way acceptable to everyone. Indeed, there are times when clashes of norms, values and interests seem to break loose with the primeval violence of volcanic eruptions. This phenomenon is a child of the late twentieth century. It is called globalisation.

Since the events of 11 September 2001 we know that we must squarely face the challenges posed by those dark and menacing aspects of globalisation, and that we cannot just sit back and enjoy its beneficial sides. We know that we must seize its opportunities and hedge, as well as we can, against its dangers. So, no matter whether we strive for progress or fight against evil, we have to *act*.

Solidarity between developed and developing countries will play an important part in this global context, enabling both the seizure of opportunities for common progress towards a more peaceful world and the fight against poverty, discrimination and exclusion. Among the means to give operational expression to such solidarity, development cooperation has traditionally occupied a prime place. If anything, then, its importance has grown dramatically in the light of recent upheavals.

This conclusion may not sound convincing to everyone. There is, indeed, a weighty body of opinion that has arrived at the opposite view: in the light of long decades of practical experience, it claims, development cooperation has proved ineffective at best and harmful at worst, a 'mission impossible' that simply does not work. This kind of radical criticism has been levelled above all at public or state-to-state development assistance. Some representatives of these development cooperation sceptics have come up with what they have called 'alternative development', advocating above all a switch from public to voluntary or non-governmental organisations. Going further, the more radical elements within that school of thought detect the same weaknesses in both public and voluntary development assistance, and so have come to advocate what they call 'alternatives *to* development'. In their emotionally supercharged attack on development cooperation, alas, they fail to realise that pleading for an alternative to development can only mean, in fact, ditching the baby of development along with the bathwater of cooperation. What they propose is just a blank, a zero, not an alternative.

It has to be recognised, however, that even the severest critics of development cooperation did have, and still have, a point: those who are familiar with development cooperation practice know that a disconcertingly high number of 'cathedrals in the desert', also known as white elephants, are among the results of development assistance and have sapped its reputation, often to the point of ridicule: roads without traffic, plantations that have returned to the bush, hospitals without doctors, nurses, medicines, water, electricity and … patients.

I still recall the apparent simplicity of the world of development cooperation (and, indeed, development) when, back in 1963, I joined the Directorate General for Development of the European Commission. As a young, enthusiastic 'technician', I was responsible for the implementation of agricultural projects in West Africa. Those were times when we thought, without really calling into question all the implicit assumptions we made, that a road, a plantation or a hospital were in and of themselves valid contributions to development. It is true that we had become a good deal more sophisticated by the time that, 25 years later, I had been nominated head of the Directorate General's evaluation division. We no longer accepted the initial technological bias. We had discovered the economic, the sociological, the cultural and the political dimensions of our work. Yet even then, or so it seems to me today, we did not entirely realise the enormous complexity of work whose final objective seems, nevertheless, so disarmingly simple: *help poor people* in less developed countries *help themselves* to lead better, richer, more prosperous lives.

Does Reidar Dale's book address that complexity? Let's investigate. First of all, and that is encouraging, there is not even a hint in the entire book suggesting that the doom and gloom philosophy of the 'alternative to development' school might pose a serious threat to the justification of development cooperation. This does not mean that the author is unaware of the formidable difficulties besetting that endeavour, as the subsequent reflections will show. But, basically, Dale assures planners, without having to say so in so many words, that their task is not a 'mission impossible'.

The picture the author paints of the planning universe starts out with a broad-based overview of the scenario planners have to deal with as well as the nature of the actors, or stakeholders, that fill it with real life. He ranges over the varying time horizons planners have to address, including the absence of any time limit when planning and acting merge into a continuous process of mutual learning, guidance and enhancement.

He then moves on to the analysis of the more operational aspects of planning, discussing the nature of programmes and projects and modes of planning that may be applied in various circumstances. In this regard he is making a truly original contribution to operationalising the concepts of *process* and *blueprint* planning. These have, of course, been widely used terms of development jargon for a long time, but generally with only very vague meanings. Furthermore, connecting the main design variables contained in policies, programmes and projects, he has recourse to the well-known tool of the *logical framework*, improving it considerably, however, through a revised terminology better adapted to practical concerns and through squarely laying the emphasis where it belongs: on the creation of sustainable benefits for the intended beneficiaries.

Next follows a detailed discussion of the problem analysis; the definition of means and ends, and the elaboration of means–ends structures; the description, through indicators closely tailored to reflect their quality and quantity, of performance and achievements; and a discussion of the context that constitutes the environment of the interventions analysed, and the assumptions to be made as a consequence. In this way he puts the necessary flesh on the bones of the logical framework. Indeed, under the persuasion of Dale's lucid pen, static *logframe analysis* seems to merge effortlessly into dynamic *project cycle management* (PCM).

But Dale does not limit his presentation to the aspects of sound planning craftsmanship once the overall objectives to be reached have been decided by political choice. He goes one step further and shows how this political decision-making process may be rationalised, presenting the tools for reasonable rather than arbitrary prioritisation.

Finally, the author shows how the planning universe will be brought to life through an active participation by all stakeholders, where each will play the role of teacher and of student in turn; where capacity building is directed at the creation of effective organisations and institutions, no matter whether they belong to the public or to the voluntary, non-governmental sector; and where planning – entirely geared towards practical action to be undertaken as a consequence – will become a natural, not an artificially imposed, function of the community.

It is precisely this amalgamation of thinking and acting that is one of the prominent features of this book and seems to merit special attention. Dale is obviously deeply involved – and that is surely an aspect that distinguishes him from many other professionals in the field of development work – in *both: planning and implementation, reflection and realisation, theory and practice.* It is therefore fair to call his book a seminal contribution to an *action-centred* paradigm of planning for development, i.e., planning directed at the achievement of objectives concerned with human welfare and betterment.

This is surely one of the reasons why this book grows on the reader (as it did on me…), as s/he starts following Dale on his voyage from thought to action. S/he participates, as it were, in the cumulative and well-connected argumentation leading him or her to anticipate, chapter after chapter, each new aspect as it follows logically (do I dare say in an Agatha Christie fashion…?) from the preceding presentation. As Dale avoids jargon and sticks to a comprehensive, unpretentious style, the reader feels more and more involved in a situation coming close to what s/he will feel is a dialogue with the author on each argument as it unfolds.

As I said earlier, my own professional background is limited to development cooperation with less developed countries around the world. The paradigm mentioned above points, however, towards a much broader perspective: Dale's approach to policy, programme and project planning and implementation is applicable to development support in general and can therefore guide planners and managers – north and south – who are devoting the resources at their disposal to promoting the welfare of their respective countries or communities, with or without financial support from abroad.

I am underlining this vital aspect of Dale's work with growing conviction, as my own recent experience points in exactly the same direction: I am currently involved in a comprehensive effort by the Italian government to improve the performance of the country's schools, a programme called Progetto di Qualità nelle Scuole and promoted by a series of specialised public agencies, the so-called Poli di Qualità, that have been installed for this purpose in several Italian regions. At the invitation of one of the gymnasia in Naples, Region of Campania, I started off the improvement process in that school by holding a seminar, in November 2002, on project cycle management, according to Dale's 'concepts and tools for planners, managers and facilitators', having previously adapted such concepts and tools, including PCM principles, to the specific requirements of the educational and formative mission of the school. This seminar was directed at the school's teachers and students, members of the parents' association, local school administration representatives and other stakeholders. It was intended as the first step on the road towards a systematic school performance improvement, conceived as a pilot project, that is currently under way and may eventually influence the entire national school improvement programme. Such hopes appear, today, more and more justified: indeed, the pilot project's feasibility study, prepared by a group of teachers along the lines of PCM methodology, was presented recently (end of June 2003) by the pupils themselves, aged between 15 and 17, to a truly rapturous audience of stakeholders, and presently the Region of Campagnia's government is giving serious thought to the introduction of PCM for improving school performance. As can be seen, Dale's work has already been bearing fruit even before it is published, and in an area he may not have been thinking about when he was preparing this book....

That is why the readership of this book may, and should, go way beyond those involved in North/South development cooperation. I would be glad to see this work in the hands of:

- teachers and students of development-focused courses in universities;
- trainers and participants in short courses on development planning, development management and good governance (a large number of which are conducted around the world, not least in less developed countries);
- policy makers, planners and managers in development-focused governmental and non-governmental organisations, in both less developed and highly developed countries;
- international and national agencies involved in development cooperation, including UN agencies and the World Bank, national governmental development agencies and NGOs;
- and, of course, public service planners and managers everywhere.

I have read drafts of Reidar Dale's book with growing interest. I have been privileged to be of assistance in sharing with him various observations formulated in the course of my own practical experience during four decades in international development cooperation. I warmly recommend this work to all those who, like myself, believe that effective development planning and action, as well as improving evidence-based performance of public services in general, are today more urgent and more important than ever before.

Hellmut W. Eggers
Brussels
bs602896@skynet.be

Chapter 1

Development and Development Planning

Conceptualising Development

'Development' is used in numerous contexts. In all these contexts, it denotes change in some sense or a state that has, normally, been attained through some noticeable change. Beyond that, the term carries a variety of more specific meanings. It may be utilised normatively (expressing a desirable process or state) or empirically (expressing a process or state without any explicit value connotation).

In this book, 'development' is used normatively. It mainly denotes a desirable ongoing or intended process of change. More occasionally, it is also used to express a desirable state (or level of development). Moreover, it is applied in a societal context. To make this clear, we sometimes add 'societal' in front of it.

In this normative sense, societal development has meaning only in relation to human beings. It is conceived by people in relation to something that they perceive as valuable – however overt or hidden that value may be, and irrespective of the kind of rationality by which the value is conceived or expressed (a point discussed later in this chapter). In short, development is viewed as a process of societal change that generates some perceived benefits for people, or as a state of perceived human well-being attained through such a process (see also Eggers, 2000a; 2000b; Dale, 2000a).

Moreover, when analysing development, we should normally be able to clarify who benefits from societal changes and, in cases of diverging opinions about benefits, who considers changes to be beneficial and who may not do so. Likewise, development as a state should be defined and specified in relation to groups of people.

This perception has substantial implications for our conception of 'development planning', as we shall clarify soon and substantiate further throughout the book. If development is a people-focused concept, its contents in specific situations must be clarified in relation to people-related problems. Moreover, in a development perspective, the problems must be of such a kind that they may be removed or alleviated through some planned action.

In any such context, we may broadly refer to human problems as 'poverty' and 'deprivation' (Chambers, 1983; 1995; Dale, 2000a). Poverty is the more overt and specific concept of the two. It is usually taken to mean few and simple assets, low income and low consumption, and sometimes also an unreliable supply of cash and food. Deprivation frequently includes poverty (in the mentioned sense), but may encompass several other features of human misery or suffering. Thus, Chambers (1983) considers deprived households to have the following typical features, in varying combinations: poverty, physical weakness (in terms of the structure of the households and abilities of household members), isolation (physically and information-wise), vulnerability (little resistance against unexpected or occasionally occurring events) and powerlessness. According to Chambers, many such features tend to be interrelated, locking households in what he calls a deprivation trap. Dale (2000a) presents a slightly more detailed framework of deprivation, in which there is also greater emphasis on individual-related problems (such as mental suffering, poor health and illiteracy).

Moreover, a distinction is commonly made between absolute and relative poverty. Absolute poverty means that people have inadequate resources to meet what are considered as basic material requirements; relative poverty means that people have a lower material living standard, by some specified deviation, than other people, usually in the same society.

Normally, wider deprivations are very difficult or even impossible to express by any objective measure; they will, therefore, usually have to be assessed through subjective judgement. To deal with such diverse manifestations of human deprivation, Dale (2000a) suggests a general typology of dimensions of development, briefly summarised below.

Economic features

Income and income-related characteristics, expressed through indicators such as GDP *per capita*, income distribution or rate of employment (at the macro or group level); and income, consumer assets or production assets (at the level of the household or, less frequently, the individual);

Social features
Various aspects of social well-being, expressed through indicators such as average life expectancy at birth, child mortality rate or rate of school enrolment (at the macro or group level); and health, level of literacy or social security (at the level of the household or the individual);

Dependent versus independent position
Degree of bondage or, conversely, freedom in making own choices about aspects of one's life, expressed through features such as degree and terms of indebtedness, degree of competition for scarce resources or degree of inequality/equality of gender relations;

Marginalised versus integrated position
Degree and terms of participation in markets, politics and social life, and type and strength of economic and social security networks;

Degree of freedom from violence
Extent to which individuals and groups may lead their lives without deliberate mental or physical maltreatment or fear of such maltreatment, within the family and in the wider society;

Degree of mental satisfaction
Degree of mental peace, and the ability to enrich one's life through intangible stimuli;

Development-related mindset
Perception of one's position and opportunities in the society, at the level of social group, household, or individual.

Obviously, the above dimensions or indicators may be used more or less normatively or empirically. At the same time, a normative usage is more likely or obvious for some than for others. For instance, the extent to which people may 'lead their lives without deliberate … maltreatment' or the 'degree of mental peace' are hardly ever among the variables that are used in descriptive presentations of a development process or state. If for no other reason, this may be because information on these variables cannot be presented on an objective measurement scale. Such variables, then, would only be expected to be explored subjectively and qualitatively in a clearly normative analysis. On the other hand, variables such as 'GDP *per capita*' and 'level of literacy' are often used in a straightforwardly empirical way, plainly describing a state (or, if stated for different points in time, change over a period). Of course, the economic and social features that are expressed may be or may reflect important aspects of well-being, and the variables may be explicitly analysed in that context as well; that is, they may also be used normatively.

Similarly, statements may express aspects of people's life situation more or less directly or indirectly (whether used normatively or empirically in the particular context). For example, in the social field at the national level, 'child mortality' (the proportion of born children who die before a stated age) is a statement directly expressive of welfare, while a 'hospital bed ratio' (for instance, the number of beds per thousand inhabitants) is, at most, a highly indirect expression of aspects of the health status of the country's population. Commonly, in a development context, the latter is primarily used as an explanatory variable for a population's overall health situation.

Moreover, development (whether perceived as a process or as a state) is characterised by a high degree of uniqueness in different settings, great diversity and high complexity. Accordingly, processes of development are often very unpredictable and liable to change in response to diverse and complex societal contexts.

The features categorised above do not include a range of institutional aspects and infrastructure facilities that may also be viewed as causal development variables. Examples of the former may be the capacity of people to form their own organisations or the effectiveness of public administration. Examples of the latter may be road density or the physical standard of various facilities.

Let us now zoom in again on our initial statement that this book builds on a clearly normative conception of development. Thus, when planning for development, it is considered necessary to incorporate an analysis of benefits for people of what we intend to do. For instance, planning the construction of a road falls, in itself, outside the scope of development planning. It is to this and other aspects of development planning that we shall now turn.

Conceptualising Development Planning

There are a multitude of perspectives on planning, and a variety of planning typologies may and have been constructed. Since this book is oriented more towards practice than theory, I offer only a brief exploration of development planning in the context of the most relevant strands of planning thought, and then clarify my own conception of the subject within that theoretical setting.

Healey (1997) distinguishes five main kinds of planning theory: economic planning, physical development planning, policy analysis and planning, interpretative (communicative) planning and collaborative planning. The first three types are presented as planning traditions, while the other two types are said to be of more recent origin. Of course, these are not exclusive categories; theoretical perspectives on planning may cut across them – as may, of course, real-world planning and plans of various kinds.

In one sense, however, we may draw a relatively clear dividing line between two main categories of planning among the types mentioned. Economic planning, physical development planning and parts of policy analysis and planning are basically concerned with substance or subject matter (such as production systems and relations, centre structure, communication networks, laws or administrative structure). Interpretative planning, collaborative planning and other parts of policy analysis and planning, on the other hand, emphasise mechanisms or processes of planning – that is, how planning is done, in the context of an institutional framework, a set of actors and a range of societal opportunities and constraints.

Planning that focuses on subject matter has commonly been referred to as 'object-centred', 'substantive' or 'technical' (Faludi, 1973; 1983;1984; Dale, 1992). Process-centred perspectives have been expressed by terms such as 'procedural' (Faludi, 1973), 'decision-centred' (Faludi, 1984), 'process-oriented' and 'institution-centred' (Dale, 2000a). 'Strategic choice' (Friend and Jessop, 1969; Friend and Hickling, 1997) and 'strategic management' (adopted into the repertoire of public planning terms from business literature) also express perspectives on planning processes (see also Chapter 3).

We may refine the mentioned general typology somewhat by subdividing the very broad and diverse 'policy analysis and planning' category into subcategories, by whether the main emphasis is on subject matter or on planning mechanisms and processes. For instance, we could then refer to the former as 'political and administrative systems planning', while we could further divide the latter into 'policy analysis and formulation' and 'programme and project management planning'.

While the above sketch of a typology seems to cover the main strands of thinking regarding societal planning reasonably well, we shall develop an alternative and much more specific terminology in the course of engaging with the various perspectives and dimensions of development planning. For that reason, we shall not explore and specify the concepts mentioned above any further.[1]

The only direct connection we shall establish between the typology just discussed and our own framework is that the emphasis in this book will be on planning mechanisms and processes – that is, on the second of the two overarching types. In a word, we may talk of *modes* of planning, and in the following text we shall refer to our perspective as *mode-centred*. Generally, then, the focus is on how to plan rather than what to plan.

This perspective involves: exploration of the problems to be addressed and related opportunities and constraints; decision making pertaining to intended beneficiaries and achievements; linking intended achievements to work tasks, resources and organisation; time horizons of plans and timing of activities; how to follow up activities and substantiate achievements; and, not least, who are or will be involved in various tasks and processes of planning. The perspective may involve notions embedded in any of the indicated subcategories of process-centred planning theory (policy analysis and formulation, programme and project management planning, interpretative planning and collaborative planning).

Proponents of a mode-centred perspective have criticised subject-matter-oriented planning theorists for (1) disregarding questions of management and stakeholder interests, and (2) being obsessed with developing general planning theory. In the words of Faludi, in reality, 'decision making [regarding societal development] involves relating empirical knowledge to goal statements in some demonstrable way' (Faludi, 1984: xx–xxi). Moreover, 'goals are normally derivatives of complex, partly unclear and often conflicting sets of values which contribute together with other problems of perception and judgement by different actors to … uncertainty and a need for mediation'. Consequently, 'one needs awareness as to the conduct of … [planning] itself, given that there is some substantive knowledge, a great deal of uncertainty and a multitude of divergent interests' (Faludi, 1984: xxi).

Our mode-centred perspective also draws on and incorporates (sometimes in modified form) frameworks, concepts and tools that have been developed more by planning practitioners than by academics. Although few of these may be said to belong to the realm of development theory, they represent very important contributions to perspectives on and modalities of planning. Unfortunately, contributions by development organisations and individuals within them have been given little attention so far in academic circles. Modes of participatory analysis and the logical framework are two examples of such contributions.

As indicated in the presentation and discussion of the preceding section, a fundamental feature of development planning, as understood and used in this book, is that it is unambiguously *normative*. This means that the planning focuses explicitly on aspects of the quality of life of people. This may, therefore, also be referred to as a *people-focused* perspective. Normally, such a perspective also implies that the groups of people who are in focus should be identified and delimited as far as possible.

In much literature, 'people-focused' or 'people-centred' development has been viewed as one specific notion of development, and 'people-centred planning' as one form of planning for development (see, for example, Korten and Klauss, 1984; Burkey, 1993). Recently, however, the normative view has gained ground in planning more generally: 'development', 'development work' and 'development planning' have now come to be widely understood as embedding the notion of benefits for people, as perceived by these people (Eggers, 2000a; 2000b; Chambers, 1983; 1993; Taylor, 1998). Eggers (2000a; 2000b) even makes 'sustainable benefits for the target group' the 'master principle' of development work (in the context of what he calls 'project cycle management').

As argued in the preceding section, this also pulls the focus towards the needs and interests of the most deprived people. At the same time, as we have seen, poverty and other deprivations may be absolute or more or less relative. This makes 'development planning' and the broader term 'development work' relatively broad concepts, extending beyond pursuits for or by the very poorest or otherwise most deprived people in the very poorest societies – although, certainly, such people ought to receive a major share of attention.

In addition, I shall demonstrate in many parts of the book that development work, to be effective and efficient, needs to be conceptualised in *means–ends* terms. That is, one has to specify – somehow and at some stage or stages – reasonably clear and well understood objectives for one's work as well as resources, tasks to be undertaken, and how the tasks are to be accomplished in pursuit of the specified objectives. Otherwise, stakeholders may not be willing to invest any resources (ranging from money from donor agencies to unremunerated time use and other inputs from deprived people) in the endeavour.

A postmodernist conception such as the one advocated by Innes and Booher (1999: 9–10) of 'moving about in a[n] … unfamiliar environment … in games without frontiers' is, in my experience, a too-loose and impractical notion of development planning in most instances. Directionless use of resources may even be ethically dubious, the more so the greater the marginal cost (in a broad economic and social sense) of the resource inputs is, for those who provide the inputs. The cost may be particularly high for intended beneficiaries of programmes and projects in poor societies, who are expected to 'participate' in various ways.[2]

The idea of means–ends formulation has been a contentious issue in much planning literature. There has been a tendency to link it bluntly with an instrumental-technical mode of reasoning. Common terms for such a conception of rationality have been 'formal rationality', 'instrumental rationality' and 'technical rationality' (Faludi, 1973; Dixon and Sindall, 1994; Dale, 1998). The inclination to link means–ends analysis directly to a relatively narrow technical perspective has been particularly pronounced among analysts who advocate interpretative or collaborative planning (for example, Healey, 1997; Innes and Booher, 1999). In the realm of programme and project planning, the same notion is embedded in the even more common conceptions of 'functional' and 'blueprint' planning.[3]

This is a too-narrow perspective on means–ends analysis and formulation. In the next section of this chapter, I shall argue (1) that other notions of rationality also need to be recognised and incorporated in development planning, and (2) that the various notions can be (and normally have to be) linked to means–ends analysis and to the clarification of means–ends structures.

Furthermore, over recent years there has been a growing recognition that a weak institutional foundation, organisational deficiencies and poor management have reduced substantially the effectiveness and sustainability of much development work. Yet even today these crucial dimensions tend not to get due attention. By contrast, our notion of development planning is *institution-sensitive*, encompassing all these aspects.

In my experience, frequently the most critical shortcoming has been inadequate attention to variables of organisation. Such variables – including organisational form, administrative systems and mechanisms of coordination – are crucial in relation to performance. In addition, they connect directly to important wider institutional aspects, internally and in the organisations' environment (such as aspects of organisational culture, relevant government regulations or interests and attitudes among stakeholders) as well as to modes of management.

We shall, therefore, apply an *organisation-including* perspective, in which development planning is explicitly viewed as an organised activity, aspects of organisation are connected to other dimensions of development work, and organisational variables are explored to some extent.[4] Thereby, attention is also directed towards related aspects of institution and management. For analysing aspects of organisation in this broad setting of interrelated dimensions and variables, a basically open-systems perspective on organisation is required (Scott, 1987).

Within the broad sphere of mode-centred planning, the book emphasises *strategic* more than detailed operational topics and issues.

Very generally stated, strategic planning for development incorporates an analysis of people-related problems (see the previous section), clarifies objectives of the envisaged intervention that correspond to significant problems, and seeks to match the objectives with contextual (environmental) factors, resources and organisational capabilities. These overriding dimensions of development planning are frequently connected to more detailed aspects, but the latter are usually not further addressed, or not explored in depth. For instance, tasks and processes of implementation (these days often referred to as 'work breakdown structure') are addressed only in rather general terms, while specific topics such as budgeting, accounting and personnel incentives are not examined at all.[5]

Reflecting typical features of development (see the previous section), development planning recognises uniqueness in specific contexts, diversity and complexity. In development practice, this recognition may be honoured only through a basically *inductive* (in contrast to deductive) mode of exploration and further analysis.

Acknowledgement of such features has made some analysts (for example, Taylor, 1998) raise the question whether societal planning – as it is practised and may need to be practised – is a scientific pursuit, an art, or some other kind of non-scientific exercise. In my view, angling the issue this way is both unfortunate and scientifically dubious.

The perspective is unfortunate in that it contributes to maintaining a regrettable divide between 'down to earth' planning practice and 'theoretical' analysis of planning in academic institutions. As already indicated, a main purpose of this book is to help break down such barriers, which prevent constructive communication and mutual learning between persons and organisations in the two 'camps'.

Scientifically, good planning is well accommodated within social science paradigms of basically inductive analysis. Of course, such analysis does not produce theory in the conventional form of hypotheses that have been tested through some kind of experiment. Like most other social scientists, analysts of development and planning need to embrace such alternative perspectives on science, and they should develop them further into paradigms that are relevant and useful for planning practice.[6]

To summarise the approach: our notion of development planning is mode-centred and normative; it emphasises the relationship between means and ends; it is institution-sensitive and organisation-inclusive; and it is primarily strategic. Together, these features require context-specific analysis in a basically inductive mode.

Conceptions of Rationality

All development planning should be rational, by normal understanding and usage of this word. However, as already suggested, one ought to distinguish between various notions of rationality. In planning and similar scientific pursuits, this largely means that one should consider other conceptions of this term than the *instrumental–technical* one. In its 'pure' form, instrumental rationality in planning is normally understood as exclusive attention to and specification of means and ways of attaining predetermined goals.

With reference to Jurgen Habermas's well-known and widely quoted typology of modes of reasoning (Habermas 1975; 1984),[7] other main forms of rationality may be termed 'value rationality' ('substantive rationality') and 'lifeworld rationality' ('communicative rationality') respectively (see, for example, Dixon and Sindall, 1994; Servaes, 1996; Healey, 1997).

In a development planning perspective, *value* rationality refers to the values that are embedded in possible or intended achievements of a considered or planned development scheme, as perceived by stakeholders of that scheme. Thus, it relates to the top level of a means–ends structure of possible or planned development work. It is incorporated in what we in this book refer to as 'normative' planning (see the previous section and later chapters).

Lifeworld rationality is the kind of reason that tends to be applied in day-to-day communication between people. It is contained in 'the worlds of taken for granted meanings and understandings, of everyday living and interaction, of emotions, traditions, myth, art, sexuality, religion, culture' (Dixon and Sindall, 1994: 303). In such reasoning, 'we frequently do not separate 'facts' from 'values' … [and] the whole process of reasoning and the giving of reasons, what we think is important and how we think we should express this and validate our reasoning claims [are] grounded in our cultural conceptions of ourselves and our worlds' (Healey, 1997: 51).

In development programmes and projects, the particular combination of rationalities 'may materialise through a combination of factors, such as: general political and administrative culture of the society; established policy of a donor agency; ideas of individuals involved in planning; and the constellation of actors in idea generation, plan formulation and decision-making' (Dale, 1998: 36).

Normally, formulation of means–ends structures (see the previous section) is easiest when the components may be specified through basically instrumental-technical reasoning. Equally normally, this is the case (1) when a clear and unambiguous goal has been set in advance, or such a goal is simply assumed or at least not substantially explored by the planners; and (2) when the planning is done by professionals in the field. This is the situation in much planning. For instance, the district unit of a national roads department will normally not explore needs of people and the usefulness for people of road building versus other development interventions. The only goal-related question they may normally address in planning is prioritisation between roads. They will mostly concentrate on how to build (or maintain) the respective roads and the resource inputs that are needed for construction (or maintenance).

However, by its very exclusion of goal analysis, this kind of planning, viewed as an entity in itself, falls outside our definition of 'development planning'.[8] In this book we shall refer to it as 'functional' planning, constituting the logical opposite of 'normative' planning (see also Dale, 2000a; 2002b).

In other words, value rationality is a core feature of development planning.

The more intricate question relating to means–ends analysis is the possibility of clarifying (and usually formulating) means–ends structures when much lifeworld rationality is involved. Commonly, this kind of rationality tends to coexist with value rationality: beyond the most basic physical needs, wants and priorities are subjectively experienced and culturally influenced, and this also means that reasoning about them will be lifeworld-based. It follows closely that the more interested parties (stakeholders) there are, the more their perceived needs and interests tend to differ. And the more the stakeholders are involved in assessing needs and interests, the more difficult it may be to agree on the relative importance of such needs and interests. The same argument goes for agreeing on objectives of corresponding development schemes, as well as ways and means of attaining whatever objectives may have been specified.

Given the stated need for clarification of means–ends relations, do we then have to conclude that genuinely people-centred or collaborative planning is impossible? We do not. If one has any purposeful, organised thrust in mind, even a numerous and diverse body of stakeholders (including prospective beneficiaries) must normally be assumed to share at least basic ideas about what should be achieved and what needs to be done to that end. Although they may be general, such ideas will usually represent important guidelines for one's work. Commonly, they may also constitute a sufficient rationale for initial allocation of at least some resources and for other initial commitments.

For example, in a broad-based institution-building programme in local communities, intended outputs could include 'people's motivation for collaborative efforts enhanced', 'people's organisations formed' and 'people's organisations functioning well' (for instance, according to the members' own judgement). A couple of intended benefits of these (and any other) outputs could be, for instance, 'increased social cohesion' and 'stronger position of women'. If the programme includes promotion of financial services by people's organisations to their members (a common element in many such programmes), other intended immediate benefits could be 'reduced indebtedness to moneylenders' and 'higher income from own production'.[9]

Much of the above may be referred to by the frequently used word 'empowerment'. Thus, even such a broad, rather abstract and usually vaguely perceived concept may be broken down into more clearly identifiable and more specific sub-entities, linked together in means–ends terms. Normally, such clarification and specification would also need to be done if empowering development thrusts are to be perceived as meaningful by those who are supposed to be 'empowered' as well as by others who may be involved in the process of 'empowerment' (see also Friedmann, 1992).

At the same time, however, ways of doing things and corresponding means–ends relations may be, and may have to be, clarified and specified gradually, for various parts of the development thrust. This may be accomplished through the mechanism of process (generative) planning. One may need to start certain activities before many aspects of the programme are fully clarified, and then draw on experiences from completed or ongoing work as well as new ideas and initiatives in the planning of subsequent activities.[10] In the present context, the essential point is that clarification and agreement must be obtained early enough to gain the necessary commitments and to ensure reasonably effective and efficient use of resources at the appropriate time.

I shall also argue, however, that most participatory planning, like other planning, should involve efforts to strengthen the capability of stakeholders for logical reasoning (induction and deduction), thereby promoting consistent argumentation about values as well as instrumental rationality whenever that is important. Instrumental logic has merit. It has been at the heart of the technological revolution in our world and is also an essential element of modern administrative and management systems. While being too narrow a conception in development planning, it should remain a duly recognised feature of such planning, normally most applicable the further down we move within the means–ends structures of development schemes.

We could have taken this discussion further into theoretical realms, linking what we have said to so-called *modernist* versus *postmodernist* thinking (see, for example, Taylor, 1998; Healey, 1997; and Moore Milroy, 1991). However, we shall leave it there. Let me just say that the focus and scope of exploration in this book cut across commonly made distinctions between the two. Modernist conceptions of logical reasoning are endorsed and considered as essential parts of planning science and practice, while basic postmodernist ideas of plurality, complexity and fluidity are considered essential in bringing out typical features of development planning situations, with far-reaching implications for planning practice. Often, this even includes a negation – emphasised in postmodernist writings – of any clear separation between subjectivity and objectivity. In planning, this clearly applies at strategic levels but may also do so at more operational levels, to larger or lesser extents. But extreme notions of subjectivity – which go so far as to question the ability to obtain intellectual consensus and, therewith, any cumulative scientific discourse – are rejected.

Notes

1 For a general overview and discussion of these concepts, the reader may consult, among others, Healey, 1997; Taylor, 1998; Servaes *et al.*, 1996 – in addition to a large number of publications on public policy and policy planning (e.g., Wuyts *et al.*, 1992), development administration (e.g., Sapru, 1994) and project planning, administration and management (e.g., Cusworth and Franks, 1993).

2 The 'games' explored by Innes and Booher are referred to as 'role playing' and 'bricolage'. The examples that are given are efforts at consensus building on big and broad societal development issues, and the actors are 'typically ... young people conscious of growing up in the postmodern context' (1999: 9). For some further reflections, see Chapter 9.

3 'Functional' and 'blueprint' planning are two among several conceptions of planning that will be addressed in Chapter 3, and then further discussed in subsequent chapters.

4 For instance, 'organisation' is a main component of a framework of strategic planning that we shall develop in Chapter 2; variables of organisation in the context of development work are addressed in Chapter 4; the interface between development organisations and their environment is explored in Chapter 8; and organisation building (in a local community context) is analysed in Chapter 10. Since this book is not primarily about organisation and management, however, variables of organisation and management are not analysed in great depth. For some further exploration and reference to additional literature, see Dale, 2000a.

5 Dimensions of strategic planning are specified and generally discussed in Chapter 2, while related notions of planning (including more operational planning) are addressed in Chapter 3. Various components of the framework that is developed in Chapter 2, in particular, are then analysed further in subsequent chapters.

6 It would fall outside the scope of this book to pursue this discussion. Reference is made to books on research theory and methodology. There the reader may find alternative conceptions of theory to the conventional one, under names such as 'grounded theory', 'pattern theory' and 'conceptual theory'.

7 Habermas refers to these modes as instrumental-technical, moral and emotive-aesthetic reasoning respectively.
8 It may, of course, be a component of development programmes or projects that also encompass analysis and formulation of goals (understood as intended improvements in some aspect of some people's quality of life).
9 Such a programme will be explored later, in chapters 6, 7 and 8. More specific terms for expressing achievements of work that is done will be formulated in chapters 4 and 6, in particular.
10 The notion of 'process planning' and its operational implications will be further clarified and discussed in Chapter 3 and in many contexts later in the book.

Chapter 2

Strategic Planning for Development

Strategy, Strategy Formulation and Strategic Planning

'Development planning' is broadly defined as the planning of any organised endeavour that aims at promoting development, as we saw in Chapter 1. It encompasses a wide range of thrusts in economic, social and institutional fields at various societal levels, from the local to the international, and usually emphasises relations between societal spheres and units. It addresses values, objectives, resources, organisational ability and a range of variables in the environment of the development organisation and its pursuit.

The main concerns of development planning may be expressed by the concept of 'strategy' and derivatives of that concept. The term 'strategy' has wide application and is used with numerous shades of meaning. Since we are concerned with organised activities, we can right away delimit our conception of the term to its application in an organisational context. With Mintzberg (1983) I shall broadly define the strategy of an organisation as *the mediating force between the organisation and its environment*: that is, it expresses how the organisation relates to its environment in achieving its aims.

Development organisations are supposed explicitly to address some *problem* in the society relating to some *people*. Consequently, the work of these organisations must be judged primarily by its influence on aspects of the *quality of life* of the intended beneficiaries. In the case of mutual benefit organisations, these people will be the organisations' members. In the case of public benefit organisations, they will be outsiders. By direct implication, in the development sphere, 'strategy' must also contain this notion of focus on and benefits for people. We may clarify this by adding 'development' to it, and speaking of *development strategy*.

We shall, then, address only the work of organisations with a direct development mission, for whom improvement in the quality of life of people constitutes the very purpose of existence. Of course, this does not mean that only such organisations may promote development. It is primarily economic production enterprises (from the small farm to the big company) that generate economic value, on which all human societies depend. However, because profit tends to be their prime motive, we do not consider their activities as 'development work', and thus they fall outside the scope of this book.[1]

In addressing societal problems those who are involved in planning need to explore which problem or problems should be emphasised, what may be done about that problem or those problems, and how any intended action may be organised and executed. These questions involve an interrelated analysis of a range of issues and variables outside and inside the organisation (or organisations) that may be responsible for the intended action, with a view to obtaining a good match between components of the thrust.

A strategy that a development organisation evolves for work that it intends to do may apply to its entire intended pursuit or to parts of it – that is, to its whole portfolio of activities, to one programme or project, or to one category of work. Obviously, the focus and scope will influence how comprehensive and detailed the strategy analysis should be, and the kinds and the number of units or persons (within and possibly outside the organisation) that should be involved in it.

We may refer to such an interconnected analysis of the main components of intended development work as *strategy formulation* for development. In slightly more specific terms, this involves identifying problems for people, making choices about the problem or problems to be addressed, and deciding on objectives and general courses of action – considering opportunities and constraints in the environment of the organisation or organisations involved, available resources and organisational abilities. These terms will be elaborated further in the next section of this chapter and again later in the book.

As thus perceived, strategy is, of course, a *planning-related* concept: that is, the aspects mentioned above will be addressed in the planning of work that development organisations intend to undertake.[2] Consequently, any strategy analysis that contributes to a plan for work to be done may be referred to as *strategic planning* or, in the development realm, *strategic development planning*.

In the sphere of development, there are also other terms that are used more or less synonymously with 'strategic (development) planning'. The most common ones may be 'framework planning' and 'overall planning', both of which tell us that the issues addressed in such planning are of a basic and relatively general nature.[3]

The terms 'strategy formulation' and 'strategic planning' may be used largely interchangeably. However, I suggest that one considers the former as most appropriate for clarifying the general purpose, scope and mode of work of development organisations, and the latter as the best term for specific pursuits, that is, development programmes and projects.

Main Analytical Categories and Variables

This book deals primarily with the planning of activities that promote development directly: that is, development programmes and projects. We shall, therefore, be using the term 'strategic planning' rather than 'strategy formulation' (leaving to the latter the somewhat broader interpretation just suggested).

To resume an argument advanced in the preceding section, the overall purpose of strategic planning – in the development sphere and more broadly – may be perceived as obtaining the best possible fit (congruence) between an intended action, the resources and abilities for undertaking it, and its societal context. This triangle of main concerns is illustrated in Figure 2.1.

The *intention* should be broadly clarified through a general statement of purpose – also called 'mission' – and must be specified through the objectives (goals) of the work that one intends to do. The objectives, we recall, should be significant in relation to a people-connected problem. In strategic planning the overriding challenge is to formulate significant objectives that may be pursued effectively (1) through a matching set of *capabilities* (resources and organisational abilities) and (2) in a *context* that makes it possible to do the intended work – that is, within an enabling environment.

In Figure 2.2, the categories and variables of strategic development planning are specified somewhat further. Generally stated, the 'objectives' category in Figure 2.2 corresponds to 'intention' in Figure 2.1; the 'environment' category corresponds to 'context' (while in addition showing the problem(s) to be addressed); and the 'resources' and 'organisation' categories correspond to 'capabilities'.

Figure 2.2 constitutes a general framework for much of the analysis in subsequent chapters. It contains the main variables that we need to

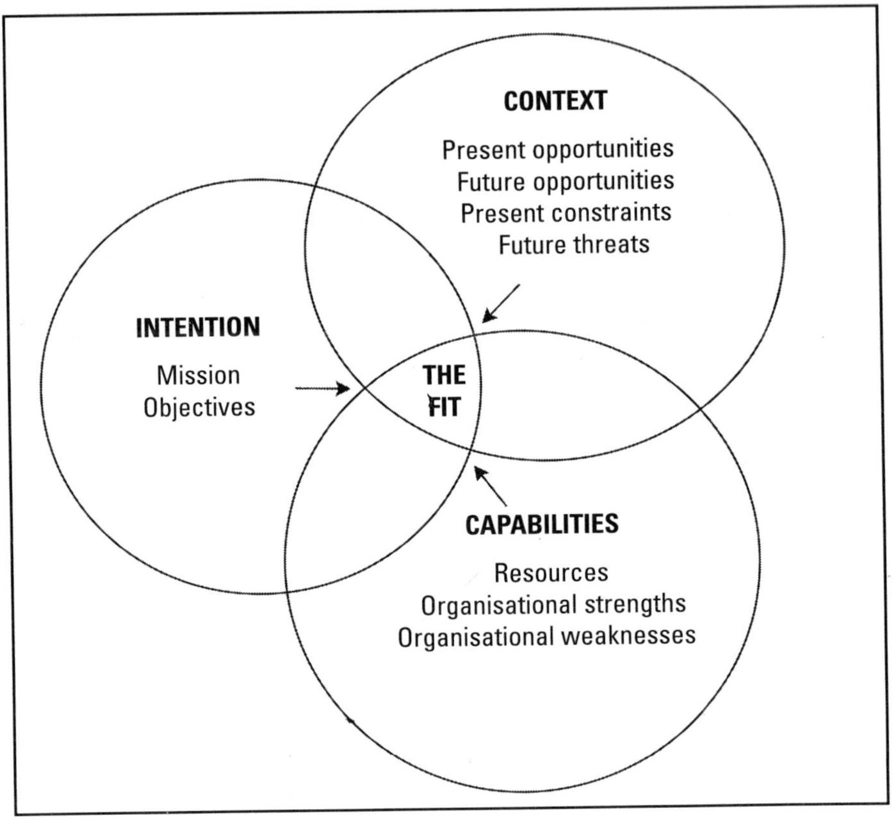

Figure 2.1 Finding the Fit in Strategic Planning

explore in order to clarify the purpose of a development scheme and specify the components of a corresponding thrust.

In compliance with perspectives that we have presented, the model assumes that development work, including planning, is done by an organisation or, in some instances, collaborating organisations. By 'organisation' we mean any body that is purposively established and designed to undertake some kind of work (in our context, some kind of development work), and whose work is regulated by a set of rules (which may be more or less formalised and more or less elaborate). In the development sphere, this body may be anything from a small community-based group to a government ministry, a national or international non-governmental organisation (NGO), or a bilateral or multilateral donor agency. In the presentation to follow, we shall refer to one organisation. More complex organisational arrangements will be addressed shortly.

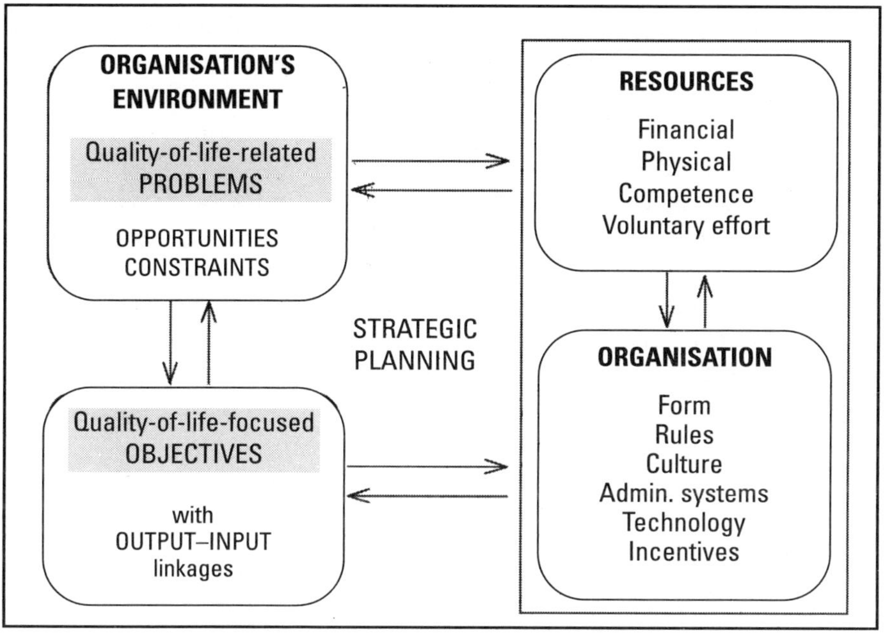

Figure 2.2 Analytical Variables and Relations in Strategic Development Planning

As already generally mentioned, the starting point for any development work is identification and analysis of one or more *problems* that one intends to address (emphasised in the figure). These problems must relate to some group or groups of people, existing in their life environment and experienced by them.

In close interrelation with the problem analysis, the planning organisation specifies corresponding *objectives* for the work that is intended to be done (also emphasised in the figure). Moreover, it identifies the types and the magnitude of *outputs* (facilities directly created by the work to be done) considered necessary for attaining these objectives.

Further, the organisation clarifies the need for *resources* (money, physical capital, competence and, sometimes, voluntary contributions), which will constitute *inputs* for the activities that are to be carried out. Resources may be provided by the organisation that will be responsible for undertaking the work (the implementing organisation), or they may be acquired from some other source or sources.

The planning organisation then tries to fit the objectives and the resources with *organisational abilities* that are needed for undertaking the planned work. If the planning organisation is to implement the work itself, these will be its own abilities; if some other organisation is to do it, they will be the abilities of that body. These abilities may be conceptualised as some synthesis of the policies and principles of work (rules) that the implementing organisation intends to follow, the technology that it has or may acquire or develop, its form and systems of administration, its culture, and the incentives it provides for people in the organisation.[4]

Moreover, in formulating a strategy, the planning organisation must analyse *opportunities* and *constraints* in the environment of the implementing organisation, in relation to the work that is to be done. Opportunities and constraints may relate to the present or to the future. For instance, a possibility to acquire some resources may be an opportunity, inappropriate laws may be a present constraint, and the possibility of a severe drought during a critical period of the growth of some plants may become a future constraint. In development planning, possible future constraints are frequently referred to as *threats*.

Such environmental factors, of course, will influence the feasibility of working on problems and how one should deal with them. Some constraints may be addressed by the responsible organisation, to various degrees, while others may not. To the extent possible, the organisation should seek to eliminate or reduce current constraints, and it should assess carefully the probability of being confronted by additional future constraints – threats – and, if feasible, devise means to counteract them. Conversely, it should seek to augment and exploit, as far as possible, opportunities for attaining the objectives, both present and possible future ones.[5]

Identifying and Analysing Stakeholders

Over the past few years, *stakeholder analysis* has been emphasised within strategic planning. For a development programme or project, we can define it generally as identifying the beneficiaries and other bodies with an interest in the programme or project, assessing their present and/or future stakes in the scheme, and clarifying any involvement by them in it (see also Grimble and Chan, 1995).[6]

A stakeholder analysis may well be considered as the most central element in the strategic planning of development programmes and projects. Stakeholders are of prime concern in their own right, and an analysis of them links directly with and integrates other components of the planning process.

Although the term 'stakeholder' is not found in our ground model of strategic development planning (Figure 2.2), stakeholders may constitute, form part of, or be connected to variables in each of the boxes in the figure.

We have emphasised that development work focuses on aspects of the quality of life of some people. Consequently, any analysis of problems and any formulation of corresponding objectives make sense only in relation to these people (which often also requires that they be involved in or even undertake the analysis). Moreover, work tasks in development schemes are the responsibility of one or more organisations and people within or connected to them; resources are provided by organisations or individuals with an interest in the endeavour; and the success of the scheme may depend on many other people.

Let us reflect a little further on each of these categories and some connected issues. Normally, in an organisational perspective, a basic distinction may be made between internal and external stakeholders, namely (1) individuals and units within the responsible organisation and (2) benefiting, involved or otherwise relevant individuals and units outside the organisation (in the organisation's environment).

The most obvious stakeholders of any development programme or project are the intended beneficiaries of the work that is done. We have seen that problems and objectives must relate to them. Normally, therefore, these people may be referred to as the primary stakeholders. As also briefly mentioned, the beneficiaries may be people outside or within the organisation that undertakes the work; that is, they may be external or internal stakeholders. This is reflected in a common distinction in literature on development organisations between 'public benefit' organisations (serving people outside themselves) and 'mutual benefit' organisations (serving their own members).[7]

Opportunities and constraints may also be stakeholders, or may be directly connected to stakeholders, as a few examples will illustrate. A school principal with high recognition, appropriate attitude, relevant knowledge and a genuine interest may be perceived as an opportunity that ought to be exploited in a community development programme. Conservative attitudes among people in a government department may be constraints on innovative ventures in fields under that department's purview. Powerful business people with an interest in cutting trees for timber may pose a threat to the long-term success of a watershed protection project.

Normally, the planning and implementing organisations will themselves consist of units and individuals (stakeholders) with more or less diverse opinions and interests, and with unequal power to promote their views and pursue their interests. Differences in these respects may depend on various features of organisation, prime among which may be organisational form, rules and culture (see the 'organisation' box in Figure 2.2 and Chapter 4).

In this connection, I want to mention in passing a matter of related importance that will be explored further later in the book. In development schemes with participation by intended beneficiaries or others outside a formally responsible organisation, the distinction between 'internal' and 'external' may become blurred. For instance, while the above-mentioned school principal may not be employed by the formally responsible organisation, he or she may appropriately be perceived as an actor internal to the programme.

Resources may be allocated by the organisation(s) responsible for planning and/or implementation, or they may be provided by some outside body or bodies that will then also be stakeholders in the programme or project.

Conceptualising Greater Organisational Complexity

Figure 2.2 displays organisation as a general analytical category in strategic planning. In the connected text we mostly assumed that only one organisation would be involved in programme or project implementation. We shall now elaborate our perspective, briefly addressing more complex organisational arrangements.

In development work, two such arrangements are particularly common: (1) two or more organisations collaborate in a programme or project; (2) a separate programme or project organisation is formed through contributions (which may be of various kinds) from two or more organisations, by which the former will be operationally linked to the latter.

The first of these alternatives – directly collaborating organisations – is illustrated in Figure 2.3. The figure shows two involved organisations. Cases of more than two partner organisations might have been illustrated by adding other organisations, without substantial changes to other parts of the figure.

Direct collaboration in the same development thrust implies that the organisations must share and contribute towards the same general objective and normally also a set of more specific objectives (while, in addition, they may have separate specific objectives). In pursuing their common objectives, the organisations will normally provide separate inputs, which they convert into separate while complementary outputs. The basic justification for contributions by more than one organisation is, usually, the comparative advantages held by each of the collaborating organisations in terms of the inputs they may provide and and/or specific

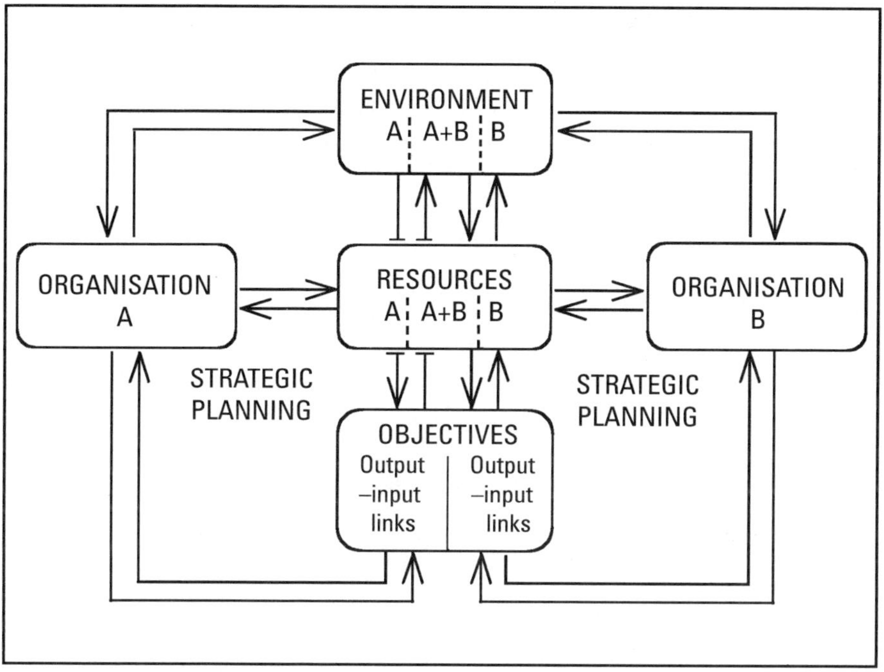

Figure 2.3 Strategic Planning for a Scheme Implemented by Collaborating Organisations

organisational abilities. Commonly, such comparative advantages are related to different kinds or levels of authority or to formal or informal recognition. These notions of means–ends relations are illustrated in the figure by the separate input–output links of the two organisations towards common objectives.

Collaborating organisations may be exposed to the same or similar environmental conditions (present and future opportunities, constraints and threats). In addition, they may be exposed and relate to separate environmental niches, posing their own challenges. This is illustrated in the figure by the indicative division of the 'environment' box into three parts: one that is common and two that are separate for the respective organisations.

As we have seen, resources may be provided by the organisations responsible for implementation or they may be acquired from outside. Commonly, there is a combination of resource providers and different arrangements for resource acquisition, for the organisations individually or together. Consequently, the figure illustrates a similar perspective on resources as on environmental factors: the 'resources' box is indicatively divided into the same three parts.

The degree of similarity or difference between collaborating organisations, their degree of exposure to similar or different environments, arrangements for sources provision, and even the extent to which the organisations share immediate objectives may vary vastly between development schemes. The following two examples illustrate this.

The first example is a water supply project involving construction of tube wells, undertaken as a collaborative effort between two departments within the same government ministry. One department is in charge of drilling, the other is responsible for installing tubes and taps. The two organisations share the immediate objectives (better access to water by the same group of people); they probably share the financial resources (a financial allocation for the project by their ministry); they prepare directly matching work plans; they complement each other directly in implementation; and they are subjected to basically the same environmental conditions in the areas where they work. In brief, common features prevail.

The second example is a diverse area development programme with only relatively general overall strategic planning, involving many government agencies and possibly other organisations in many fields. These fields may be as diverse as irrigation, crop marketing services, health care, road construction and natural resource conservation. The organisations must be assumed to share an overall objective and sometimes more specific (immediate) objectives, but they will also have separate more specific objectives for the kinds of work they do. They may get resources from a common pool, but may also have to supplement these with resources that they acquire on their own. Moreover, the organisations may work out entirely separate operational plans; they may have weak or no functional linkages in implementation; and they may be faced with largely different opportunities and constraints. In short, the individual organisations tend to share only framework plans of a very general nature, and their work will normally be subjected to only relatively weak mechanisms of coordination.[8] By and large, they tend to work largely independently in quite different kinds of projects.

The second common type of more complex organisational arrangements – a separate programme or project organisation formed through common commitment by and contributions from two or more independent organisations – is illustrated in Figure 2.4. In this case, three organisations are shown to contribute.

The programme or project organisation may be closely tied to and governed by the parent organisations, and may therewith also be entirely

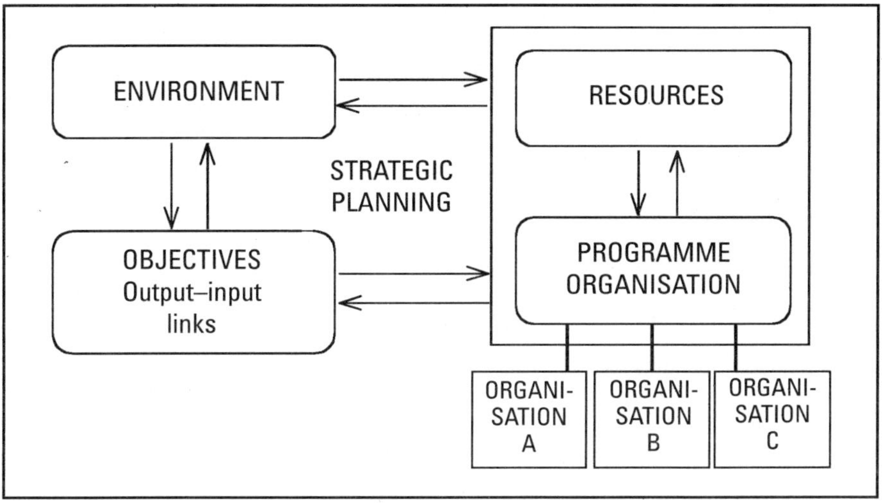

Figure 2.4 Strategic Planning with a Joint Overlay Organisation

dependent on the resources and abilities of the latter. One example of this might be a body established by a number of farmers' organisations in an area for the purpose of planning, on their behalf, the use of resources that are allocated to the farmers' organisations for some specific purpose (for instance, rehabilitation of local irrigation facilities). Another example might be a disaster relief organisation that is formed with personnel and other resource inputs from several non-governmental organisations, in order to deal more quickly and effectively with an emergency situation than the support organisations could have done individually.

Alternatively, the programme or project organisation might be a more independent body, to which other organisations contribute larger or lesser amounts of expertise and possibly other resources. The contributions might be regulated through a long-term plan of collaboration or they might be provided on an on–off basis, depending on specific needs and/or abilities.

Under this second alternative, an example of a relatively long-term and firmly committed arrangement might be an organisation established by the government for conducting a countrywide adult education programme, with inputs from several existing government departments. The established organisation would then probably be mandated by the government to formulate its own strategy and pursue its work largely independently of the contributing departments. The latter might nevertheless be obliged to contribute regularly to the programme or project organisation in specified ways.

An example of a more *ad hoc* approach might be arrangements within a broad-focus area development programme with flexible planning, in which overall planning and implementation is the responsibility of a separately established programme organisation.[9] Commonly, in such cases, the programme organisation may, whenever this is considered necessary or desirable, draw on various contributions by several other organisations – such as various government departments, other government agencies, non-governmental organisations and people's organisations.

Variables and Linkages in Comprehensive Strategic Planning

Table 2.1 provides an outline of the main analytical categories and variables that may have to be addressed in strategic planning and the main linkages between them. The table elaborates and supplements information given in Figure 2.2. Still, it should be seen as a broad, generalised and flexible framework of variables and linkages, serving the function of a checklist.

In reality, the emphasis that will be placed on different dimensions and issues and the depth and complexity of the analysis will vary greatly. Thorough analysis of all the listed variables may be needed in rare instances only. Any exercise will depend on or be influenced by numerous factors. The most important ones may be: the type, size and complexity of the development scheme; the kind of planning and implementing organisations and their degrees of freedom of action; the capability of the planners and implementers; and numerous aspects of the external environment (including stakeholders). Such aspects of scope and applicability will be further discussed in the next section.

The main analytical categories in the table correspond directly, or almost so, with those in Figure 2.2. The main difference is that stakeholders are explicitly incorporated in Table 2.1 but not in the figure (an absence accounted for on pp. 20–1 above).

Some important additional issues to those presented in the table should be mentioned. First, before starting any planning exercise, one needs to know *who are to be involved* in it, at least initially. This may mean to clarify:

- who is to be in overall charge of the planning (the organisation and the unit or person within this);
- how broad the participation is to be within the overall responsible organisation;
- which other organisations, if any, are to be involved;
- which other groups and individuals, if any, are to be involved.

Table 2.1 Comprehensive Strategic Planning

1 Problem analysis

- Identify the general problem that is intended to be addressed or general problems that may be addressed;
- If more than one general problem is considered, prioritise between them and decide on the one that will be in focus in the present planning exercise;
- Try to agree on and specify a component of the general problem that most clearly expresses the difficulty for the people who are affected;
- Identify cause–effect links to/from this subproblem (core problem), resulting in a structure of subproblems in cause–effect terms (sometimes called a problem tree).

2 Analysis of external stakeholders

- Identify the stakeholders by their stakes – they may include:
    - those who are affected by the problem
    - those who cause the problem
    - those who may be affected by measures against the problem
    - those who may contribute in dealing with the problem
    - those who may work against envisaged measures
    - any other organisation, programme or project that does or may do the same or similar work as envisaged, partly or fully;
- Categorise the stakeholders by main relevant criteria (individuals, interest groups, private organisations, government agencies, etcetera);
- Get an overview of the needs and interests of each category of stakeholders;
- Discuss and decide on whose needs, interests and views should be given priority;
- Analyse further the needs and interests of the prioritised individuals, groups and/or organisations and, if needed, clarify further who should be beneficiaries of the planned scheme;
- Analyse the strengths and weaknesses of potential external contributors – individuals, groups and/or organisations that may be involved in or otherwise contribute to the envisaged work;

- Analyse the constraints or threats posed by any hostile individuals, groups and organisations.

▶ *Feedback to the problem analysis*

3 *Formulation of objectives with linkages*

- Reformulate components of the cause–effect structure into positive statements, i.e., into intended benefits (objectives) for the intended beneficiaries and underlying perceived requirements for attaining these benefits (means–ends structure);
- Discuss and decide on any deletion, addition or revision of objectives and underlying requirements, in the light of
  - the legitimacy and importance of any objections by any stakeholders to intended measures;
  - whether or to what extent any objectives may be attained through development work that is being or may be undertaken by others.

▶ *Feedback to the stakeholder analysis (particularly, decision on beneficiaries)*

4 *Assessment of resources*

- Estimate generally the requirement for money, expertise (personnel with the needed competence), equipment, and any other resources for attaining the intended objectives;
- Clarify the feasibility of acquiring these resources.

▶ *Feedback to the stakeholder (actor/beneficiary) analysis*

▶ *Feedback to objectives /means–ends formulation*

5 *Analysis of external influencing factors*

- Explore external factors (in addition to supportive stakeholders) that may facilitate realisation of the programme or project (opportunities);
- Explore external factors (in addition to hindering stakeholders) that may constrain or prevent the realisation of the programme or project (present constraints);

- Explore external factors (in addition to hindering stakeholders) that may pose problems for the continuation of the programme or project, for maintenance of facilities created, or for the upkeep or augmentation of benefits generated (threats);
- Examine and determine whether, to what extent and how the programme or project organisation or organisations may exploit identified opportunities and counteract identified constraints and threats.

▸ *Feedback to the problem analysis*

▸ *Feedback to the stakeholder (beneficiary/actor) analysis*

▸ *Feedback to objectives /means–ends formulation*

▸ *Feedback to the resources assessment*

6 Assessment of organisational ability

- Undertake an internal stakeholder analysis: i.e., examine the interests, views and capabilities of units and individuals in the responsible organisation(s);
- Clarify, in general terms, necessary or desirable structures, rules, work systems and incentives of the responsible organisation(s) for undertaking the intended work;
- Explore necessary or desirable measures (such as formal training, workshops, and on-the-job training) for creating the necessary or desirable organisational capabilities and, if needed, for harmonising the interests and views of units and individuals in the organisation(s);
- Determine the eventual organisational ability for implementing intended measures, and undertake any corresponding prioritisation.

▸ *Feedback to the external stakeholder analysis*

▸ *Feedback to objectives /means–ends formulation*

▸ *Feedback to the resources assessment*

If one finds, in the course of the planning, that others should be involved than those included from the beginning, one may consider bringing them in subsequently.

Moreover, it may be desirable or even necessary to undertake an *initial scanning* of the whole planning field: that is, to conduct a general, relatively quick assessment of all the main aspects that one thinks need to be addressed in the course of planning. The purpose of this is to be confident that one continues to plan with a reasonable degree of certainty. For instance, it may be futile or unproductive to embark on comprehensive problem, stakeholder and objectives analysis if there turns out to be no possibility of financing any measures, or if money may be found only for activities for which little strategic planning is needed.

In compliance with the people-centred nature of development planning, the *core problem* – mentioned in point 1. in the table – should express a quality-of-life deficiency of identified people, normally one or more population groups that are from the inception of the strategy analysis intended to be the beneficiaries of the planned programme or project. Commonly, the core problem may be referred to as the 'development problem', being on a level with the 'development objective' of a corresponding development thrust.[10] Sometimes, however, it may be easier to start disentangling the problem structure[11] from a more specific problem. In such instances, 'core problem' may not be the most suitable term for this immediately identifiable phenomenon.

One should, in any case, have a practical approach to this. The main concern should be to select a starting point that will be as helpful as possible for a constructive analysis, by which in the end one should arrive at a cause–effect structure that makes sense for everybody.

Timing, Time Horizon and Scope of Action

There are essential aspects of time, scope of action, and relations between the two that need to be addressed in a discussion of strategic planning.

Much of this issue-complex connects to 'sequence' and 'sequencing'. The general question is how various activities are linked to one another over time. In the present context, there are two main subquestions or issues: (1) the time-wise relation between, on the one hand, strategic planning and, on the other hand, other general work categories of a development thrust, and (2) the timing of the analysis of main categories and variables (outlined in Table 2.1) within the strategic planning exercise itself.

Let us first examine issue 1.

A common perspective on strategic planning is that it precedes any other activities of a development programme or project, in the absolute sense that it has to be completed before any other activities may be started. This reflects a notion of linearity in development work, in the following general sequence: strategic planning → operational planning → implementation and monitoring → operation and maintenance (depending much on what has been created) → evaluation (often optional).[12] Others argue that the various activities of a development thrust tend to be too intertwined to be conceptualised in such clear-cut sequential terms and undertaken accordingly.

This contradiction may reflect different ideologies about the nature of societal changes and about planning for such changes. Using planning concepts that were operationalised by Faludi (1973), the perspective of linearity reflects a 'rational-comprehensive' perception of planning, while the opposite perspective corresponds to the idea of 'disjointed incrementalist' planning.[13] Crucial here is the extent to which and how the planner is considered to be able to control or modify organisation-external factors that influence (or may influence) the development work.

Obviously, different perspectives may also be closely related to the kind of development work that one plans for. Normally, work of a technical nature may be more directly controlled and its direct outcome much more reliably predicted than may be the case for more complex people-centred work – for instance, a programme of institution building involving deprived people.[14] This will clearly influence the mode of planning that may be feasible or suitable, including perspectives in and the timing of strategic planning.

Writers on 'disjointed incrementalism' and on 'collaborative planning' in complex environments have questioned the very notion of strategic planning, associating the term with the 'rational-comprehensive' perspective, that is, with a belief in the ability to establish a comprehensive and reliable image of all that one intends to do, in advance of further detailed planning and implementation.

This negation of strategic planning is unfortunate. In order to create a fuller understanding of this concept, the ubiquitous need for such planning, and how it may be related to other work categories, we shall pursue our argument a step further. We shall do so by sketching two different scenarios.

In the first scenario, upon request from the Ministry of Agriculture of a country, a donor agency has expressed willingness in principle to promote the income of farming households in a district, through an envisaged three-year project for furthering cultivation of a potentially wide range of marketable crops. Support will depend on better justification, clarification and specification, including a work programme and budget over the three years.

Presumably, nobody would argue against the need for strategic planning in this case. And, for this project, such planning needs to be undertaken initially. The justification for such a project needs to be well ascertained and documented; objectives need to be specified and intended beneficiaries identified; the viability of cultivating various potential crops must be generally ascertained, involving examination of opportunities, constraints and threats of many kinds; the magnitude and kinds of resources that will be needed must be clarified; and main aspects of organisation have to be assessed and determined. Moreover, all these dimensions need to be examined in an interrelated manner, through which the components of the plan are made to fit together.

The second scenario is the planning, by an NGO, of a community-based institution-building programme for highly deprived people. The programme includes, among other components, generation of savings and management of the accumulated money by member organisations in individual local communities.

Although many similar programmes may have been undertaken elsewhere – even by the same NGO – the performance and achievements between and within those programmes will certainly have varied widely, largely depending on a range of context-specific variables. So, one may have to start from only a general ideology and certain indications of what may work and what may not. Consequently, one will mostly have to find one's own way as one proceeds, even within individual communities, or at least be open to making substantial modifications of some more general model. Such a programme should, therefore, start on a relatively modest scale, and its evolution must be influenced by experiences that will be gained as one proceeds.

Obviously, the initial round of planning will be much more general and indicative than in our previous case. It is nevertheless strategic. Even the very conceptualisation of such a programme, as a suitable thrust for promoting development among deprived people in the respective communities, involves strategic analysis, irrespective of the extent to which the basic development concept may be formalised and elaborated.

Moreover, and more significantly, such a generative, learning-based programme will require recurrent strategic planning in the course of the programme period (which initially may be unspecified). This may relate to the orientation of the programme at large and to individual components within it – ongoing and new. Frequently one has to ask a range of basic questions that need to be explored individually and in relation to each other.

Some examples may be: Are initially formulated specific objectives still appropriate, or should they be modified? Are we managing to build sustainable organisations under existing circumstances (abilities, opportunities and constraints)? Are these circumstances changing and, if so, why? Are we managing to promote organisations of the most deprived people? Are we achieving our aim of strengthening the position of women? Are we providing the right kind of support in the best possible way to all the programme communities and organisations? Is there a need to change, over time, the components of support and the way it is rendered? Are we going too slowly or too fast?

Of course, these are questions of strategy, the examination of which may be followed by subsequent operational planning relating to various components and aspects, at various points in time.[15]

We can now turn our attention to the previously posed – and partly interrelated – issue 2, namely, the time-wise relation between activities within the general category of strategic planning itself. Table 2.1 may give the impression that the main analytical categories in that table, numbered 1–6, are to be analysed in a simple linear sequence, starting with the first and ending with the sixth.

I have tried, in the table, to modify this impression by specifying feedback links. In the connected text, I may have managed to weaken the impression of linearity even further by stating the need for initial broad-based scanning, that is, for a general overview of the situation or prospects in all the main dimensions before each of them is more comprehensively examined. Still, the reader may perhaps interpret these as mere modifications of a basically linear process.

Commonly, in reality, planning may not address each of the stated dimensions systematically in a step-wise manner, from the first to the last, with or without formalised feedback loops. A wide range of options exists for deviating from the sequence that is presented in the table. One may, for instance, explore funding possibilities comprehensively while still having only a general idea about objectives, or the analysis of problems and prospective beneficiaries may be so closely related that the exploration of the two becomes entirely intertwined.

Yet it is essential for clarification of the focus and scope of any development thrust to distinguish between main analytical categories, and there is a basic logic in the sequence in which they have been presented in the table. For instance, detailed formulation of objectives makes sense only after one has got a fairly clear idea about the problem to be addressed and whom it affects; external opportunities and threats relate directly to the type of intended intervention; and aspects of organisation will largely depend on the nature of one's aims.

Thus, in brief, the table is to be considered as nothing less and nothing more than a framework of main dimensions and common variables of strategic planning and common relations between them, while also indicating the logical sequence of much of the analysis that may need to be undertaken.

Finally, I want to stress that for many small and relatively simple thrusts, strategic planning (whether it is done once or recurrently) need not be either comprehensive or long-lasting. The exercise must also be made to fit the abilities of the people who are involved in it.

Notes

1 Of course, development strategies may and frequently do include the planned promotion of economic enterprises that are thought to have a development-enhancing effect.

2 One often sees 'strategy' used more broadly, with a meaning similar to 'approach', in which cases its meaning is usually less well clarified than it has been above. The term is sometimes even used in relation to other main activity categories of development programmes and projects than planning: in the combination 'implementation strategy', for example. Alternative formulations for the last-mentioned term might be 'implementation approach', 'mode of implementation', or something similar – reserving 'strategy' for its more precise meaning.

3 More detailed planning is commonly referred to as 'operational planning'. We shall briefly address that in the next chapter.

4 We shall elaborate these and other variables of organisation in Chapter 4.

5 In Chapter 8, we shall analyse further types of environmental factors and how one may relate to them.

6 The concept of 'stakeholder' has been developed primarily in the context of business management. Carroll (1989) made a seminal contribution. The article by Grimble and Chan (1995) contains an insightful discussion of the application of stakeholder analysis in development work, with direct reference to natural resource management.

7 For elaboration and discussion of these and related concepts of organisation, see Dale, 2000a. In that book, typologies are formulated of development organisations, on different dimensions and by different criteria. 'Public benefit'–'mutual benefit' constitutes one organisational dimension. Typically, public benefit organisations are bodies within the statal and private spheres, while mutual benefit organisations exist mainly within what Dale (2000a) refers to as the voluntary sector. For further exploration, see also Salamon and Anheier, 1997 and Uphoff, 1986; 1996.

8 Dale (2000a) elaborates a typology of coordination mechanisms considered to be suitable for development programmes and projects. In Chapter 4, we shall present those mechanisms in brief, as one important dimension of development organisation.

9 This is a quite different arrangement for overall management from the diverse area development programme discussed on p. 24.

10 In plan documents, the 'development objective' is the highest-level (and the most general) statement of intended achievements of the respective programmes and projects. Linking to that, objectives of more specific kinds should be clarified and formulated, as already suggested. For further elaboration and discussion, see chapters 4 and 6.
11 Problem structures will be analysed in Chapter 5.
12 Most of these concepts will be clarified further in later chapters of the book. Of most direct significance here is the relationship between strategic planning and operational planning. For now, it suffices to say that operational planning specifies further what one needs to be clear about before starting to use resources in implementation.
13 These and related concepts will be further clarified and discussed in Chapter 3.
14 See the various conceptions of rationality addressed in Chapter 1.
15 In chapters 3 and 10 we shall examine in greater detail how such recurrent strategy analysis may be done in practice, under the heading of 'process planning'.

Chapter 3

Diversifying Perspectives on Planning

Linking to More General Concepts of Value and Intent

The strategy of a development organisation – which may encompass all or some of its activities – is normally embedded in more basic ideas about the intention of the work the organisation does or plans to do. Such ideas, in turn, usually reflect general values on which the organisation's work is founded. Common words for expressing such fundamental conceptions are 'vision' and 'mission'. They may be perceived and expressed more or less explicitly and clearly.

More specifically, *vision* denotes *a desired outcome that the organisation intends to help create*, such as 'equal opportunities for women and men' or 'a society without malnourished children'. *Mission* stands for *the general contribution that the organisation intends to make towards fulfilment of its vision*: 'advocacy work for greater gender equality', for example, or 'improving the nutritional status of children' in specified social groups. Thus the overall mission of a development organisation will clarify the very justification for its existence. An alternative, commonly used word is the organisation's 'purpose'. While any development organisation should be able to specify a vision and a mission, these terms are at present most frequently used by non-governmental (private and voluntary) organisations.

If a vision and a mission are to wield significant influence, they must become institutionalised throughout the organisation. In other words, they must become broadly agreed mechanisms for regulating behaviour, permeating the activities of the organisation in a predictable manner.[1] This implies a close link between vision, mission and organisational 'rules'. Such rules may be more or less formalised. If they are primarily or entirely informal, rules may be interfaced with and may even be difficult to distinguish from organisational 'culture' (see also Chapter 4).

'Policy' is another common term in the development sphere and more broadly. *Development policy* may be defined as a coherent set of general development priorities, formulated by well-institutionalised organisations and relating to the general public or to specified groups of people, along with the kinds of measures that are needed for working effectively according to these priorities. 'Policy', then, is a more general expression of intended action than 'strategy'.

Strategic versus Operational and Adjustive Planning

Strategic planning, as conceptualised in Chapter 2, normally needs to be supplemented with planning of a more detailed nature. And detailed plans frequently have to be modified in the course of implementation of activities. Common terms for such additional planning are 'operational planning' and 'adjustive planning'.

Operational planning means further specification of components and processes that one has decided on during preceding strategic planning (which may have been more or less formalised and more or less comprehensive). A good operational plan should be a firm, detailed and clear guide for implementation. Normally, in operational planning, further elaboration is needed mainly of intended outputs and aspects of organisation and resource use.

The following is a somewhat more detailed, while not exhaustive, list of aspects that commonly need to be elaborated and specified through subsequent operational planning:

- geographical area/localities and intended beneficiaries;
- outputs, commonly with detailed design;
- implementation: tasks, actors and their roles, procedures of work, time schedule;
- technology to be applied in implementation;
- finance: detailed budget, payment system, expenditure recording system;
- reward system, personnel training and other personnel-related matters;
- benefit–cost relations;
- sustainability: of organisations, systems of planning and management, facilities and/or benefits;
- monitoring: tasks, actors and their roles, procedures of work, progress recording and reporting system;
- evaluation arrangements.

Adjustive planning means modification of existing plans, normally in the course of implementation, within a framework of aims, tasks and modes of operation that has been established in those plans. Thus, the scope of adjustive planning to modify plans is usually strictly limited.

Planning is a highly multifaceted activity, which may cover aspects from general societal values underpinning a development thrust to details of design, budget and management of that thrust. These aspects are most appropriately seen as located on a continuum from the most general to the most specific.

Our categories of strategic and operational planning relate respectively to the more general and more specific parts of this continuum. However, while the two concepts convey differences of perspective and approach that are normally crucial for good planning, there is rarely any clear dividing line between the two. In other words, one may rarely say exactly where strategic planning of a development scheme ends and operational planning begins.

Any idea of a clear line of separation between the two categories of planning may be particularly untenable in cases where all the aspects of a plan (from the most general to the most specific) are addressed during one relatively continuous exercise, sometimes even by the same persons. In such instances, all that is planned is commonly presented in the same document as well.

As we saw when discussing strategic planning in the last section of Chapter 2, the distinction between strategic and operational planning may also become very blurred in programmes that involve ongoing processes. In such programmes, the scope and contents become, to different extents, determined in the course of the programme period, normally through an interplay between (1) experiences gained from ongoing and completed work, and (2) additional relevant information and ideas. Typically, at any point in time, components of such programmes tend to be at different stages of conceptualisation, plan formulation or implementation. Thus, within such programmes, planning of a relatively general and a relatively specific nature will normally proceed simultaneously, for varying numbers of programme components.

In other cases, the distinction between strategic and operational planning will be clearer. For instance, relatively general aspects of a broad development thrust may be addressed in a framework document, while the various programme components (which may, normally, be referred to as projects) may be planned separately and presented in additional, while connected, documents. The first-mentioned document, then, is clearly a strategy document, while the connected documents address operational aspects of the respective thrusts – possibly in addition to specific aspects of strategy pertaining to those thrusts. The planning of a regional development programme offers an example: normally, in such a programme, an overall plan document is prepared, under which various component plans are worked out. Such exercises may be done once or sequentially (see also later in this chapter).

In much project planning of a relatively standardised nature (usually sector-delimited), very little strategic planning may be done. In Chapter 1 we mentioned the example of planning by a regional unit of a national roads department. We made the point then that little normative planning will be undertaken by such a unit, limited perhaps to prioritisation of road projects within the department's geographical area of authority.

Conversely, sometimes little or no formalised operational planning may be done, as in the case of programmes for providing support to local organisations or individual persons for small-scale activities that they are intended to undertake themselves. Examples of support items may be credit, other production inputs or housing materials. In such cases, the programme plan (formalised in a document) will normally be primarily strategic in nature. In addition, of course, the programme organisation needs to specify at least some criteria for the support and procedures for providing it – that is, it needs to conduct operational planning of what it does. On the other hand, plans for the activities to be undertaken using the allocated resources may not be specified extensively (or at all) in writing. Commonly, the outputs and particulars of implementation merely exist in the minds of the individual users of the resources provided.

It falls outside the scope of this book to address aspects of operational planning comprehensively. That would bring us into the realm of substantive planning and plans, the contents of which will depend on the particular field of intervention. Still, many of the relatively general aspects and concerns of operational planning that we have mentioned will be revisited in later chapters.

From Long-Range Planning to Continuous Strategic Management

In the last section of Chapter 2, we reflected on the scheduling of strategic planning in relation to other activities of a development thrust. We shall now elaborate this and connected issues somewhat further.

As indicated in Chapter 2, the scope and the specificity of strategic planning tend to be related to the time horizon of the planning exercise. Commonly, there are complex interconnections between these main dimensions of planning. For example, the envisaged time horizon may directly influence what may be covered (that is, the scope of the programme or project); the time horizon and/or the scope may influence the degree of specificity that may be possible; and conversely, the intended level of specificity of a plan may have bearings on the time horizon that may be applied. A related dimension is often the degree of connectedness between topics and issues that are addressed in planning. Simultaneously, all these aspects of planning will be interfaced with the societal context of the respective programme or project and how one intends to relate to opportunities and constraints.

The notions and perspectives involved may be better clarified through an examination of the following set of terms found in literature on societal planning:

- long-range planning;
- issue-focused planning;
- strategic management;
- environmental scanning.

These categories constitute an uneven continuum of time horizons, from the relatively long-term to the relatively short-term, with related differences of scope, specificity and interconnection of variables.

Addressing the first three of the listed categories, Bryson and Einsweiler (1988) consider only the first two to be planning pursuits and only the second of these to be strategic planning. Among the two categories, *long-range planning* focuses primarily on the 'specification of goals and objectives and their translation into current budgets and work programmes', while *issue-focused planning* 'typically relies more on the identification and resolution of *issues*' (1988: 4).

This distinction is fruitful, in that it reflects a common difference in the extent to which interests of different stakeholders and related conflicts are addressed in planning. Usually, long-range planning is done without much stakeholder analysis and assumes broad consensus about objectives. This may even be justified by the general nature of the objectives that are formulated. Issue-focused planning, by its more selective, probing and action-orientated nature, is 'more suitable for politicised circumstances, since identifying and resolving issues do not presume an all-encompassing consensus on organisational purposes and actions' (Bryson and Einsweiler, 1988: 4). Thus, exploring interests and trying to resolve interest conflicts may be major concerns of issue-focused planning.

An example of long-range planning may be the formulation of a general plan spanning many years (also referred to as a 'perspective plan') for development of an economic or social sector, a region, or a town. For instance, general town development plans may contain guidelines for physical expansion of the town, development of housing and infrastructure, and location of economic enterprises of various kinds. And these guidelines will be based on numerous assumptions, which in this case may be about such matters as population growth, the composition of in-migrants or the usage period of various types of infrastructure.

Sticking to the example of town development, issue-focused planning may be applied to many aspects, normally involving the expression of and mediation between conflicting interests. One example might be efforts to integrate an ethnic group better into the social and political life of the town; another might be efforts to reclassify zones within the town by their main function (such as residential and industrial). Both examples relate directly to the present and future interests of several groups of people.

Unlike Bryson and Einsweiler, I see no good reasons for considering only issue-focused planning as 'strategic'. Both long-range and issue-focused planning fit within our framework of strategic planning, while tending to emphasise different components of that framework. We must also assume that such planning of societal changes is justified by envisaged improvements in the life situation of some people (although this may not always be deeply analysed). On this basis, we should be able to refer to manifestations of both these types as development planning as well.

The third category listed above, *strategic management*, is a much-used though highly adaptable and commonly elusive concept. It used to be applied primarily in the business world, but is now being used increasingly in the public realm also. It conveys the notion of exploring changing opportunities and constraints in complex environments and responding with appropriate measures as and when this is deemed necessary or desirable, in contrast to proactive plan formulation and decision making (Crow and Bozeman, 1988). Consequently, in strategic management, one tends to apply shorter time horizons and to emphasise more specific issues in a less coherent manner than in either of the two previously mentioned forms of planning.

Within the broad conceptual scope of 'strategic management', a clearly planning-focused perspective is provided by the term *strategic choice*. This concept was to a great measure operationalised by J. K. Friend and W. N. Jessop more than three decades ago, and has since been widely used by planners in public agencies and development organisations. Friend and Jessop developed their perspective from a comprehensive analysis of decision making in a municipality in England (Friend and Jessop, 1969).

Later, the concept was further elaborated by Friend in collaboration with A. Hickling (Friend and Hickling, 1997).

Central to the analysis developed by these authors are the various *uncertainties* with which the public planner has to contend. Friend and Jessop (1969) specify three main kinds:

- uncertainty about the planning environment – regarding its characteristics at the time of planning, future changes in it, and responses from it to interventions;
- uncertainty about future intentions of related actors – for instance, intentions by other government agencies;
- uncertainty about value judgements – because values, as held and expressed by different people in the society, cannot be directly measured and objectively compared with each other.

The planner's main challenge, according to Friend and Jessop, is to cope with these uncertainties as constructively as possible, in order to provide the final decision takers with an analysis comprehensive and clear enough to constitute a solid foundation for their decisions. To do so the planner must first comprehensively explore the uncertainties relating to alternative courses of action through an interactive process of analysis. Next, the uncertainties must be clearly exposed: they must be made easily discernible; they need to be as clearly delimited and specified as possible; and they should be presented to the decision takers in a well-structured form.

The decision takers should then express *immediate preferences* and identify *short-term courses of action* that are judged to be relatively safe. This is important (1) to ensure, as far as possible, that resources are used wisely, and (2) to maintain the public agency's accountability to its constituency (the people whom it is intended to serve). At the same time, they should usually *keep several options open* for action in the longer term, in order to provide the space and flexibility to exploit unforeseeable future opportunities and cope with future threats as effectively as possible. It is also essential to *coordinate* the choices of agencies whose activities are related. Equally, any agency should be able to adjust its priorities and its mode of work in response to decisions and actions by other agencies.

Thus, good strategic choices will normally have to be made incrementally. Similar perspectives have subsequently come to be widely referred to as incremental planning, generative planning, or, even more commonly, process planning.[2]

Environmental scanning is another common strategy-related term in planning and management literature, particularly in the business realm. It expresses a relatively general and broad-focus assessment of external opportunities and constraints of importance for an organisation's work or some part of that work, particularly in rapidly changing environments. The main aim of the scanning, then, is to be able to respond as quickly and effectively as possible to external changes that are important for performance. In the sphere of development planning, this term is sometimes used to denote the earliest steps of a strategic planning exercise, synonymously with 'initial scanning of the whole planning field', a formulation I used in the section on comprehensive strategic planning in Chapter 2.

The term may also be utilised to denote frequent assessments of opportunities and constraints in programmes that are planned and implemented in a genuine process mode. The scanning will then be a relatively continuous function. As will be further clarified later, such programmes may be adjusted, expanded or contracted, more or less frequently, in response to additional relevant information. Of course, changes or adjustments of approach may not only be needed or desirable because of changes in the environment of an organisation or a programme or project. They may also be warranted because of internal changes of some kind (increased or reduced organisational capability, for example), or some combination of external and internal changes.

Process versus Blueprint Planning

Our focus has been and will remain on the act of planning and the context within which planning takes place. We have referred to this as a *mode-centred* perspective on planning. The perspective was conceptualised and advanced in the 1970s, in the course of a general debate among planning analysts on the ideological and theoretical foundation of societal planning. Initially, the main ideological divide in this debate was between a Marxist (*historical materialist*) and a more liberal school of thought. From the late 1970s, however, the credibility of orthodox and even modified Marxist notions of societal development was being eroded, leading to a sharp decline in genuinely historical materialist analyses of planning. Simultaneously, another debate emerged among more or less liberal scholars in which a *subject matter* perspective was ranged against the mode-centred perspective.

The Friend–Jessop analysis of strategic choice (summarised on pp. 41–2 above) is widely considered to have been the most seminal early theoretical contribution to mode-centred societal planning. Their book (Friend and Jessop, 1969) was followed by other contributions from many authors. The most important overall contributor was probably Andreas Faludi, through several publications (Faludi, 1973; 1979; 1983; 1984). He developed a typology of dimensions of what he referred to as 'procedural' and 'action-centred' planning, operationalised as pairs of juxtaposed 'planning modes'.[3]

The most significant of Faludi's dimensions – spurring substantial further thinking and writing – was the dimension of 'process–blueprint' planning. *Process planning* basically means that plans are not finalised or specified fully prior to the start-up of implementation; that is, greater or lesser amounts of planning are done in the course of the implementation period of the development scheme, interactively with implementation and monitoring. *Blueprint planning*, in its extreme or pure form, means that one prepares detailed plans for all that one intends to do before implementing any of the work. Thereby, the implementers will know exactly what they are to do, in which sequence and at what cost, until the scheme is completed.

Implicit in the process–blueprint conception is that planning may be more or less process or more or less blueprint; that is, actual planning events should be viewed as located somewhere along a continuum between extreme process and extreme blueprint. Uncertainty and uncertainty management are central notions in *process* planning (Faludi, 1973; Korten, 1980; 1984). This planning mode is particularly appropriate in complex environments, where no firm images may be created, or when the planners' control over external factors is restricted for other reasons. Korten also refers to process planning as a 'learning process approach', and he thinks that 'planning with people' needs to be done in this mode (1980: 498–9). The concept of 'process' is partly related to the idea of 'disjointed incrementalist' planning, used by Faludi (in the texts already cited), Lindblom and Cohen (1979) and others. However, the latter concept also contains notions of fragmentation in planning that may not necessarily be the case with process planning (Dale, 2002 b).

With *blueprint* planning, all possible efforts must be made during a single planning effort to remove uncertainties regarding implementation and benefits to be generated. Ideally, then, blueprint planning is 'an approach whereby a planning agency operates a programme thought to attain its objectives with certainty' (Faludi, 1973: 131). To that end, the planner must be able to manipulate relevant aspects of the programme environment, leaving 'no room for the environment or parts of it to act in other ways than those set by the planning agency' (1973: 140).

We see that Faludi uses the term 'programme' for the set of activities that are planned and implemented. Korten, however, stresses that, in blueprint planning, it is 'the *project* [my emphasis] – its identification, formulation, design, appraisal, selection, organization, implementation, supervision, termination and evaluation – [that] is treated as the basic unit of development action' (Korten, 1980: 496).[4]

Connections exist between these notions of planning and the notions explored in the preceding section, in terms of time horizons in planning and related plan specificity and firmness. Some categories are, in fact, more or less overlapping. In particular, long-range planning tends basically to be of blueprint nature, while, as stated, strategic management and, even more, specific notions of environmental scanning will be of process nature.

We shall now operationalise 'process' and 'blueprint' somewhat more, with reference to programmes with many components – for instance, comprehensive regional development programmes. In this endeavour, we shall also link up with our previously clarified concepts of 'strategic', 'operational' and 'adjustive' planning. Further analysis of this planning dimension will then be undertaken in some subsequent chapters, most comprehensively in Chapter 10, in the context of participatory and empowering programmes.

Our specifications of this planning dimension are illustrated in Figure 3.1. For simplicity's sake, we show only three programme components, referred to as X, Y and Z. We have also limited the time period to three years, although most such programmes go on over a longer period. Actual or possible continuation beyond the three-year period is visualised by arrows and question-marks respectively, on the right side of the diagram. The arrows for individual components, already under implementation, tell that work on these components will continue – either under a current phase or in a new phase, after a new round of planning. The question-marks indicate that it is an open question whether or how many additional components will be planned and implemented after the three-year period.

In the figure, four models of planning are shown (1, 2, 3 and 4, in the first column). Model 1 signifies blueprint planning and Models 2, 3 and 4 varieties of process planning. These models illustrate only some out of a wider range of potential approaches. The entire range would have shown more of a continuum of modes, between extreme versions of blueprint and process planning, than is illustrated here.

We have distinguished between four categories of planning, by the kinds of issues that are examined, the degree of detail of the exercise, and the further action that the exercise is intended to induce. Together, these aspects are in the figure title referred to as the 'action scope' in planning. We have already addressed three of these planning categories: 'strategic', 'operational' and 'adjustive' planning. Earlier in this chapter, we also introduced the fourth category, 'environmental scanning'. In the present

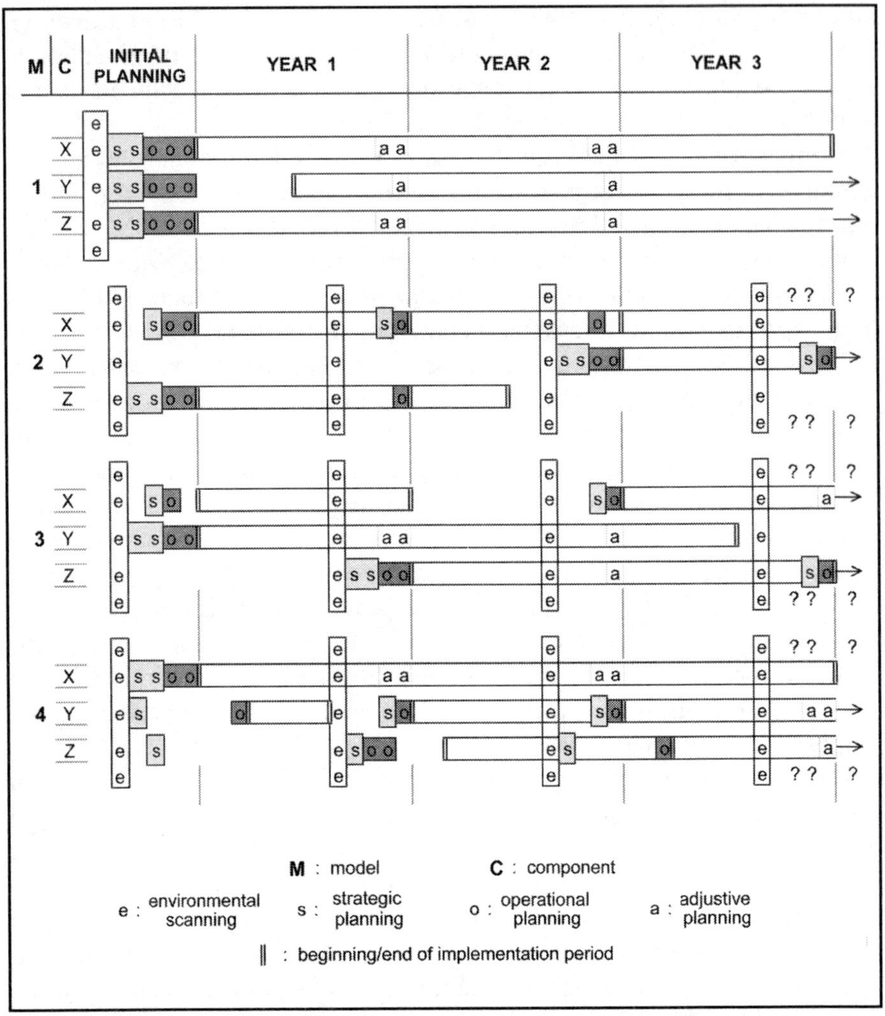

Figure 3.1 Action Scope and Time Horizons in Planning

context, we have seen that this stands for a broad-focus, relatively general assessment of the context (environment) in which the programme or a component under it is envisaged to operate.

Additionally, the planners will have time horizons for the work to be done, manifested in the subsequent intended periods of implementation of the components that have been planned. These operational entities may, alternatively, be referred to as projects (see later). Note that the points of commencement and end of implementation of any project are visualised in the figure by double vertical lines.

Model 1 expresses a quite clear-cut form of blueprint planning, in which all substantial planning is done before the implementation of any component starts and covers the entire programme period. With blueprint planning, strong efforts need to be made at the planning stage to help ensure controlled use of resources and processes of work throughout the programme period and, concomitantly, creation of the specified outputs. Normally, this becomes the greater challenge the further ahead one plans. Consequently, with relatively long-term perspectives, some uncertainty is virtually bound to remain. In recognition of this, annual rounds of adjustive planning are incorporated in the model. In other words, a possibility is instituted for correcting initial mistakes or inaccuracies of design and costs, and for removing or steering clear of hurdles that one may unexpectedly meet.

In this case, component X is planned for implementation over a three-year period (corresponding to the period shown in the figure), whereas the other components will continue to be implemented beyond that period. The implementation of two components will start as soon as the operational planning of them has been completed, while the work is intended to start a few months later for the third component.

Models 2, 3 and 4 are all versions of process planning, as this mode has been defined in this chapter. The outstanding difference between Model 1 and the others is that, in the latter, priorities as well as aspects of operation are re-examined regularly – in these cases annually. This is shown by recurrent (annual) rounds of environmental scanning, followed by strategic and operational planning. The planning may encompass (1) any new phases of or additions to components that have been implemented or are under implementation, and (2) any additional components.

Model 2 is conceptually the simplest and also the least flexible among the three models of process planning. Its characteristic feature is strictly annual work programmes. This means that no component or phase of a component (both of which may be referred to as 'projects') may be planned for a longer period than one year, and new sets of components (projects) will have to be approved annually.

Model 3 is characterised by annual planning cycles as well. At the same time, it allows projects to be planned for longer periods than one year, according to the perceived need for longer time horizons. Extended time horizons in operational planning may often be advantageous, and even necessary for relatively big and indivisible (or hardly divisible) projects. For instance, it would not make sense to plan one half of a bridge one year and the other half the following year. Before allowing the construction of such a facility to start, one needs to be sure that the whole facility is soundly designed and realistically budgeted. A closely related point is that one normally needs an initial commitment for funding the entire facility, which usually requires approval of details of design, cost and other matters for the whole entity (in this case, the bridge).

In *Model 4*, even greater flexibility is accommodated, by a provision for operational planning of approved components at any time during the year. With this model, too, resources for planned and approved projects usually need to be committed for the entire period of implementation. As with Model 3, as long as this requirement is met, the resources may still be allocated annually.

With both Models 3 and 4, such annual allocations will then be based on (1) existing (possibly revised) cost estimates for ongoing projects (for which resources have already been committed), and (2) cost estimates for any new projects that have been fully planned by the time of resource allocation. In addition, with Model 4, allocations may be made based on (3) indicative cost estimates for any projects that have, by that time, been generally conceived and prioritised, but still have to be planned in detail.

Issues of process planning are further illustrated through the case presented in Box 3.1. This case clarifies the nature of overall plan documents that may have to be prepared in programmes with a high degree of process planning, and it focuses attention on some questions of management and information generation that are not addressed in the figure.

Normally, a main justification for a process mode of work is that it provides opportunities for learning from experience and concomitant improvement of the programme as one proceeds. The learning may relate to anything from overall prioritisation to details of design and organisation, and involves the collection of good information about aspects of the programme environment.

The case emphasises fairly continuous generation of information in the course of implementation of the different components, and various means of generating that information are indicated. In this particular programme, frequent and flexible reviews came to constitute a crucial part of the system of information generation.

This model functioned well and became increasingly effective during a period of years in which the programme enjoyed a favourable combination of internal promoting factors and a permissive environment for process planning. The favourable factors included effective leadership, an innovative and collaborative spirit among involved personnel, substantial freedom of action and a reasonable degree of surrounding political and administrative stability. The system then largely disintegrated, along with other innovative management practices in the programme. This was

Box 3.1
Managing a Programme with Process Planning

The Hambantota Integrated Rural Development Programme (HIRDEP) in Sri Lanka, implemented from 1978 to 2000, was an unusually dynamic and flexible development endeavour. During the 1980s, in particular, it operated according to a well-elaborated model of process planning. A core aspect of this was annual programme documents with the following main components:

- review of the previous year's work and past experience;
- outline of a future general strategy;
- proposals for new programme components (projects) to be started the following year;
- a work programme for the following year, encompassing ongoing and new projects;
- indications of project priorities (beyond already planned projects) over the next three years.

Information for planning was generated from various sources, largely depending on the nature of the respective projects. For instance, much information for the planning of infrastructure projects tended to be available with the respective sector agencies, and might be supplemented with additional information acquired by responsible officers at the field level. Community-based schemes, on the other hand (some of which are most appropriately referred to as flexible subprogrammes), required a more participatory, step-wise and cumulative approach to generating information.

The most innovative part of the system of information generation was a provision for flexible evaluations – termed reviews – instituted as a supplement to current monitoring. The reviews were important tools for feeding back information from ongoing and completed work into further planning. Salient features of this system were:

- the focus and comprehensiveness of the reviews were situation-determined and varied greatly;
- reviews could be proposed by any involved body (in practice, mainly the overall planning and coordinating body, sector departments, and the donor agency) at any time;
- the planning of reviews was integrated into the planning process outlined above, resulting in annual programmes of reviews;
- the review teams varied with the specific purpose of the particular reviews, consisting of one or more insiders, outsiders or – commonly – a combination of internal and external persons;

- a system of follow-up of the reviews was instituted, with written comments from involved agencies, a common meeting, decisions on follow-up action and reporting on that action (mainly in the next annual programme document).

Adapted from: Dale (2000a)

mainly due to changes of programme personnel, strains imposed on the programme by two years of political turmoil, and a change of policy and new bureaucratic imperatives on the part of the donor.

Planning Categories by Functional Level and Type of Area

Development planning may often be categorised according to the administrative level at which it is undertaken (this is often a political level as well) or the type of area to which the planning relates. Level-wise, we may broadly distinguish between national, regional and local community planning.

National planning may be broad-focus or delimited to administrative sectors, social groups, natural habitats, fields of production, etcetera. It may be undertaken entirely at the national level, or it may be deconcentrated, to larger or lesser extents. In the latter case, units of the central government at one or more subnational levels (such as provinces and/or districts) are responsible for at least some of the planning confined to their geographical areas, within frameworks of rules and regulations provided by the head office of the respective national agencies. Still, the planning thrusts are basically national concerns, and the implementation of the resultant plans is the overall responsibility of national organisations.

Likewise, *regional planning* may be undertaken at a specified regional level only (such as a province or a district), or it may be deconcentrated, more or less, to units below that level. Frequently, even if all the planning is done at the regional level, the plans may apply to only one part or some parts of the region, delimited by some criterion/criteria. Examples of such criteria may be the assessed degree of poverty, certain ecological features, or a dominant land-use pattern. These aspects are elaborated below.

Local community planning is taken to mean any planning thrust that is wholly or mainly undertaken within the community itself. It may be done entirely through local initiative and organisation or through interaction with one or more external bodies. In the latter case, the effort in a particular community may be self-standing, or it may be part of a programme covering a number of adjacent communities or a set of communities with some specific characteristic or characteristics.

Local community planning will normally have an explicit emphasis on the quality of life of people in the respective locality or localities. Thus, while we may not want to refer to all kinds of national planning as 'development planning', and not even consider all kinds of regional planning in that light, typical local-level planning is unambiguously 'developmental'.

Regarding the type of area that is addressed, planners have commonly distinguished between *urban (development) planning* and *rural development planning*. Historically, however, the two have hardly been corresponding categories.

Urban planning has tended to emphasise physical planning of cities and other urban settlements. It then deals with the design of numerous urban facilities, commonly with reference to general standards of those facilities and their use. Specification of such standards may sometimes be a planning concern in its own right. Examples of standards may be the physical quality of various kinds of buildings, safety measures, criteria for usage of facilities, or aspects of aesthetics. The standards may be more or less firm or indicative. Physical urban planning ranges from the formulation of highly general perspective plans for whole settlements, via regulation plans for parts of settlements, to detailed plans for specific pieces of infrastructure.

Of course, urban physical planning ought to be based on some strategy analysis and related strategic planning, linking these aspects of design to more basic considerations of development. However, in much urban planning, functional perspectives have tended to dominate over normative ones. This may relate in part to the academic disciplines of most urban planners – mainly engineering, architecture and, less frequently, geography.

'Rural development planning' has been a much-used term, in particular favour with donor agencies of programmes and projects in developing countries. Yet it is very difficult to find a common denominator for schemes that have carried this nametag. Commonly, the focus and approach of rural development programmes and projects have tended to reflect loosely founded (or, at least, little elaborated and poorly documented) ideas of individuals involved, rather than any organisation-permeating conception of development. This is well illustrated by the large variety of stated priorities of such programmes, even those that have been implemented or supported by the same organisation. Some common examples of stated priorities have been: higher quality of life of the poorest people, development of agriculture, improved natural resource management, rural industrialisation, and promotion of rural institutions of various kinds.

Moreover, rural development schemes have ranged from very broad-based (comprehensive) to highly selective thrusts, planning has spanned highly prescriptive and highly flexible modes, and a range of organisational arrangements and modes of management have been applied. In other words, rural development and, consequently, rural development planning have been fields wide open to interpretation, and programmes and projects of rural development have accommodated very different kinds of development work.

Some analysts and planners have advocated a more general ideology of 'rural development', including a direct and unambiguous focus on the quality of life of people, with the main emphasis on particularly deprived groups. Deprivation has then tended to be interpreted broadly, encompassing much more than poor livelihood (in its normal meaning of inadequate access to material resources for living). This focus is commonly connected with participation by people in problem analysis and decision making, and with the strengthening of local development institutions.[5] These features, however, have tended to be typical of 'community development' as well. Moreover, they may often be as applicable in urban as in rural communities, and may even be features of some regional development programmes (see below).

Thus, the term 'rural development planning' contains hardly anything of specific analytical value. We shall therefore not use it subsequently in this book. Its semantic (although not substantive) counterpart, 'urban planning', will not be much used analytically either, since its most characteristic feature (design of urban facilities and space) largely falls outside our scope of analysis.

Notwithstanding such considerations, the bottom line of our argument is that the analytical categories and modes of analysis that are presented and discussed in this book are applicable for most planning across the levels and settings that we have outlined. The various planning terms we have used (national, regional, urban, rural and local community planning) may be more or less good identification tags for exercises leading to different – sometimes vastly different – kinds of plans. Still, planning in all these highly different contexts may be guided by our general analytical framework, to the extent that it is reasonably normative and emphasises action. Moreover, more specific features and methodologies relating to this framework, to be elaborated subsequently in the book, may be applicable to varying extents.

There are some additional aspects of regional and community development planning that I want to address more specifically. They are important in their own right, while also highlighting issues and linking to arguments in subsequent chapters.

Regional planning

Planning that focuses on a contiguous and relatively big area (region) within a country is commonly referred to as regional planning. The spatial planning units are usually so-called functional regions. They may range from a basically rural area with a hierarchy of small centres located within it, via a major town with its hinterland, to a bigger area of basically urban nature having more than one town (an urban agglomeration). In most cases falling within the first two categories, the planning area is some administrative entity as well, such as an administrative province or district.

Much regional planning has aimed at producing comprehensive long-term plans for development of such areas. Yet its scope of action has also tended to be limited to the activities of government agencies, having normally been closely linked to a 'public interest' view of the state and work that it undertakes (Mackintosh, 1992; Dale, 2000a; 2000b).[6]

Regional planning is primarily strategic. It addresses relatively general aspects more than specific ones, the latter being normally dealt with subsequently through more detailed project planning. Yet the conception of 'strategy' has tended to be a narrow one. As noted by Dale (2000b), regional planning has mostly been confined to relatively overt, tangible and clearly delimited matters. Main components of regional development programmes have usually been various kinds of physical infrastructure (often related to an overall settlement plan), land-related projects (sometimes connected to land-use zoning), and standardised support facilities for individuals and groups, along with connected tasks such as compilation and processing of statistical data and statistical population projections.

Thus broad-focus analysis of problems, stakeholders and environmental factors – a crucial feature of most strategic planning – has often not been undertaken or not pursued with much purpose and vigour. Accordingly, regional development plans have tended to be comprehensive only or mainly in the sense of providing the framework for relatively independent sector plans and individual projects.

According to Bryson and Einsweiler (1988), these priorities and features are largely explained by the macro-institutional context of the planning, such as the location of the planning agencies within government and the legislation that regulates the planning. Commonly, the characteristics noted above have also been reinforced by an inadequate institutional basis at regional levels for comprehensive planning – in spite of the fact that a political foundation may exist and regional planning agencies may have been instituted. Subnational political bodies, on which the planners depend for effective work, are commonly weak and often lack clout and accountability both upwards and downwards; the planning agencies may not have the required expertise or the authority they need for effective leadership and coordination; and the regional agencies tend to be highly dependent on the resources of line agencies of the central government.

Another explanatory factor, no doubt, is a heavy emphasis in much training in regional (and urban) planning on physical features and spatial planning techniques, which tends to be linked to functional (in contrast to normative), blueprint (in contrast to process) and top-down perspectives.

Dale (2000b) argues that conventional regional planning, largely owing to the factors discussed above, has tended to be a less-than-effective mechanism for directing or guiding changes in the regions where it has been applied. This contrasts with the lofty ambitions that have often surrounded such planning, in terms of steering courses of development according to rational principles espoused by the planners and the agencies that they represent.

But in the same article Dale also argues that there is scope for adjusting or even radically changing existing approaches in regional development programmes. The need for some long-range planning and for relatively firm plans for investments in physical and social infrastructure is recognised. Yet alongside these, it is argued, other initiatives for the development of regions may be planned and implemented in a much more generative manner, with more emphasis on facilitating processes of change. Efforts in that direction have indeed been made, mostly in a few so-called Integrated Rural (or Regional) Development Programmes (IRDPs), emphasising process planning, institution building and broad stakeholder participation.

Dale also proposes that recent innovative strands of development thinking should be incorporated into an alternative paradigm of regional development programmes, emphasising 'flexible facilitation'. Such an approach could encompass support to a range of organisations and groups of the state, civil society and the market. Emphasis should be placed, he suggests, on measures such as:

- strengthening local government;
- training decentralised units of the central government;
- promoting community-managed development work;
- promoting cooperative services of various kinds;
- strengthening entrepreneurship and business management;
- facilitating the formation of interest and advocacy groups.

Community development planning

Most often, 'community' refers to a local area, the inhabitants of which are socially and emotionally related to one another, to larger or lesser extents: from this they derive a sense of belonging to the place where they live. This meaning may be more unambiguously expressed by adding the word 'local', i.e., in the term 'local community'. 'Neighbourhood', 'village' and 'locality' are other common terms for denoting a place where a group of people live. The first term is defined as a small group of adjacent households, while the two others normally denote somewhat larger areas, consisting of a number of neighbourhoods.

Alternatively, 'community' may refer to any group of people who share a social or cultural feature or a cluster of such features, examples of which may be ethnic origin, religion and/or occupation. Here we use 'community' in the first-mentioned sense or in a combination of the two senses. In the latter case, we refer to groups of people in one or more local communities who also share some other feature or features. Examples may be poor women, landless households or members of a local organisation. By 'community development' work we then mean work to improve the life quality of all or some people in one community, or in a number of communities.[7]

On this basis, we may make a distinction between three broad notions of community development planning. The first notion may be referred to as *regular community-wide planning*. This is some approximation of regional planning, done at the local level, normally by a local government body. It is an important part of the planning repertoire in most countries of Europe and other economically advanced countries with strong and relatively independent local governments. Commonly, the plans cover larger spatial units than we normally consider as local communities, but they also tend to be broken down by such communities within the local government area.

Such planning is referred to by specific national terms, most of which may be translated into 'commune planning' in English. The planning system normally consists of a nested set of long-term framework plans, intermediate action plans and annual work programmes. A noteworthy feature, normally, is an emphasis on physical planning, including formulation of detailed land regulation plans, particularly for densely populated areas and for new residential and industrial zones. In economically advanced countries, commune planning, anchored in a local government body, has tended to be much more important and effective than any regional planning that may have been done (Dale, 2000b).

In less-developed countries, this kind of planning has been much weaker or even absent. This is related to weak local governments in the large majority of such countries. Moreover, local government bodies in most less-developed countries are located at a regional rather than a locality level, and they tend to have weak (or no) links with any other locality-based organisations that might have helped them perform an effective community development role.[8]

The above applies primarily to areas outside cities. City planning is in large measure a field of its own, determined by specific challenges posed by big population agglomerations. In all countries, such planning is at least partly anchored in a city government (urban municipality).

A second main notion of local-level planning is what we shall call *participatory community-focused planning*. Regular community-wide planning, just addressed, ought to be participatory as well, in some substantial sense. In such planning, the interests and views of the community's inhabitants are incorporated indirectly, through representation, and commonly also through additional direct involvement in specific situations or for specific purposes.

Ideas of more direct participatory planning (and implementation as well) have primarily been conceived and pursued in countries and situations where local governments are non-existent, unrepresentative or poorly functioning. Such participatory planning has occasionally been promoted through regional and local units of the central government. For instance, in Sri Lanka, participatory local community planning has been incorporated in some of the country's IRDPs and even in other programmes that have been coordinated or managed by central government agencies.[9] More commonly, however, genuine participatory planning has been promoted by NGOs. In some instances, links have been established with government agencies as well – for their approval of plans, various kinds of support, and even implementation of specific components.

In such planning, a range of participatory methods of problem analysis and prioritisation may be applied (see chapters 5 and 9). Strengthening community-based organisations for planning and implementation is often an important part of the approach (see, particularly, Chapter 10).

In most instances, participatory community-focused planning is broad-focus and flexible. Sometimes, it in principle encompasses anything that the participants prioritise, within existing abilities and constraints. In other instances, the planning is limited to specific concerns or sectors. One example of the latter is the formulation of rules and regulatory measures in community forestry, another the planning of local irrigation facilities. Even in such instances, planning is mainly intended to benefit all or the majority of the community inhabitants.

The third main notion of community development planning may be referred to as *group-based planning*. This normally emphasises empowerment, in some sense, of the intended beneficiary group or groups. Group-based development work has become a very common approach, used particularly by NGOs. Fundamental to it is the belief that organised efforts may generate more benefits for the group members than the sum of benefits through the same persons' individual efforts. To that end, the participating persons should have the same basic needs and interests and be like-minded in other important respects as well. The focus is normally on people who are particularly deprived, in one or more senses. The approach involves institution building, frequently including the formation or strengthening of formal organisations of the involved persons (commonly referred to as 'member organisations').

A common example is community-based programmes with micro-financial services as a core component. Dale (2001) refers to the typical combination of activities in such programmes as a 'mobilisation–organisation–finance nexus'. Another example is programmes that focus on the life situations of women. They may address a broad range of issues, more or less freely, or they may focus on one or a specified cluster of issues. Such programmes are participatory in the deepest sense of this term, sometimes expressed through the concept 'empowering participation' (Oakley *et al.*, 1991; Dale, 2000a). Normally this is coupled with highly generative planning. This approach will be further explored in Chapter 10.

Connecting Planning to the Concepts of Programme and Project

In previous pages, I have already used the words 'programme' and 'project' several times. This is because they tend to be the most frequently utilised terms for denoting planned and organised work for societal development. For this reason, and because the terms are not synonymous and should not be used interchangeably, we need to clarify their meanings further.

Programmes

A programme is not easily defined. It is normally regarded as a less specified and/or less clearly bounded entity than a project, in terms of its focus, scope of activities, time horizon, etcetera. Many development programmes also tend to be relatively broad-focus and long-lasting.

In terms of the main planning categories we have specified, a programme may be designed through strategic planning only or through some combination of strategic and operational planning. For instance, in a development programme, strategic aspects may be formulated in a separate document, which will usually be referred to as the programme document. Parts of the development thrust may then be further operationalised in one or more additional plan documents, more appropriately referred to as project documents. Alternatively, strategic and operational planning may be undertaken as parts of one comprehensive exercise and formulated in the same document. In some instances, as we have seen, little or no operational planning may be undertaken or formalised by the planning agency, as this is done informally by the users of the allocated resources. In such cases, we have unquestionably a programme, under which these users undertake their own, normally very small, schemes (which may be referred to as programme components or projects).

We may distinguish between two main types of development programmes by their scope: one-sector programmes and multisector programmes. 'Sector' is normally defined by the general type of activity performed or the service rendered. A few examples are education, primary health care, fisheries, irrigation, financial services or social mobilisation. To the extent that these activities are also concerns of governments, sector categories normally coincide with public administrative responsibility as well.

Both one-sector programmes and multisector programmes may be more or less flexible or rigid. That is, they may be planned in more or less of a process or a blueprint mode. Most development programmes require a substantial amount of process planning. In particular, this applies to relatively diversified programmes, programmes with broad stakeholder participation and programmes that aim at capacity building. We have already clarified this to some extent, and shall substantiate it more in later chapters. In addition, multisector programmes may be more or less disjointed or integrated; that is, they may consist of components that are functionally unrelated or more or less interconnected.

There may also be hierarchies of programmes. For instance, a development programme covering one district may contain several divisional programmes, each of which may contain local community programmes. Within this hierarchy, projects may be planned and implemented at any level.

Please note that 'programme' is also used with a different meaning in the phrase 'work programme'. A work programme spells out implementation details of a project or parts of it. Linked to this is 'programming', meaning detailed sequencing of activities.

Projects

Definitions of 'project' abound in business management literature and in literature on public planning and management. When signifying a formally organised endeavour – also in the development field – a project is normally stated to be a clearly delimited and relatively highly specified undertaking. A synthesis of typical definitions that have been presented gives us something like: a planned intervention for achieving one or more objectives, encompassing a set of interrelated activities that are undertaken during a delimited period of time, using specified human, financial and physical resources.

The idea is that development projects, like other endeavours that use resources that must be accounted for, should be well specified before one may start implementation, leaving as little uncertainty as possible about the quantity and quality of the outputs and their costs. The logical implication of such a conception is that a development intervention, to be termed a project, should be formulated in blueprint mode and specified through operational planning.

In reality in the development sphere, 'project' tends to be used more broadly than this, encompassing endeavours that ought to be called programmes according to most formal definitions of 'project' and the argument above. In my view, a more restricted and stringent usage of 'project' than has been common (and a corresponding more frequent use of 'programme') would be advantageous. This would help unify perceptions about characteristics of various kinds of development thrusts and, therewith, facilitate communication about modes of planning.

Notes

1 For further clarification of institutionalisation, as well as relations between institution and organisation, see Uphoff, 1986; Dale, 2000a; Brett, 2000; and Narayan *et al.*, 2000. The terms will also be explored further in Chapter 10.

2 It should already be clear to the reader that process planning is a major analytical concept in this book. It will be better defined and elaborated in the next section of this

chapter and explored further in later chapters.

3 Dale (2002b) discusses this typology and formulates a set of more specific dimensions and modes.

4 See the last section of this chapter for a further discussion of the terms 'programme' and 'project'.

5 Robert Chambers has been a main proponent of this ideology. See publications by Chambers in the Bibliography.

6 According to this view, in the words of Dale (2000a: 57), 'the government, by its politicians and civil servants, is considered capable of defining the *common interests* of the people (being frequently referred to as the "public interest"). On this basis, government agencies should formulate policies and plans and use the powers of the state to further those interests.... Many measures need to be implemented, as well, by agencies of the state, such as taxation, provision of a wide range of welfare services, and regulation of production.'

7 'Community development' has also been given a more specific meaning, emphasising changes in people's attitude and connected behaviour. See, for instance, Dale, 1992.

8 A further discussion of this highly important topic for development would bring us beyond the scope of this book. For a brief discussion, see Dale, 2000a. For a more comprehensive analysis relating to Asia, see Aziz and Arnold, 1996.

9 Dale (1992) examines such development thrusts in Sri Lanka and their underlying political rationale.

Chapter 4

Elaborating Linkages in Development Work

Connecting Design Variables, Work Categories and Intended Achievements

In the preceding chapters, we have explored concepts of and perspectives on development planning. In addition, for fuller conceptualisation of development work, we need to connect planning to other work categories of programmes and projects and to the intended outcome of the latter, and we need to specify further some variables of design and achievements. This will be our thrust in the present chapter.

Strategic and operational planning are generally applicable planning categories in the development sphere.[1] In Figure 4.1, planning, expressed by these concepts, is connected to other main tasks and activities and to intended and actual achievements of the planned work. For easy conceptualisation of the figure, the presentation of strategic planning is simplified from that in Chapter 2: we have here omitted specification of analytical categories and linkages between them. Also note that 'objectives', used in the strategic planning framework presented earlier, is in this version replaced by the more general term *intended achievements*. This term should be understood as corresponding to all three levels of objectives specified in the upper half of Figure 4.1.

In the figure, *strategic planning* is shown as followed by *operational planning*. Sometimes, however, the two may be more or less interrelated: this is shown by the feedback link from the latter to the former. Operational planning may encompass a large number of variables, as briefly outlined in Chapter 3. Two of them, *implementation tasks* and *inputs*, are specified here because they connect directly to the implementation of the work that has been planned and the intended outcome of that work. They also correspond to main categories in the logical framework, a much-used

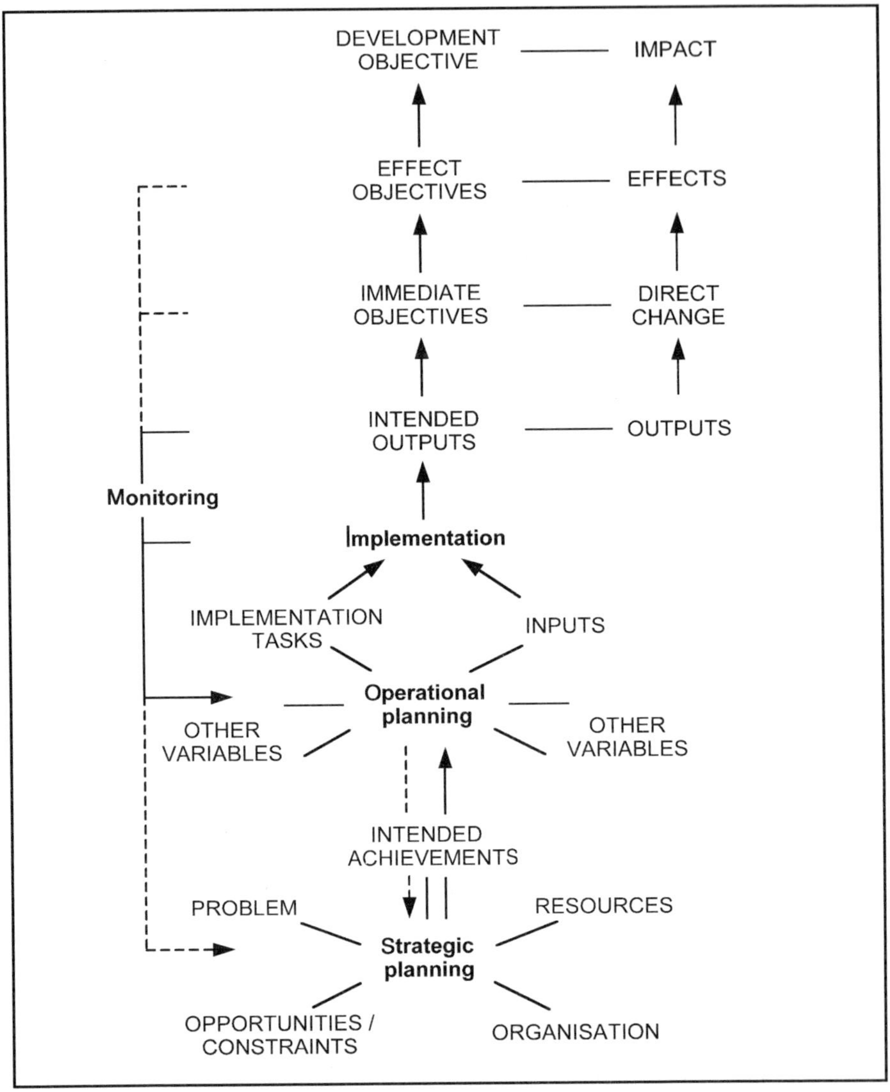

Figure 4.1 Connecting Variables of Development Work

tool for structuring major variables of development programmes and projects. We shall soon present the logical framework and make use of it later in the book.

Implementation is intended to be done in accordance with the planned work tasks (implementation tasks) and the planned inputs for these tasks. The direct (or relatively direct) outcome of the work that is done is referred to as *outputs*. Commonly, the managers of the respective development schemes should be able to guarantee the outputs, since they ought to be in control of the resource inputs and the work that directly produce them. We shall see later, however, that the matter is often not so straightforward.

During implementation, one will *monitor* the resource use, work processes, outputs and, possibly, fairly direct changes caused by the outputs. The purpose of monitoring is to know whether or to what extent the programme or project proceeds according to the plans and creates what it is intended to create, and to provide information that may be needed for any changes – regarding plans, mode of implementation or outputs. This is shown by a feedback link to planning – particularly operational planning, but sometimes even strategic planning.[2]

As emphasised several times, the very purpose of development work is to enhance the quality of life of one or more groups of people. The overall intended improvement in people's life quality (the intended ultimate benefit) is expressed by the highest-level objective, referred to as the *development objective*. Thus, it is essential that this objective is people-focused and expresses the intended improvement for the intended beneficiaries in explicit and unambiguous terms.

A major challenge in development planning is to explore and substantiate logical chains of linked variables from the level of outputs to the level of development objective. This is what we refer to as means–ends analysis, to be most comprehensively addressed in Chapter 6. As we have already mentioned briefly, however, some planning does not incorporate any analysis of consequences of the planned work for people's quality of life. Following Faludi (1973; 1984) and others, we refer to this as 'functional' (juxtaposed to 'normative') planning.

For example, part of a project for enhancing the income for farmers under an irrigation system may be to replant the water catchment of that system, in order to reduce soil erosion, negatively affecting irrigation and therewith cultivation and income. It would make sense if another body than the overall planning agency was placed in charge of planning what to do to have the area planted (and normally also implementing the plan). That body would then consider any benefits for people of these activities to be outside its field of concern. This would be a clearly functional planning thrust, which may not in itself be referred to as development planning. It emanates from a development planning thrust (for the project as a whole), and would need to be seen in the context of that wider thrust to be given development significance.

There are some kinds of programmes with highly indirect relations between outputs and benefits for people that must be considered as development schemes. In particular, some institution-building programmes fall into this category. In these, the links from augmented institutional abilities to improved quality of life may be cloudy and hard to ascertain. Let us illustrate this with another example.

A government intends to augment the competence and capacity for managing public development work by establishing a national Institute of Development Management, for which it may also seek donor funding. The overall objective of the institute may be formulated as 'promoting economic and social development' in the country. However, for both the government and any donor agencies that may support the enterprise, this objective will, for all intents and purposes, remain an assumption, rather than an intended achievement against which any investment may be explicitly analysed.

In other words, the operational planning of the institute and any subsequent investment in it will have to be based on relatively general and indicative judgement of its relevance and significance, rather than any rigorous means–ends analysis. Still, I would think that few people, if anybody, would hesitate to refer to such an institution-building thrust as development work. The building of the institution is undertaken with the ultimate aim of benefiting parts of the population of the country in which the institution is established.

In our analysis of means–ends relations in Chapter 6, we shall explore a case of institution-building in greater depth. However, in that case, links between intended outputs and objectives can be analysed much more directly. That is primarily because the case is a local community-based programme, in which intended beneficiaries are clearly identifiable (and in addition comprehensively involved in the scheme).

The next questions we need to address are how many levels we should specify between the outputs and the development objective and what we should call those levels. In most versions of the logical framework, which tends to be the main tool for formulating such means–ends chains, there are two levels of objectives: that is, one category between the 'outputs' and the 'development objective'. In other versions, a third level of objectives has been incorporated (see, for example, Cracknell, 2000). In practice, we may often construct means–ends chains above the outputs at more than three levels. In Figure 4.1, I have specified three levels of objectives, that is, two categories of objectives below *development objective*. I have termed them *effect objectives* and *immediate objectives* respectively.[3]

Conceptualising and formulating clear means–ends relations is often a challenging task. Persons who seek advice on this point in writings on planning and in programme and project documents will easily get confused by the variety of perspectives and even inconsistencies and cloudy statements that they may find. A main question is how directly objectives should express benefits for people: that is, who are to benefit and how. In many cases of projects that are envisaged to promote development (and often referred to as 'development projects'), even a stated top-level objective (by whatever name it goes) does not express intended improvements in people's quality of life, or does not do so in clear or unambiguous terms. However, since such improvements are the very justification for any development programme or project, this intention needs to be clarified by the highest-level objective of that thrust. If we compromise on that, we cloud the very idea of development work. Thus, we can readily agree with Eggers (2000a; 2000b; 2002), who calls this requirement the 'master principle' of such work.

Even an experienced development analyst such as Cracknell (2000) clouds the issue. As examples of development objectives (called 'goals') he mentions 'improving foreign exchange earnings' and 'integrating a remote region into the rest of the political and economic structure' (2000: 109). While, in such kinds of programmes, benefits for people may largely remain assumptions (see the argument a couple of pages back), one should not just replace statements of benefits (assumptions though they may be) with statements that are, in a means–ends perspective, of lower order.

With reference to the conventional goal–purpose constellation (see footnote 3 and later discussion), Eggers (2000a; 2000b) argues that the statement of purpose, too, must directly express benefits for people. Converted to our terminology, this means that all objectives of lower order than the development objective should also express improvements in the quality of life of the intended beneficiaries.

I agree with the view that links should be clarified and shown between the ultimate intended benefit and more specific and immediate intended benefits for people. The former will invariably be generated through the latter. Substantiating such connections is also important for monitoring and evaluation: achievements of more specific nature are normally easier to ascertain than is the general achievement expressed by the development objective.

Here, however, we are into the trickiest part of the means–ends analysis of most development schemes. At the level right below the development objective – that is, at the level of effect objectives, in our terminology – one should always be able to formulate directly people-focused achievements: that is, intended benefits for intended beneficiaries. For example, 'people drink clean water' may be a statement of benefit at that level, in a water supply scheme for a population group. Assuming that drinking of unclean water has been a main cause of poor health, the new practice should then lead to improved health of the target population. The latter may then be the project's development objective.

As mentioned, we may normally formulate more specific objectives as well, below these two levels. As should become clearer later, if we limit ourselves to only two levels, we are commonly left with the problem of a fragmented means–ends structure. That is, the gap between the outputs (signifying the direct or relatively direct outcome of implementation) and the effect objectives tends to become so big that causal links between them may get blurred. Consequently, I consider it useful to formalise at least a third level of objectives, referred to as 'immediate objectives'.

At this level, we may be somewhat less strict regarding benefit formulation, allowing a wider repertoire of less directly benefit-expressing statements. However, to be at all referred to as objectives, even statements at this level need to express some link with people. Examples of immediate objectives from cases presented in this book are or could be: 'cultivation is stabilised' (for our case of reforestation, mentioned on pp. 63–4), 'more hygienic household routines are practised' (Table 6.1) and 'informal loan taking is reduced' (Table 6.2). All express features relating to people, as a result of more directly created provisions (in our examples: area reforested/erosion reduced; information about household hygiene provided; and financial services instituted by people's organisations).

In another version of the logical framework than the presently popular one, there are three levels of objectives as well: 'development objective', 'intermediate objectives' and 'immediate objectives'. In the development field, I consider 'effect objective' to be a better term than 'intermediate objective', since, in this field, 'effect' is normally taken to denote relatively direct benefits for people.[4]

On the right side of Figure 4.1, I have formulated a set of parallel terms to the intended outputs and the set of objectives, just addressed. These are expressions of achievements that are actually being or have been generated. Such actual achievements are in focus when we monitor or evaluate what we are doing or have done. 'Outputs', 'effects' and 'impacts' are now fairly conventional terms of the development vocabulary, and are mostly understood the way they are used here. 'Direct change' is considered to express well our concern at the level of immediate objectives. With reference to our preceding discussion on this, a more accurate but more complex formulation would be 'relatively direct changes relating to people'.

One thing we must keep in mind is that changes that are induced by a development programme or project may not only be positive. There may be negative changes also. Such outcomes, too, should be examined during monitoring and evaluation.

The Logical Framework

The above discussion leads us directly to a presentation and discussion of the logical framework, which has now been mentioned in passing several times. The logical framework was formulated over 30 years ago as a tool for clarifying means–ends relations and other linkages in development work (Eggers, 2000b; Cracknell, 2000). In somcwhat different formats, it has become the most widely used tool for structuring main features of development programmes and projects. For that reason, we shall also apply it in our analysis in subsequent chapters. The purpose at this stage is to clarify the basic structure of this planning tool and briefly explore its strengths and limitations.

Table 4.1 shows the logical framework in the form we shall be using it in this book. At the upper levels, it is somewhat more elaborate than the version that is presently in vogue. The rest of the framework is in basic compliance with that version. The cells of the left column and the bottom cell of the middle column show the basic *means–ends structure* of the formulated programme or project. As we have seen, in the present conventional format there are only two levels above 'outputs', normally referred to as 'purpose' and 'goal'. The meaning of and the rationale for the three levels of objectives in our version have been given above and will be substantiated further in Chapter 6. Basically, this format gives more information in more coherent form than the conventional format, making the framework a more useful tool for planning, monitoring and evaluation.

Also note that I have made one more change from the conventional terminology regarding the means–ends structure. The most common term in the bottom cell of the first column has been 'activity', not 'implementation task', used here. My reason for this change is that 'activity' contains a notion of process, which one does not find anywhere else in the framework. Work processes are a much more comprehensive matter, involving a range of organisational and management issues that in any case need to be addressed in other ways. The corresponding process notion is more appropriately expressed by the word 'implementation' (see Figure 4.1).

The logical framework summarises means–ends relations that will normally have been analysed earlier in greater detail, using other methods and techniques. Such tools of more comprehensive analysis will be addressed in later chapters.

The first four cells of the second column show *indicators*. In both scientific and more common usage, an 'indicator' is normally understood as a brief expression of a more comprehensive and usually more complex

Table 4.1 The Logical Framework

DEVELOPMENT OBJECTIVE	INDICATORS	ASSUMPTIONS
The overall intended improvement in the quality of life of the intended beneficiaries	Measures to ascertain to what extent the intended improvement is materialising or has materialised	Requirements in the society for sustainability of the generated improvements
EFFECT OBJECTIVES	INDICATORS	ASSUMPTIONS
Relatively specific intended benefits for the intended beneficiaries, considered necessary to attain the development objective	Measures to ascertain to what extent the intended benefits are materialising or have materialised	Requirements in the environment of the programme or project for attainment of the development objective
IMMEDIATE OBJECTIVES	INDICATORS	ASSUMPTIONS
Expected people-linked changes, considered necessary to attain the effect objectives	Measure to ascertain to what extent the expected changes are occuring or have occurred	Requirements in the environment of the programme or project for attainment of the effect objectives
OUTPUTS	INDICATORS	ASSUMPTIONS
The planned direct results of the work that is done, considered necessary to attain the immediate objectives	Measure to ascertain to what extent the planned outputs are being created or have been created	Requirements in the environment of the programme or project for attainment of the immediate objectives
IMPLEMENTATION TASKS	INPUTS	ASSUMPTIONS
The pieces of work that have to be undertaken to create the expected outputs	The resources that are needed to undertake the intended work	Requirements relating to the programme or project for creating the planned outputs

phenomenon.[5] In order to be useful, an indicator should fulfil certain basic requirements. Most importantly, it should be a good reflector of the phenomenon it indicates – or, at least, of some part of the phenomenon; it should express an important feature of the phenomenon; and it should be as unambiguous and trustworthy as possible. Additionally, in planning and other scientific pursuits, an indicator should be reasonably convenient to use.

In development work, we use indicators to substantiate whether or to what extent we have created the outputs or attained the objectives that we have planned for. We may then refer to indicators as 'measures'. By this we mean any number or any brief and concise verbal statement that serves the purpose of substantiation.

Numbers may be arrived at through direct measurement or through manipulation of verbal statements (for example, the frequency distribution of answers to a question, by specified categories of answers). Since numbers are concise and unambiguous, they tend to be good indicators whenever they also meet other requirements. As we shall make clear, that is often not the case, because development realities are commonly too complex to be adequately expressed by simple numerical statements. Therefore, we often have to use verbal expressions. We shall devote Chapter 7 to a further analysis of indicators.[6]

The third column of the logical framework addresses factors in the environment of the planned programme or project of importance to its performance and achievements. Thus, the statements in this column express conditions under which attainments at one level of the means–ends structure are expected to be converted into attainments at the level above. We shall refer to these conditions as *assumptions*.

Most often, assumptions are actual or potential influences on which the organisation (or the set of organisations) responsible for the programme or project has very limited or no influence. This notion is directly expressed by the common alternative terms 'external factors' and 'external conditions' (see NORAD, 1990/1992/1996; Dale, 1998; Cracknell, 2000).

Some examples of possible external factors that should be easy to understand are: the weather (over which hardly any single development scheme has any influence); religion (hardly ever directly addressed in planned development work); and relevant national legislation in relation to a community development programme (normally beyond the scope of such programmes).

What will be internal, and what external, to a development scheme is directly related to the purpose and design of the scheme, and is a major consideration in strategic planning. For instance, an urban slum development project may be limited to the provision of physical infrastructure, leaving aspects such as the residents' perceptions, community institutions and relevant official regulations unconsidered and unaddressed. Such factors may then influence the performance and achievements of the project, in various and often hardly predictable ways. Alternatively, one may broaden the scope of the project to encompass components such as social mobilisation, organisation building and relevant aspects of municipality legislation. Thereby, one may not only remove constraints relating to the construction and operation of infrastructure, but also create synergy effects of various kinds and obtain larger overall impact. On the other hand, the project will become more challenging to plan and manage.

Even if variables such as weather, religion and legislation may be entirely external – framework conditions that may not be influenced at all – the interface between a development scheme and its environment may not be a clear-cut dividing line, but a rather porous, blurred and sometimes also changing boundary. A project for promoting the nutrition of undernourished children, for example, may not influence the ability of households to spend money on food at all, but it may influence people's acceptance of alternative food items, through training on nutrition. At the same time, the acceptability of food will be influenced by numerous factors beyond the scope of the project, and it will be impossible to draw a clear boundary between influence and non-influence.

The assumptions, as understood in the logical framework, relate directly to the concepts of 'opportunity', 'constraint' and 'threat', introduced in Chapter 2. In Figure 2.1, these terms were linked to time, broadly categorised as the present and the future. The resultant categories – 'present opportunities', 'future opportunities', '(present) constraints' and '(future) threats' – constitute a typology of contextual variables that is highly useful in planning. The typology helps structure an exploration of factors that the programme or project organisation may have to relate to, and it promotes constructive analysis of ways and means of exploiting or adjusting to various relevant contextual factors. The context of programmes and projects and relations between internal and external variables will be further explored in Chapter 8.

The *strengths* of the logical framework ought now to be reasonably clear. The main ones are: emphasis on clear objectives, promotion of a logical and internally consistent means–ends structure, linking of intended achievements to measures for substantiating the achievements (indicators), and explicit attention to assumptions on which the programme or project is based. Moreover, the simple format makes the framework attractive both as a planning tool and as a means for conveying basic information about a programme or project to organisations and persons that are not directly involved in planning and management of the scheme. Examples may be funding agencies, the top tier or person of involved organisations (for instance, the general director of a government department) and the general public.

The logical framework has strict *limitations* too, with related risks in the use of it. Unfortunately, due to its simplicity and relative ease of application, uncritical usage has been common (Eggers, 2000a; 2000b; Cracknell, 2000; Dale, 2003). Basically, while much essential information is compressed within very limited space, important dimensions of planning are not incorporated in the framework. First, there is no mention of problems and stakeholders. The logical framework builds on the assumption that adequate analysis of these has been undertaken, as a basis for the means–ends relations that are specified. Second, the framework excludes altogether the crucial planning dimension of organisation. Third, there is no provision for clarifying unintended effects.

The omission of underlying problems, stakeholder interests and aspects of organisation may have had substantial negative implications for conceptions of development planning and related practices. It has probably contributed to a notion of planning as a rather mechanistic exercise, not sufficiently connected to the ever-present complexity of needs, interests and power structures, as well as requirements of organisation and management.

Whether we should consider these omissions as shortcomings in the logical framework itself is the additional question we ought to ask. The attractiveness of the framework largely lies in its structural clarity and simplicity, being closely related to its brevity and restriction of coverage. Thus, the main challenge may not be to change the logical framework substantially, but to promote a better understanding among its users of the framework's limitations, and of the need to consider it as only one tool (albeit often a major one) within a broader thrust of development planning.

Of course, many promoters and users of the logical framework recognise such shortcomings. Some trainers of logical framework-related planning have even incorporated problem analysis and stakeholder analysis into their training programmes. Unfortunately, such broader exercises have still tended to be too much connected to the logical framework (as a schema), indicated by the commonly used term 'logical framework analysis'. This is certainly a good indication of the superior status that the logical framework has attained in development organisations (particularly donor agencies of various kinds, but also others). In addition, however, it may reveal an uncritical perspective on development work.

The logical framework was devised within the tradition of a technocratic notion of development and a corresponding approach to planning for societal change. As conventionally used, the framework is the more applicable and helpful the more technical, clearly delimited and predetermined the intervention is. First, these features facilitate the formulation of inputs, tasks, outputs and objectives at the level of specificity that is usually expected in conventional planning. Second, highly specified achievements facilitate the formulation of quantitative indicators, another requirement of such an approach. By implication, we may also conclude that the conventional logical framework catches more of the reality of projects than of programmes, and may be more suitable for some types of projects than for other types.

A pertinent question is whether specific conventions relating to the framework may be modified or at least loosened somewhat, in order to make the framework meaningful and useful for more open and flexible development thrusts as well. We have already indicated that we may use a broader spectrum of indicators than has normally been considered as appropriate. This question will be further explored in Chapter 7. In Chapter 6, we shall explore how and to what extent basic concerns and features of broader and more flexible programmes may be structured in means–ends form, suitable for incorporation in the framework.

Irrespective of such considerations, the logical framework should not be viewed as the centrepiece of development planning, around which every other concern and all other activities revolve. The more appropriate perspective is to consider development planning as a much broader and more complex thrust, only limited parts of which may be connected to and structured in the logical framework.[7]

Adding Dimensions of Organisation

Organisational ability in development work

As already mentioned, the logical framework has nothing to say about organisation. Even the broader 'logical framework analysis' does not purport to examine this dimension of development work substantially. Still, as we have mentioned in many contexts, aspects of organisation are crucial for the performance and achievements of development programmes and projects. The main work processes of planning, implementation and monitoring, and frequently also operation and maintenance, are organised activities.

'Organisation' includes two interrelated notions: *responsibility* and *capability*. One or more organisations are responsible for planning, implementation and monitoring, and commonly for any operation and maintenance that may be done. In order to be able to perform these functions, the organisations structure themselves physically in specific ways, and they apply rules, systems of administration, technologies and personnel incentives. All these features are, to varying extents, interconnected with the culture of the organisations, and they influence the way the work is managed and coordinated.

Figure 4.2, building on Figure 4.1, illustrates links between organisational ability and the work that is performed in a development programme or project. The main general message is one of interconnections. The ability of the involved organisation or organisations influences, directly and strongly, the processes and the quality of work – and, therewith, the achievements – of any development scheme. This is shown in the figure by arrows from 'organisational ability' to the various work categories.

Organisational ability is no constant, however, but may change or be changed substantially. It may be augmented by increasing the competence and work capacity of individuals in the organisation and/or by adjusting or changing organisational rules, structures or systems. Individual competence and capacity may be enhanced by recruiting additional qualified personnel, through formalised training of already employed personnel, or by creating a learning environment that encourages staff to increase their ability through work experience. Normally, the last-mentioned mechanism is very important for organisational development. In dynamic organisations, learning (by individuals and groups) will, in turn, often influence other features of organisations (rules, form, work systems and/or incentives, together with aspects of organisational culture). Such feedback from work performance to the ability of the respective organisation or organisations is shown in the figure by arrows from planning and other work categories to 'organisational ability'.

There are two categories of work in Figure 4.2 that do not appear in Figure 4.1, namely, operation and maintenance. They are shown as influencing the transformation of outputs into benefits for people (attainment of programme or project objectives). Normally, these activities, too, need to be organised, and the same basic links exist between them and organisational ability as for the other work categories.

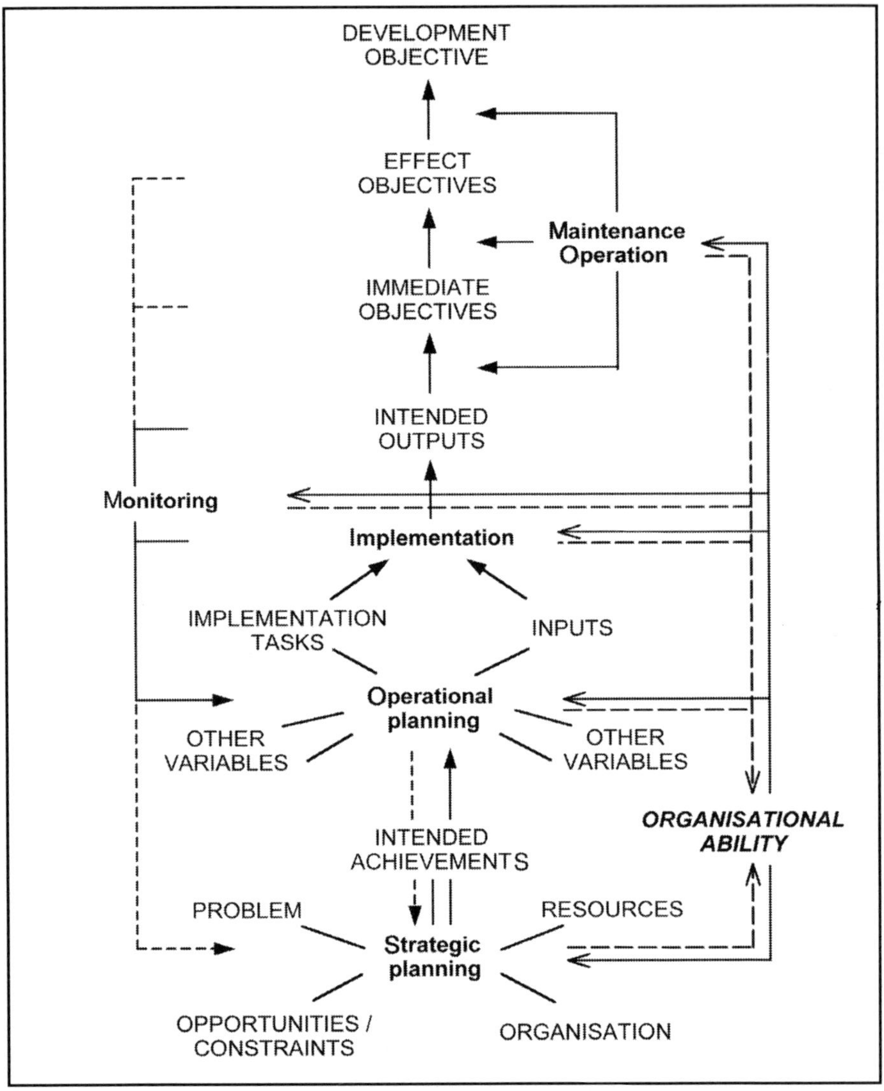

Figure 4.2 Linking Development Work and Organisation

Main variables of organisation

I shall here give a concise overview of main features of organisation that frequently need to be considered and analysed in the planning of development programmes and projects.[8] We have already met, in Figure 2.2, a set of basic organisational variables that are widely applicable to development organisations. Brief definitions and elaborations follow.

An organisation's *form* stands for the number and types of units within the organisation and main relations of work between these units. It reflects the purpose and sphere of work of the organisation and predominant patterns of communication, responsibility and power. Dale (2000a) distinguishes between the following main forms of development organisations:

- *collective*: a group of people who work together for a common purpose, more than casually, on relatively equal terms;
- *one-leader body*: an organisation, usually small, in which one person directly guides and oversees all major affairs;
- *hierarchy*: a firmly structured organisation, having one person in overall charge at the top and an increasing number of units at successively lower levels, each of which has a manager, being responsible for the work of that unit as well as any linked units at lower levels;
- *loosely coupled network*: an entity, often of changing size, consisting of people who primarily work together on a case-to-case basis, often through changing partnerships and normally relating to one another on fairly equal terms;
- *matrix*: one organisation or a constellation of organisations or parts of them in which individuals are responsible to two managers (or sets of managers) for various parts of the work that they do.

All these forms have their strengths and their weaknesses, and may be suitable for different pursuits and environments. For example, the collective may be appropriate for relatively simple activities done by small numbers of equals; some form of hierarchy will be needed for work according to bureaucratic principles; and the loosely coupled network, by its flexibility, may respond best to challenges in uncertain and changing environments.

Like most typologies, this one represents an approximation of more complex realities. While most development organisations are at least primarily characterised by features of one of the mentioned forms, a few may be more difficult to locate in this framework. One reason may be that they are changing. For instance, a one-leader body may gradually be transformed into a hierarchy as it grows, because the leader may no longer have the capacity to be in direct charge of all that is done.

The concept of organisational *culture* has its roots in the anthropological concept of 'social culture'. Generally stated, an organisation's culture is the set of values, norms and perceptions that frame and guide the behaviour of individuals in the organisation and the organisation as a whole, along with connected social and physical features (artefacts) constructed by the organisation's members. All these facets of culture are usually strongly influenced by the customs of the society in which the organisation is located.

Values are closely linked to the organisation's vision and mission (see Chapter 3). They may be very important for development organisations. Many such organisations are even founded on a strong common belief in specific qualities of societies, which then becomes an effective guiding principle for the work that they do. Usually, the ability to further such qualities will then also be perceived by the members as a main reward for their contribution. Commonly, people may not even get any payment for the time they spend and the efforts they put in.

Examples of important *norms* and *perceptions* in organisations may be: the extent of individualism or group conformity; innovativeness and attitudes to new ideas and proposals for change; the degree of loyalty *vis-à-vis* colleagues, particularly in directly work-related matters; the extent of concern for the personal well-being of colleagues; perceptions of customers or beneficiaries; and perceptions of strains and rewards in one's work.

In a study of people's organisations with micro-financial services as a core activity, Dale (2002a) found that the following features of culture were particularly important for good performance and sustainability of the organisations: open access for everybody to organisation-related information; regular (commonly formalised) sharing of information; active participation by all (or virtually all) the members in common activities; respect for and adherence to agreed formal and informal rules of behaviour; sensitivity to special problems and needs of individual members; and a willingness to sacrifice something personally for the common good.

Values, norms and related perceptions of importance for organisational performance may, of course, differ among the organisation's members. Influencing and unifying an organisation's culture is often one of the main challenges for the organisation's leader or leaders.

Rules are provisions for regulating the behaviour of individuals in the organisation and of the organisation as a whole, in internal matters and in dealings with outside bodies. Rules are needed for two main purposes: (1) to properly institutionalise organisational values and norms, by which they will permeate the organisation's pursuits; and (2) to promote work efficiency. Rules may be formalised to larger or lesser extents. Normally, they are then formulated in writing, in greater or lesser detail. Highly formalised rules for processes of work are commonly referred to as 'procedures'. But rules may also be less formal and sometimes even entirely informal. In such cases, they may be quite direct manifestations of the organisation's culture, and the distinction between culture and rules becomes blurred.

Administrative systems encompass all formally designed and established routines and formats for coordinating and controlling the organisation's work. In most organisations beyond a minimum size, main examples of administrative systems are: management information systems (including monitoring systems), financial accounting systems and personnel management systems.

An organisation's *technology* encompasses the set of tools that the organisation uses to plan, implement and monitor its work, along with the knowledge in using the tools. In development organisations, concepts, methods and techniques of planning programmes or projects are essential, as are guidelines for implementing and monitoring planned activities. More specific tools for converting inputs into outputs are also needed. Examples may be: a teaching methodology, techniques of organisation building, and physical things such as hand tools, machines and energy. More specific aspects of a monitoring technology are methods and techniques of generating, processing and using information about performance.

Of course, the degree of sophistication of technologies varies vastly. Moreover, in some kinds of development work, planning, implementation and monitoring may be so closely interrelated that one may not easily distinguish clearly between technologies for each of them. In particular, this may be the case for simple or recurrent activities of collective organisations and for programmes with predominantly process planning. As we have seen, a characteristic of the latter is the use of monitoring as a mechanism for generating information for subsequent planning.

Incentives are the rewards that the organisation's personnel get from the work that they do, in terms of money, other tangible benefits, and intangible benefits (such as work satisfaction). Formalised reward mechanisms may be referred to as a reward system, which may be considered as one of the organisation's administrative systems. Most organisations have some reward system. However, as mentioned, in many development organisations, non-formalised, intangible rewards may be at least as important as the tangible ones, and sometimes they are even the only kind of reward.

In addition to the basic organisational variables that have been outlined above, I shall briefly mention some other highly important dimensions of organisation that we may consider to be of a more derivatory nature. In other words, they are variables that are influenced or even largely determined by the variables already addressed. At the same time, there may be some influence in the other direction also; in other words, there may be more or less complex interrelations between the variables.

Management and *leadership*, while not easy to define precisely, are crucial for the performance of organisations, including development organisations. The two terms are sometimes used interchangeably, or largely so. In other instances, management is considered as the wider term, embedding leadership. For example, Mintzberg (1989) refers to the leader role as one among several management roles. It involves motivating and inspiring the people in the organisation, for which the leader needs vision, a good sense of judgement, and ability and clout to guide. Beside this leadership role, the manager is also expected to play the roles of figurehead, liaison person, monitor, disseminator of information, spokesperson, entrepreneur, disturbance handler, resource allocator and negotiator. Others consider leadership to also encompass endeavours such as developing a clear vision of the organisation's future, building a supportive organisational culture, and creating and responding to opportunities in the organisation's environment (see, for example, AIT, 1998).

Coordination is an important concept of organisation. Unfortunately, in the development field, the term has tended to be used rather loosely. This has reduced its analytical value correspondingly. Drawing on work by Mintzberg in the business sphere (particularly, Mintzberg, 1983), I have in other contexts (Dale, 1992; 2000a) formulated a typology of means of coordination that should be of direct relevance and applicability for most development organisations in relation to most of the work that they do. Basically, the typology should help promote an understanding of mechanisms of interaction and corresponding measures to improve collaboration towards common aims.

Dale (2000a) broadly defines coordination as the harmonisation of work that is done by various units within an organisation or by collaborating organisations. It is accomplished through a range of alternative or complementary mechanisms that are brought into play in specific tasks. The mechanisms specified by Dale are:

- promoting a common vision;
- establishing common objectives;
- standardising outputs;
- standardising skills;
- routinising work;
- direct supervision;
- mutual adjustment.

The most effective combination of coordination mechanisms in any particular programme or project depends on numerous factors. They may be summarised broadly as: the size and complexity of the development scheme; the mode of planning that is applied; the size, form and other features of the organisation or organisations that are responsible for the scheme; and opportunities, constraints and threats in the environment of the responsible organisation or organisations.

Participation is another main dimension of organisation that has received increasing attention in much development work. Linked to the concept of stakeholder (see Chapter 2), it may be used with a variety of meanings, largely depending on its scope. In the development sphere, it is most often applied in the sense of 'people's participation'. This is broadly understood as participation in some development work by ordinary people in local communities, who are frequently also the intended beneficiaries of the development work that is intended to be done or is being done.

Participation by intended beneficiaries and other stakeholders may be promoted for a range of reasons and may have various effects, for the development thrust and for the persons involved. The potential scope of people's participation is well expressed by the following three notions, presented by Oakley *et al.* (1991):

- participation as contribution;
- participation as organising;
- participation as empowering.

People's participation may be analysed along several other axes as well. Examples are: free–forced, spontaneous–induced, direct–indirect, comprehensive–selective (partial) and intensive–extensive. People-centred development work, including the rationale, modes and processes of participatory planning, will be analysed further in Chapter 10.

Notes

1 Adjustive planning has much less substance and is disregarded here.

2 The role of monitoring may vary substantially between types of programmes and projects. It tends to be particularly closely related to the planning dimension of process–blueprint. See Chapters 3 and 10.

3 Another set of terms for denoting objectives is now fashionable, namely, 'goal' and 'purpose' for objectives at the first and second level respectively. In particular, this is the case among proponents of the so-called logical framework approach. For reasons that will be clarified in Chapter 6, I consider 'goal–purpose' to be a poor pair of terms for expressing means–ends relations in development work.

4 At this point in the book, the discussion above may have appeared theoretical, and the practical implications may not have been easy to grasp. The issues involved should become clearer when we present examples of cause–effect and means–ends structures in following chapters.
5 In our daily lives, we think of fever as an indicator of illness; a laugh as an indicator of joy; and the barometer stand as an indicator of certain aspects of the weather.
6 Among trainers of the so-called logical framework approach a peculiar habit has crept in of using the 'indicator' column for elaborating the components of the means–ends structure to which they refer – contrary to ordinary usage. For a further critique of this and other aspects of the logical framework and how it is used, see also Dale, 2003.
7 For a further discussion of this issue, see Dale, 2003.
8 It falls beyond the scope of this book to examine in detail relations between organisational variables and the performance of development schemes. For further reading on this topic, see, for example, Cusworth and Franks, 1993 and Dale, 2000a.

Chapter 5

Problem Analysis

Conceptualising Development Problems

Development work aims at improving the quality of life of people. In order to achieve such improvements, the work must be based on an adequate understanding of problems that afflict the intended beneficiaries. The problems to be addressed will depend on the mission of the respective development organisations and any additional overall aims of programmes or projects that they undertake. These factors will also influence the breadth and depth of the problem analysis that will be required or desirable.

For instance, a national Department of Primary Education will have a relatively narrow, clearly defined and stable purpose for its work. The Department addresses a specific development aspect for a clearly defined and little-changing target group, usually over the whole country. The Department will consider the focus of concern to be basically the same everywhere (a need for children of specific ages to acquire certain attitudes and knowledge). Normally, the Department will undertake no specific problem analysis in individual communities.

An NGO with a broad community development mission faces quite different challenges. This organisation may undertake various activities for different groups, in response to different problems, within and between communities. Consequently, the problems must be explored more typically 'from the ground up'. Moreover, to the extent that process planning is applied for the work that is done (as is normal in community development programmes), problems and measures may be re-examined frequently, often over a long programme period.

In a development perspective, human problems may be perceived as *deprivations* of various kinds. As stated in Chapter 1, a deprivation may be defined broadly as a material and/or non-material state of an individual or a household that is below a level considered to be acceptable. Certain material dimensions of deprivation are normally referred to as *poverty*.

Deprivations should be seen as existing along a more or less continuous range, from the strongest absolute deprivation to increasingly relative ones (see also Chapter 1). The three following examples should succinctly illustrate this:

- a mother who is desperately looking at her child dying of hunger without having any means of feeding it;
- a mother and head of household who just manages to provide her children and herself with the basic necessities of life, but who can obtain hardly anything beyond that;
- a single woman employed in the public sector in a highly developed country, who feels underpaid compared to most other employees of that country, but who still enjoys much greater material comfort than the large majority of women in most countries.

As we move towards deprivations of increasingly relative nature, we may feel that the very term 'deprivation' becomes more and more watered down and even inappropriate. In reality, individual persons' perceptions of acceptable standards of living will be influenced strongly by variables such as the society they live and work in, the work they do, many other aspects of their life situation, their knowledge of other realities and their degree of personal empathy.

Generating Information about Problems

Qualitative and quantitative approaches

In development planning, as in many other professions, it has become common to distinguish broadly between *qualitative* and *quantitative* modes of searching, processing and presenting information. In the former, words and sentences are the only or main analytical tool; in the latter, statements in numerical form are primary.

These categories of generating and managing information – searching, processing and presenting – are normally closely related, in that the approach that is applied in one of them has strong bearings on the approach in the others. As in most conventional science, much development research and planning is undertaken in a series of clearly designed steps: data collection is succeeded by data processing and then presentation

Table 5.1 Qualitative and Quantitative Approaches to Information Generation and Management

QUALITATIVE	QUANTITATIVE
Sampling of study units through personal judgement	Sampling of study units through predetermined criteria and techniques
Flexible overall research design	Predetermined and unchangeable research design
Enquiry through more than one method	Enquiry through one method only
Facilitates incorporation of a broad range of research variables and allows high complexity of variables	Reduces the field of investigation to what is statistically controllable
Allows direct exploration of processes of change	Confinement to the contemporary or to different points in time
Information recorded in flexible formats	Information recorded in fixed form in predetermined categories
Substantiating relations through reasoning and interpretation	Verifying relations through statistical testing
Participation in analysis by non-professionals possible	Analysis by professionals only

Source: Based on: Dale, 1998

of the findings. With such a design, there will be a one-way dependency chain, from the first to the last step. Alternatively, one may apply a more generative design, in which the perceived need for information and the gathering and processing of that information are interrelated and evolving, through processes of cumulative learning and, commonly, increasing capacity for managing the information.

The clearly step-patterned design is a hallmark of quantitative analysis, particularly when statistical testing is involved. Reliable statistical associations may only be produced from relatively large numbers of directly comparable data of unambiguous and specific nature. Such data may, in turn, only be collected through a pre-determined approach. A basically qualitative design, on the other hand, allows much greater flexibility in searching and analysing information and substantial interaction between the two.

The main general features of qualitative and quantitative approaches to information generation and management are summed up in Table 5.1. This conceptual framework helps guide the design and pursuit of any systematic problem analysis in any society. In problem analysis relating to development work, a purely quantitative approach is hardly ever either useful or feasible. This is mainly because the topics and issues that are addressed are too complex and fluid for rigorous quantitative analysis. Another reason may often be that one wants to involve people who are not skilled in such analysis.

While qualitative approaches are needed to analyse human problems, the analysis may include some quantification. For instance, some qualitative information may be converted into quantitative categories on an ordinal measurement scale (discussed in more detail later). Often, certain primary data of a quantitative nature may be collected as well, usually to supplement specific parts of the analysis. I shall not elaborate this general framework through further theoretical reasoning here, but proceed more indirectly through practice-related exploration in this and later chapters.[1]

Methods of generating information

The scope of this book does not permit any comprehensive exploration of methods for gathering and analysing information. For that, the reader is referred to textbooks on research methodology. The purpose of the brief presentation to follow is to give an overview of the variety of methods at one's disposal and the main strengths and weaknesses of each of them.

One intention in this overview is to sensitise readers to differences that commonly exist between, on the one hand, approaches in practical development work and, on the other hand, academic conventions about information gathering and processing. The latter tend to dominate in textbooks on research methods, and they are still reflected in much development research. Information for planning is normally, and often necessarily, generated through a more varied and flexible menu of tools than the rigid methodology that tends to be promoted in textbooks, even for development-focused studies.

Informal and formal observation

In our context, 'observation' means carefully looking at or listening to something or somebody, with the aim of gaining insight for planning. A range of phenomena may be observed: physical facilities, for example, or the work done by some people, or organisational performance.

Observation may be informal or more or less formalised. Informal observation may be more or less casual or premeditated. An example of casual informal observation may be an unplanned assessment by the head of a district roads department of the quality of a road under his or her purview, as the person drives on it; an example of formal observation may be a scheduled trip on the road by that person for the purpose of getting information about the road's quality.

Sometimes, observation may be the only or the main method for generating information for planning. More commonly, observation is a more or less important or necessary supplementary method.

Lobbying

With the possible exception of some action research, lobbying can hardly be referred to as a research method. This is because the initiative for communication is taken by the information provider, normally also meaning that this person or body sets the agenda and may largely determine the mode of communication. Still, in many instances lobbying is an important mechanism by which information is provided to planners and decision takers (such as politicians). Its importance and acceptability may vary greatly across societies and specific settings.

Commonly, stakeholders may view lobbying as a necessary or opportune means of getting their views across, often in competition with other views. Paradoxically, this may be the case in contrasting political and administrative environments: under authoritarian regimes open to unequal treatment of groups or individuals, and in highly democratic societies with a tradition of broad participation. In the former, lobbying constitutes part of and reinforces a culture of disguise and favouritism, which open-minded development planners and facilitators would consider as unfortunate or even unacceptable. In the latter, lobbying may be positive within certain limits. Beyond such limits, however, it may lead to greater inequality in the possibility of being heard and may even, in extreme situations, choke rational decision making.

Meetings

In democratic societies, meetings are often major events for generating information about development problems for planners and decision takers. Depending on the composition of the audience and the matters discussed, the meetings may also be forums for discussion among the participants. Another strength is that ideas and opinions tend to be widely disseminated and known, usually also through some kind of subsequent written report (minutes). A main limitation of meetings as information-generating events is their formal nature, which may influence the composition of participants as well as limit active participation to the most vocal persons.

Facilitated group discussions

In group discussions, the participants are expected to communicate actively on relatively equal terms, in an open and secure atmosphere. Such events are, therefore, facilitated rather than led by somebody. To be effective, the groups should be of limited size, and the participants may be purposively chosen. Sometimes, parallel groups of relative equals (for instance, female and male or long-term and new settlers) may address the same matter. Information may be generated for use by an organisation of the discussants or by others.

If well planned and facilitated, group discussions are in many instances a particularly effective (and often underutilised) method of generating, within a short time, much information of high relevance, significance and reliability.

Casual conversation

While hardly recognised as a method in most scientific research, casual conversation is often an important means of generating information for planning. It may substantially augment the planners' understanding of the environment they work in and even of the performance and effects of development schemes. For instance, it may be the main resort of a facilitator in generating the basic information that she or he needs for subsequent support to community-based people's organisations, and it may provide important feedback from intended beneficiaries to programme personnel during field visits by the latter.

Collective brainstorming

This is intensive and open-minded collective communication that a group agrees to embark on in a specific situation. It may be a useful method for analysing a problem that is clearly recognised and shared by all the participants. The method may be particularly effective if the problem occurs or is aggravated suddenly or unexpectedly, in which case the participants may feel an urge to solve or ameliorate it. It may be resorted to in organisations (particularly, collective ones) or in non-organised contexts.

Questionnaire surveys

Here, several persons are asked the same questions. The questions may be closed or more or less open. That is, they may require precise brief answers or they may invite some elaboration (for instance, a judgement) in the respondents' own words. Depending on its nature, the information is then further processed quantitatively or qualitatively.

This method is superior whenever one wants information of the same kind from large numbers of people as a basis for planning. It also enables the study of statistically representative samples of units. This extensive coverage may also be the method's main weakness, particularly if one is under time pressure. The information that is generated may then be too shallow to provide adequate understanding, because of limited opportunity to explore in depth, and often also because different persons may be employed to gather the information, restricting cumulative learning.

Surveys that comply with textbook requirements of representativity and rigour are, normally, comprehensive thrusts. In most planning contexts, they are therefore considered to be too time-consuming. Thus, whenever such surveys are done by planners, simpler and more open versions tend to be used. The simplest are often referred to as checklist surveys (exploration guided by a pre-specified list of topics or issues to be covered).

Systematic rapid assessment

This is the equivalent of what is more commonly called rapid rural appraisal (RRA). I use this alternative term because the method is applicable beyond appraisal (as normally understood), and because it may be used in both rural and urban settings. By rapid assessment is meant, in the present context, a composite approach for generating information for planning within a short period of time. That information may be all that we think we need, or it may constitute part of that information.

The method may involve the use of many techniques such as quick observation, informal communication with key informants (casual or preplanned), brief group discussions and, sometimes, checklist surveys. The assessment is often undertaken by a team of persons, each of whom may have different professional background and a prime responsibility for exploring specific matters. Broader judgements and conclusions are then normally arrived at through frequent communication among the team members.

When used by a team, this method may create synergies of knowledge generation among the information gatherers. For this reason and because simple techniques are used, it may also be cost-effective. A common weakness is that the generated information may not be as representative as desirable. Even more importantly, if one is not careful, important matters may be left unattended or inadequately analysed.

Participatory analysis

This is also the equivalent of a more conventional term, participatory rural appraisal (PRA). Another familiar term is participatory learning and action (PLA). These terms have come to be applied as a common denominator for an array of techniques by which non-professionals jointly explore problems, plan and/or evaluate in a workshop setting.

The people who participate in the problem analysis (in focus here) are most often intended beneficiaries of an envisaged connected programme or project. The scheme may be planned and implemented by the participants themselves, by one or more external organisations, or by a combination of the two. Commonly used techniques of participatory analysis are simple charting and mapping, various forms of simple ranking, grouping of phenomena (in simple tables, for instance) and – less frequently – oral accounts (including community stories and individual life stories).

The general justification for participatory problem analysis in the present context is quite obvious. It is to involve ordinary people in analysing problems in their environment (and frequently affecting themselves) that may be addressed in some way. Commonly, this is also based on a general ideology of democratic development. A more specific justification may be to generate more valid and reliable information than one thinks may otherwise be possible.

Main limitations may be the organisation-intensive nature of such exercises and the long time that the participants are often expected to spend in the workshops. Moreover, in my experience, the purpose of some visual techniques (such as village mapping and listing of ranked phenomena) is often unclear, for both the initiators and the participants, and the outcome of such exercises may be of uncertain use.

In-depth case studies

These are thorough and often long-lasting explorations. Common tools of analysis are long formal interviews, in-depth informal or semi-formal communication with key informants, focused group discussions and participatory observation. Most of the information will be qualitative and requires further analysis of qualitative nature.

A familiar method in certain types of social science research, in-depth case studies are rarely used in problem analysis in relation to planned development work. This is primarily due to the amount of time (and sometimes other resources) that is required for it. One example of the useful application of the method may be anthropological exploration in some local communities in preparation for an envisaged community-based development programme, for instance by an NGO in a new programme country.

Direct measurement

For planning certain kinds of physical facilities, in particular, the planners may have to acquire information through measurement. When planning an irrigation scheme, for instance, they need to know such things as the size of the water catchment, the amount of precipitation (including its average, distribution and variability over specified periods), the rate of run-off and numerous measurable land features. If this information has not already been acquired or is not accessible for some reason, the planners will have to collect raw data, through appropriate methods of measurement, and process those data as needed.

Examining already documented information

In most cases of problem analysis for planning, parts of the information that is needed are acquired from existing documents, usually referred to as secondary sources. Common examples are reports of various kinds (from brief notes to scientific documents), maps (general and thematic) and statistics (such as census data and other statistical data produced by government agencies).

Verbal Analysis

We shall now explore means of further analysing information that has been gathered through one or more of the above methods. Expressions through words and sentences – verbal expressions – are by far the most common and most widely applicable mode of analysis in the development field. This includes, of course, analysis of problems that one may intend to address.

Let us start by looking at brief excerpts from three pieces of verbal analysis. They have been done by the same person (myself, sometimes with others) and relate to the same country. The excerpts are modified from the original versions to a limited extent in order to make some arguments more succinct.

1 The interviewed persons were asked to say what they thought were the main obstacles to development in their local community. The large majority emphasised damaging or constraining interpersonal relations. These included jealousy towards one another, a habit of stealing, a general lack of interest in matters that would need collective effort, poor leadership and a divisive effect of party politics. Beyond this set of factors, most respondents of the poorest households emphasised lack of land. Most respondents of households with irrigable land, who tended to be relatively well-off, expressed dissatisfaction with the state of the irrigation facilities, while farmers with no irrigable land deplored skewed benefits of existing irrigation systems. A few persons mentioned poor physical infrastructure other than irrigation facilities, such as bad roads and inadequate water supply. Only a couple of the respondents mentioned problems relating to health or education. (Modified from: Dale and Hesselberg, 1979)

2 For understanding social differentiation and its consequences for the quality of life of people, we need to study aspects of social and economic power, the distribution of resources, and the decision-making processes that determine the control of and access to resources.... Access to land and related resources along with the terms of and conditions for such access are crucial. They constitute much of the basis for the social structure and are commonly the primary source of power for the rural élite. This land-based élite determines terms of relations between people that are crucial for the persistence of poverty. Another feature is the structure of the markets and the intermediaries who largely control them, yielding considerable power to the latter over the material status of people. Merchants, moneylenders and village traders are the main intermediaries.

Exploitation of poor people in this context takes many forms. Crucial is dependence on financial capital on terms that many cannot cope with. Unable either to accumulate their own savings or obtain loans from formal institutions, poor people borrow from merchants and other persons who lend money at very high interest rates. In order to get such loans, many have to mortgage their land and some lose it. (Slightly modified from: Iddagoda and Dale, 1997)

During this period, the Village Councils were suppressed by the central government, through regulations and control and through the promotion of alternative local institutions, having standardised roles specified by the central government. The three main types of alternative institutions were Rural Development Societies, organisations for agricultural development and various kinds of cooperatives.

The Rural Development Societies had long existed and had been supported by alternating governments. They now became even more politicised, in the sense that their leaders were in reality required to be active supporters of the governing political party. The Agricultural Productivity Committees at the divisional level and the corresponding Cultivation Committees at the village level took over the role of the Vel Vidane [traditional local community institution] and the Village Councils, particularly in irrigation management and paddy cultivation. Although supposed to be farmers' organisations, they largely came to be made up of persons nominated by the government. Among the set of cooperative organisations, the multipurpose cooperatives were particularly actively promoted and developed into a state trading network with monopolistic features.

A positive aspect of these institutional changes was greater opportunity for sections of the population to partake in decision making about local affairs. However, this mainly applied to politically favoured people. The political affiliation of those with power also tended to make them biased for or against other people, with negative consequences for distribution of benefits and communal unity. (Slightly modified from: Dale, 1992)

The above statements provide some pointers to main dimensions and issues of problem analysis. First, excerpt 1 indicates, in highly general terms, the *relative importance* of problems, in this case as perceived by local community inhabitants. The statement also indicates *different perceptions* of problems among different groups of people, according to their economic standing and/or occupation. This links to additional issues of social stratification and structure, exemplified in excerpt 2. Obviously, the importance of problems and who experiences them are crucial in relation to development planning.

Second, excerpt 2, in particular, indicates *interrelations* of factors, constituting what we may call a problem structure. Such interrelations are of a cause–effect nature, and are often referred to as cause–effect structures. In this case, access to cultivable land, the terms of such access and the structure of markets are said to generate social differentiation and poverty. These, in turn, may reinforce the dependency on powerful people, through indebtedness and loss of assets. Societal problems tend to be complex and may only be effectively combated if we can trace and understand relations of cause and effect. Components of problem structures and relations between them may be more or less overt or difficult to discern.

Third, problems or problem components may be more or less direct or indirect expressions of deprivations of people. Consequently, problem analyses may differ greatly in terms of their *focus and emphasis on people*.

Earlier, we briefly distinguished between 'normative' and 'functional' perspectives in planning by the degree of focus on people's well-being. Here we may talk of more or less normative or functional perspectives in problem analysis, too. For example, in excerpt 3 the perceived problem (although not much analysed here) is an inadequate institutional foundation for community development, to which the government responds. Probably, the government will have only a vague idea about any benefits that their change might bring about, in terms of improved living conditions of people. We may even suspect that such benefits may not have been the main motive behind the change. It may instead have been undertaken primarily to strengthen the power base of the governing party. This would be a manifestation of a functional perspective.

Fourth, societal problems may need to be studied in a *time perspective* to be properly understood: that is, we may need to trace changes and why they occur or have occurred. In excerpt 3 changes in local community institutions are described, forces behind those changes are stated, and some consequences of the changes are indicated. In this case, the changes are basically brought about by the ideology and interests of a new government. Excerpt 2 describes processes of change as well, although no time length is indicated.

Moreover, verbal analysis may be *linked with numerical or graphical analysis*. As we have seen, the extent to which quantitative analysis may be applied varies hugely. For example, in relation to our text excerpts, the ranking of problems – indicated in excerpt 1 – may be presented in numerical form, usually as the frequency of answers given to questions about problems. Cause–effect analysis – most explicitly done in excerpt 2 – may also be undertaken through some kind of charting. On the other hand, the information given in excerpt 3 can hardly be analysed through any other mode than the verbal one.

Ranking

In the rest of the chapter, we shall explore the two more specific techniques of problem analysis that are most frequently used, namely, quantitative problem ranking and cause–effect charting. The presentation of the two tools connects directly to the use of the same tools in later chapters, namely, means–ends analysis in Chapter 6 and prioritisation of development measures in Chapter 9.

The techniques that may be used for ranking problems and for prioritising development efforts are largely the same. Since we shall address such techniques more comprehensively in the latter context, we shall here illustrate problem ranking through two examples only. Before presenting the examples, some general reflections about the ranking of development problems are warranted.

Quantitative ranking of problems may be done in different contexts. Most commonly, the ranking is intended to reflect the views of afflicted people. It may then be done by those people themselves, through some group exercise, or it may be done by outsiders, based on answers the people make to questions. Occasionally, the ranking may be based on the views of others than those who experience the problems. For instance, health problems in a population may be discussed and then ranked by health workers at a workshop of such workers.

Ranking that is done by *outsiders* (whether independent researchers or programme or project personnel) is most often based on answers by persons to questions that are posed to them. It may also be based on information collected through other methods, such as observation or physical measurement. For the sake of clarity, we shall limit the immediately following reflections to the most typical scenarios. That is, we shall consider the information on which the ranking is based to be collected through a questionnaire survey, and we shall consider the information providers (the respondents) to be people who are afflicted by the problems.

We have seen that the information constituting the input for the ranking may be generated through one of two main types of questions, namely, open or closed. *Open questions* may be asked for one of two main reasons or some combination of the two: (1) one knows too little about the reality that one wants to explore to decide on firm answer categories in advance; (2) one wants the respondents to reflect on the issues that are addressed relatively freely, by which one hopes to get more elaborate answers, enabling a more insightful analysis.

Before quantitative ranking of problems based on an open-question survey can be done, the answers will need to be further processed. Open questions will lead to answers all of which are different, and will have to be grouped by the analyst into some standardised categories before they can be counted and ranked. This is often a big challenge in studies of this kind. In practice, the analyst may have to develop his or her set of categories gradually, in parallel with the information he or she receives from the respondents. In other words, collection and analysis of information goes hand-in-hand, at least to some extent.

For instance, in a field study that extends over several days or weeks, the researcher or development worker may have to examine each day's answers carefully after finalising that day's interviews. As the analyst extracts and interprets the information, the answers will gradually be fitted into an overall format (in practice some table) that will get its final form only after the fieldwork has been completed. Of course, the information in such a table will be a highly generalised framework only. Sensible analysis of qualitative information will involve much more than fitting the information into a tabular format for the purpose of ranking.

Ranking based on *closed questions* is a much more straightforward exercise. The answers can then be directly counted and entered into a table that directly corresponds to the questionnaire format, after which the answers are ranked by category.

One kind of quantitative problem ranking is illustrated in Table 5.2. The ranking is assumed to be done by an external analyst, based on a questionnaire survey with closed questions. The table shows the main problems of 120 women, as experienced by those women according to their own reporting. The respondents have been asked to identify, from the list of specified problems, the three problems that they consider as being most severe for them. Next, they have been asked to rank the selected problems by their perceived severity. For example, the table shows that altogether 52 of the 120 respondents mentioned 'low household income' as one of their three most severe problems. Of those 52, 22 consider this to be their problem of highest concern (entered in the first column), 20 as their problem of second highest concern (in the second column) and 10 as their problem of third highest concern (in the third column).

The problems have then been weighted accordingly: in this case, the most severe problem has been given the weight 3, the second most severe problem 2, and the third most severe problem 1. On this basis, a severity index of problems has been calculated, using the following formula:

$$\text{Severity index} = [(f_{ONE} \times 3) + (f_{TWO} \times 2) + (f_{THREE} \times 1) / r$$

where: f_{ONE} = frequency of the most severe problem
f_{TWO} = frequency of the second most severe problem
f_{THREE} = frequency of the third most severe problem
r = the total number of respondents.

Finally, the problems have been ranked by their perceived severity, in the last column. For instance, we see that 'low household income' is considered to be the most severe problem overall among those listed,

Table 5.2 Weighted Ranking of Women's Perceived Problems

Problems	Scores				Severity index	Rank
	Weight			Total		
	3	2	1			
Inadequate housing	14	10	10	34	0.60	***4***
Few/poor household facilities (utensils, water, toilet, etc.)	14	12	15	41	0.68	***3***
Low household income	22	20	10	52	0.97	***1***
Little reliable household income	10	8	5	23	0.43	***6***
Little influence on the use of the household income	2	4	4	10	0.15	*15*
Indebtedness	10	9	9	28	0.48	***5***
Poor own health	8	4	5	17	0.31	*8*
Poor health of other family members	8	8	2	18	0.35	*7*
Inadequate own knowledge	1	4	8	13	0.16	*14*
No/inadequate education of children	16	15	16	47	0.79	***2***
Other problems regarding children	4	5	6	15	0.23	*10*
Difficult personal relationship with the spouse	4	4	4	12	0.20	*11*
Difficult personal relationship with other people	2	6	6	14	0.20	*11*
Little help to the household from others	3	3	6	12	0.18	*13*
Poor external services (public and private)	2	8	14	24	0.30	*9*
Total	*120*	*120*	*120*	*360*		

while 'little influence on the use of the household income' is considered to be of least importance (mentioned by 10 women, only 2 of whom regard it as their most severe problem). For easier visualisation of the problems by their perceived priority, in the table the three highest ranked problems are emphasised by larger numbers and bold type, while a second group (ranked 4–6) is emphasised by bold type only.

In many planning contexts, the information that is contained in such a simple table may be very useful, by assisting the planners in directing and focusing the development work. In most instances, however, this will constitute only a limited part of the information about problems that is needed. For instance, the table says nothing about cause–effect relations (to be addressed shortly).

Cautionary comments are also warranted about the list of priorities itself. First, it hides differences between subgroups of the sample of 120 women. Second, the three identified problems may not be of equal severity for different respondents. Third, even problems that appear far down on the list may warrant attention – owing to their severity for some people, because of implications for other problems, or for other reasons. For example, 'difficult personal relationship with the spouse' may cover incidences of severe suffering that may warrant further examination and possible counter-measures. One should also be conscious about under-reporting of problems – for instance, the just-mentioned one – because they may be regarded as sensitive or inappropriate to talk about.

Problem-affected people, and sometimes others, may also undertake ranking as part of a joint problem analysis. Among techniques of participatory ranking, pair-wise ranking is one of the most frequently used. This is a technique for determining the order of pre-specified categories by juxtaposing pairs of them, until each category has been compared with all the others. In the present context, the categories are, of course, problems. The problems to be ranked may have been determined through a separate preceding exploration (for instance, a survey among individuals or households), or by the participating persons themselves in advance of the ranking.

Pair-wise ranking is exemplified in Table 5.3. Here, occupation-related problems of a group of farmers are analysed through a joint exploration by those farmers themselves. The categories to be ranked (the problems) are listed both vertically and horizontally, for direct comparison of each category with all the others. The number in each cell signifies the prioritised category of the two that are juxtaposed in that cell. For comparing the problems once, only half of the diagram space will be needed. For instance, the table shows that 'low affordability of cultivation inputs'

Table 5.3 Pair-Wise Ranking of Occupation-Related Problems of Farmers

	Problems	1	2	3	4	5	6	7	8	9	10	Score	Rank
1	Little land for cultivation		2	3	4	5	1	1	8	9	10	2	
2	Constraining terms of tenancy			2	2	2	2	2	8	2	2	8	***2***
3	Low land fertility				4	5	3	3	8	3	10	4	*6*
4	Insufficiency/ irregularity of water					4	4	4	8	4	4	7	***3***
5	Low outside demand for the produce						5	5	8	9	10	4	*6*
6	Inadequate marketing services/facilities							6	8	9	10	1	
7	Restricted availability of cultivation inputs								8	9	10	0	
8	Low affordability of cultivation inputs									8	8	9	***1***
9	Inadequate labour										9	5	*4*
10	Limitations regarding management											5	*4*

(problem 8) is ranked highest. We arrive at this conclusion by counting all the 8s (vertically and horizontally). Consequently, we have given this problem the number '1' in the 'Rank' column.

The usefulness of participatory problem ranking lies partly in the ranked list of problems. Assuming that such exercises are done in some development context in which people's own opinions are considered as relevant and important, the resulting list would be expected to influence priorities of subsequent development work. In addition, the process of joint analysis may be important in itself: it may augment people's awareness of discussed matters, clarify any differences of interest and opinion, and even help promote an eventual consensus that may be needed for any related development programme or project.

Cause–Effect Charting

The next technique we shall address is cause–effect charting. The purpose of this technique is to visualise main relations of cause and effect between components of a problem structure. Problems that are addressed in development work are normally multi-dimensional and complex. They consist of sub-entities that are connected to one another, to larger or lesser extents and more or less directly or indirectly. This also means that what is perceived and described as 'the problem' is rarely any objective or obviously bounded entity, but reflects the breadth and depth of the analyst's perspective. In other words, one normally focuses on and delimits one's scope of analysis to certain parts of a more comprehensive and complex reality.

A set of linked entities may also be called a 'cause–effect structure'. By implication, explanation of any component of the structure involves identifying other components that are causally linked to it. One may undertake such cause–effect linking in basically three ways: verbally (by reasoning through words and sentences), graphically (through cause–effect charting) and statistically (by inferring causal relationships from statistically tested associations). We have already addressed verbal problem analysis. As we have seen, this is by far the most widely applicable mode, and may be used alone or in some combination with other modes. Statistical cause–effect linking is a specialised exercise that is applicable under specific conditions only. We shall not address that in this book. What remains, then, is graphical linking, to which we turn our attention in this section.

One kind of cause–effect chart is shown in Figure 5.1. The chart is influenced by a story presented in Bernstein (1992). Using very few words, it illustrates how a household enters into a deficiency of resources by three inducing factors: frequent purchase of medicine for a chronically ill household member, division of family land among the husband's brothers (at the time of their marriage) and the birth of many children. It then shows how this resource deficiency leads the household to adopt strategies for survival that keep it in a poverty trap. The loops in the figure show what are commonly referred to as 'vicious circles of poverty' (for example, Chambers, 1983; Burkey, 1993). The chart is confined to variables of a relatively overt nature, basically variables of poverty (as defined in Chapter 1) and factors directly connected to them. It would also be possible to include additional aspects of deprivation (see Chapter 1). They could either be linked to the whole visualised structure or to parts of the structure.

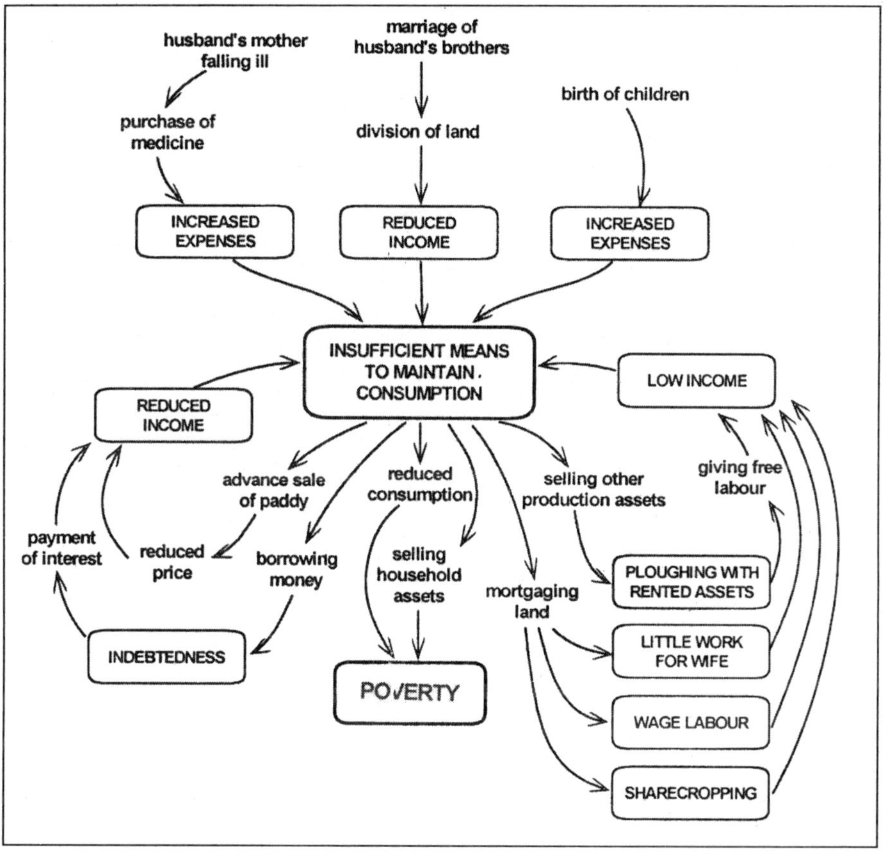

Figure 5.1 Problem Structure A

In Figure 5.2, the information contained in Figure 5.1 is presented in a slightly different, more linear form, with cause–effect links drawn vertically from the bottom upwards. Interrelations, shown in the previous figure in a circular form, are here visualised by two-way relations. We may refer to the broken lines with arrows as feedback links.

While most of the categories are the same in the two figures, the category 'insufficient means to maintain consumption', presented in a centrally placed box in Figure 5.1, has been removed altogether in Figure 5.2 – and this has been done without any significant loss of information. This illustrates the degree of flexibility one has when formulating categories of problem structures and constructing diagrams of such structures. What one ends up with will be influenced by personal perception and preferences.

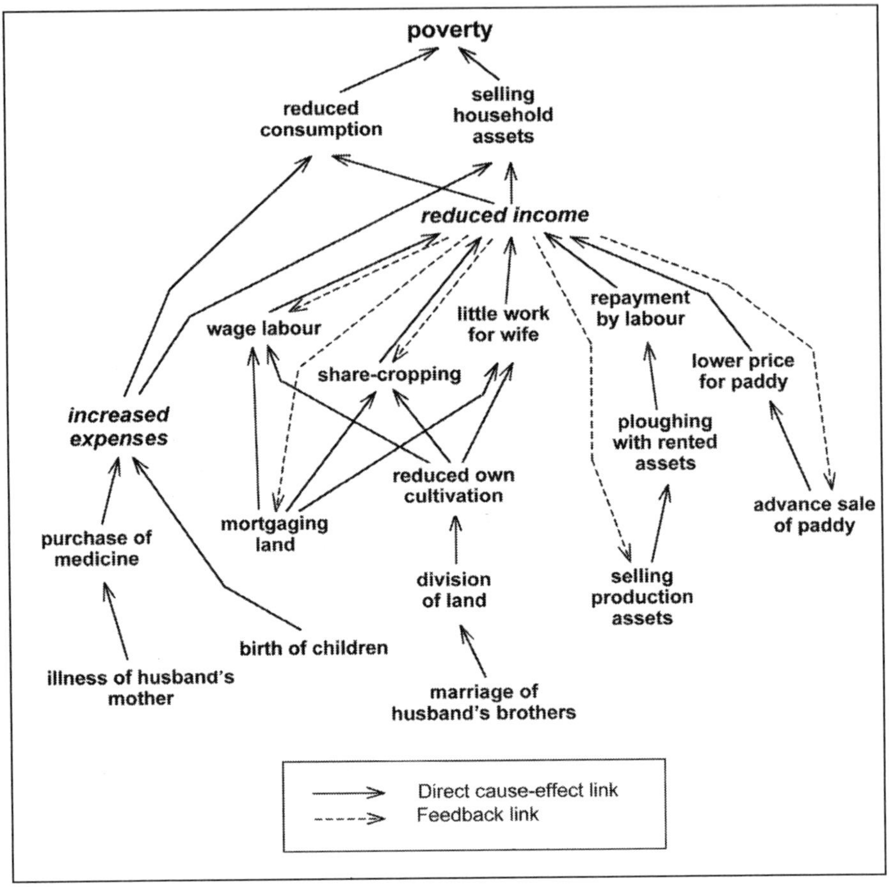

Figure 5.2 Problem Structure B

At the same time, there are basic general principles of cause–effect charting. The main ones are the high relevance of one's categories, the relatively exhaustive coverage of variables (within the scope of the analysis) and internal consistency. If these requirements are met, even diagrams of rather different form may convey basically the same message.

Such linear diagrams are much more frequently used than diagrams of more circular form, even if one considers 'vicious circles' to be important elements of the problem structure. The main reasons are that (1) linear charts are normally easier to comprehend and (2) they correspond more directly with conventional means–ends diagrams, visualising relations between elements of development plans (to be addressed in the next chapter). When important, interrelations may be visualised through feedback links, as in Figure 5.2.

Figure 5.3 is a cause–effect diagram without any feedback links incorporated. Most of the relations in this diagram are unambiguously one-directional. For instance, the absence of fencing allows cattle to drink from people's water sources, by which these sources become polluted, which in turn causes consumption of contaminated water by the children. Here, no cause–effect relations in the other direction would make sense.

If we search thoroughly, we may still identify a couple of possible feedback links. For instance, there could be a two-way relation between, on the one hand, no or small own farms and, on the other hand, low income among people: that is, poor people may sell off their land to get money in the short term but thereby reduce their income in the long term. Another example may be an interrelation between access to schooling and education of the population. While the level of education is shown to be low owing to a poor local school, the quality of the school may perhaps be influenced by low recognition of the importance of a good school, which may, in turn, be linked to low level of education of the population. However, none of these possible feedback links may be so likely or so significant that they ought to be shown in the diagram.

This diagram may also be used to illustrate an issue briefly addressed earlier in this chapter that needs conscientious attention and reflection: the question of objectivity versus subjectivity. Certain problems are clearly objective: that is, there are phenomena that everybody considers to be negative for people. Obvious examples are starvation, freezing and other manifestations of direct physical suffering. Other problems are of a more subjective nature: their perceived severity, or even whether they are considered to exist or not, may depend on personal values, perspectives or insight. One example might be the role of women inside and outside their household respectively; another the clearing of forested land for agricultural production. Usually, problems (or possible problems) may most appropriately be viewed as located somewhere on a continuous range from the obviously objective to the strongly subjective.

In Figure 5.3, the children's consumption of contaminated water, for instance, is objectively bad. The access to those sources by cattle would probably also be considered as a problem among people who are aware of the water-polluting effect of this. Yet the reason or reasons for the cattle's access may be perceived differently: some may emphasise lack of fences, others factors such as the long distance to alternative water sources for the cattle or poor herding practices. The view of misuse of money through the use of stimulants may not be shared by everybody either, or this may not

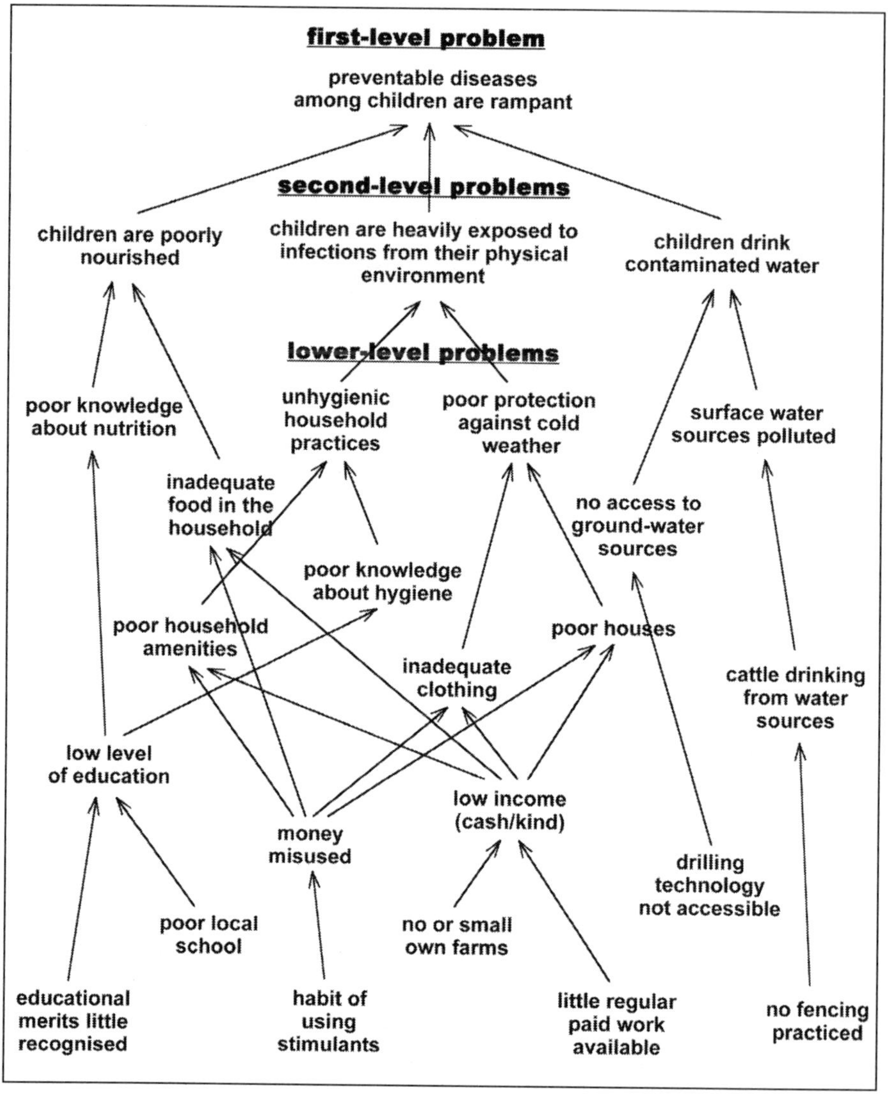

Figure 5.3 Problem Structure C

be equally emphasised by all. If the issue is raised, some may, for instance, claim that they restrict their use of stimulants to 'a minimum' or to what is customarily accepted. Others may try to avoid the question of stimulants altogether, focusing on other reasons for inadequate money for food.

In the last figure, I have also made an indicative distinction between three levels of problems. This is done in order to facilitate comparison with corresponding means–ends structures of planned development work, to be addressed in the next chapter. Broadly stated, the first-level problem corresponds to a development objective, the second-level problems to effect objectives, and lower-level problems to lower parts of the means–ends structure.

Notes

1 At a general level, a further exploration would lead us into examining fundamental differences between natural and social sciences and between disciplines within the latter. While the natural sciences rely, wholly or mainly, on experimental designs and related quantitative analysis (including statistical testing), there are big differences of paradigm and approach between and within social sciences. In the latter, analysts also have different views about the desirable degree of exclusiveness or combination of qualitative and quantitative approaches. Creswell (1994), for example, argues for a clear separation between the two.

In the development field, a rather pragmatic view has tended to prevail, particularly when academic pursuits have been interrelated with practical development work. Mostly, qualitative analysis is considered as fundamental and primary, while quantification is regarded as a possible and potentially useful supplement, to larger or lesser extents. This conforms to my general view, expressed above. For further elaboration and substantiation of such a perspective, see Moris and Copestake, 1993.

Chapter 6

Means–Ends Analysis

Basic Concepts and Relations Revisited

In Chapter 4, we explored means–ends relations in development work in general terms. Two points were emphasised. First, means–ends structures may be more or less elaborate and may extend over a varying number of levels. Second, in order to facilitate planning and planning education, elements of means–ends structures should be grouped into standardised named categories that carry the same meaning for all.

Among these categories, it is particularly important to distinguish clearly between what we have referred to as 'outputs' and 'objectives'. *Outputs* stand for the direct or relatively direct results of implementation of the work that has been planned. Assuming that relations between outputs and their benefits for people have been well substantiated in planning and that no unforeseen external factors intervene too strongly, the created outputs should lead to attainment of the objectives of the respective programme or project, at least to some extent. *Objectives* should, as explicitly as possible, express intended benefits for the people whose problems are to be addressed (the intended beneficiaries). In Chapter 4 this basic notion underpinned our discussion of the formulation of objectives.

To provide reasonable clarity about the purpose of planned develop ment work, one needs to formulate objectives at two levels at the very least. This is common practice in the logical framework, which has become a major tool for structuring main aspects of development schemes. In Chapter 4 I suggested a third level of objectives for incorporation in that framework. The lowest of the three levels may then be used to express people-related achievements in less explicit benefit terms than is required at the two highest levels. I have used, and will continue to use, the terms 'development objective', 'effect objective' and 'immediate objective' for these three levels.

There are two main interrelated reasons for formulating a relatively comprehensive set of objectives, including relatively specific ones below the general development objective. First, as repeatedly stressed, creating benefits for people constitutes the rationale for development work of any kind. Consequently, in order to facilitate rational decision making, we should understand as clearly as possible what the intended benefits are and who are expected to get them. Second, as we have also seen, specification of means–ends relations between subcategories of benefits (that is, within the entire 'objectives' category) greatly helps to clarify connections between outputs and their intended effects on people's quality of life. In other words, it helps clarify the steps through which the outputs are expected to lead to attainment of the ultimate goal (the development objective). Thereby, the conversion of outputs into improved quality of life may also be monitored and evaluated more effectively.

Keeping these reflections in mind, I can now clarify better a comment I made in note 3 of Chapter 4, regarding an alternative set of terms that is conventionally used at the upper levels (the levels of objectives, in our terminology) of the logical framework. These terms are 'goal' at the top level and 'purpose' at the level below. While 'goal' may be a good term for denoting the highest-level aim, I consider 'purpose' to be a too vague and too broadly used word to appropriately express more specific intended achievements. The problem is aggravated by the commonly given advice (sometimes even stated as a requirement) that one should formulate only one purpose. This creates a conceptual gulf between a set of outputs, on the one hand, and a highly general statement of 'purpose' on the other hand, clouding linkages between the outputs and the benefits they are intended to generate for people.[1]

Moreover, the high level of generality and often vagueness of the two terms (goal and purpose) means that statements of them tend to be similar or only artificially different. The extent to which this goal–purpose constellation may impoverish means–ends analysis will be illustrated by an example from a workshop on the logical framework approach, conducted as part of the planning of a regional development programme.

Based on a draft programme document prepared beforehand, the workshop facilitators suggested the following statements of goal and purpose:

Goal: *Improvement of the economy of [X] Province*
Purpose: *Improvement of the living standards of poor people in coastal communes of [Y] District, [X] Province*

After a long discussion, most workshop participants felt that there was a flaw in the structure: namely, that improved living standards of people could not reasonably be considered as a means to an improved economy. The facilitators then suggested the following formulation:

Goal: *Improvement of the social and economic status of people in [Y] District, [X] Province*

Purpose: *Improvement of the living standards of poor people in coastal communes of [Y] District, [X] Province*

This change somewhat rectified the earlier flaw, but this was achieved by making the statements of goal and purpose almost identical. The only substantial difference that seems to remain between them is one of geographical level (the purpose statement specifying the communes in addition to the district and province). In the present context, even this remaining difference was irrelevant. In a means–ends perspective, it might have been so only if the changes in the specified communes (on which the programme was to be concentrated) were to cause similar changes in the district more widely. Nothing in the document presented indicated that anyone had such spread effects in mind.[2]

The other main general categories of means–ends analysis of development work, 'implementation tasks' and 'inputs', are less problematic. They have been clarified sufficiently in Chapter 4.

Relating Problems to Abilities, Opportunities and Constraints

As we saw in Chapter 5, when we talk about a 'problem', we usually refer to a specific manifestation that exists within a more comprehensive structure. Normally the latter may be formulated as a set of more or less complex cause–effect relations. Moreover, for problems that one intends to address through development work, no formulated cause–effect structure will ever be an exhaustive expression of the entire problem complex.

There may be several reasons for what one covers in a problem analysis and what is left unconsidered. Most basically, one may not be able to trace or conceptualise all the factors involved, or one may consciously limit the analysis to what one thinks may be significant in relation to an intended connected development scheme. These reasons may, in turn, be linked to several more specific factors, such as the perception of participants of the problem analysis, what the participants know or are familiar with, the thoroughness of the exercise, and so on.

This perspective on problem complexes connects to perspectives on programme and project structures. Like formulated problem structures, means–ends structures of development schemes will encompass only portions of an imaginable relevant field, and the selection of components will be influenced by many factors during the process of analysis.

Moreover, the process of planning is, normally, more circumscribed and constrained than a process of problem analysis, and it is influenced by partly different considerations. In brief, these considerations are primarily the variables and interconnections that we have addressed under the concept of strategic planning (see Chapter 2, in particular).

Obviously, individual competence, organisational capacity and available financial and other resources are crucial in determining to what extent problem structures (and which parts of them) may be addressed. For clarifying the intended intervention and what will be needed for it, we also have to relate rationally to present and expected future opportunities, constraints and threats. Moreover, resource inputs and organisational abilities should be made to match, as well as possible, the mission and the mandate of the organisation or organisations in charge of the respective programme or project.

By implication, formulation of the components of a programme or project involves much more than responding directly to the set of interlinked components of the problem complex that may have been specified. Delimitation will virtually always be required in relation to the components of any comprehensive problem structure. Conversely, the programme or project may extend beyond the scope of the preceding problem analysis. This may be because planners have different perspectives or more information than persons involved in the problem analysis (if they are not the same persons), because additional information may be generated during plan formulation, or because specific resources or capacities are available.

From Problem Structures to Means–Ends Structures

In Chapter 5, we conceptualised development problems, explored how to generate information about such problems, and presented various approaches and techniques for clarifying and expressing the problems. We emphasised a broad requirement for verbal analysis. In addition, we gave examples of how information may be sorted, simplified and presented more concisely in tables and charts of various kinds. In particular, we elaborated tools for ranking and specifying cause–effect relations of problems in a more concise and comprehensible form than a piece of text.

Ranking exercises may help us decide on the problem or problems to be addressed. In any case, whether any ranking has been done or not, we have to analyse the structure of identified problems before exploring how we should work to solve or alleviate them. In order to act, we need to conceptualise and try to agree on a means–ends structure that relates to the problem structure.

At this stage, let me reiterate a general relation between clarification of means–ends structures and the blueprint–process dimension of planning (see Chapter 3). When we plan in a clear-cut blueprint mode, the focus and scope (and, therewith, the means–ends structure) of the entire development thrust must be clarified before implementation. When we favour a process approach, the focus and scope may change, depending on the degree of flexibility that is encouraged or allowed. This may involve recurrent cause–effect and means–ends analysis, commonly for additional or new programme components. We shall explore this issue further in Chapter 10.

In Chapter 5, we elaborated different kinds of cause–effect charts. We concluded that charts of a basically linear type are most common. Normally, these also have a hierarchical form. The problem structures thus visualised tend to resemble the means–ends structures of any corresponding development schemes.[3] Further, in Figure 5.3 we grouped the elements of problem structures into three broad categories and indicated a correspondence between these categories and commonly formulated categories, or levels, of means–ends structures.

The first-level (highest-level) problem normally corresponds, in a means–ends structure, to what we ultimately want to achieve. We have referred to that as the 'development objective'. At the next level or levels come problems that normally correspond to objectives of lower order. We have already clarified that such lower-level objectives are often specified at one sub-level, but also argued that one should add at least a third level. The categories of means–ends structures that correspond to 'lower-level problems' in Figure 5.3 will be clarified further later.

We have said that relations between problem structures and means–ends structures will vary. Sometimes, we may convert problem statements into positive statements fairly directly. In other instances, we may have to deviate from or even disregard statements. Let us illustrate this point by briefly reflecting on what we might do about problem components that we presented in Figures 5.1 and 5.2.

Obviously, it would be meaningless simply to convert all the negative statements into statements of intended achievement and corresponding action. For instance, there is nothing we could do about the past expenses on medicine for the deceased mother. Most probably, we could not reverse the process of subdivision of land either. On the other hand, we might try to break the circles of further erosion of income and assets, possibly even reverse them. The elements of these circles include borrowing money (at high interest rates), selling paddy before it is ripe and harvested (at only half the price for harvested paddy) and selling and mortgaging assets. Thus, for these phenomena, we might formulate directly corresponding positive statements, in terms of halting the respective practices. Of course, we also need to go beyond those statements to clarify further what we could do. We might, for example, think of promoting access to a new source of income, giving advice on new cultivation practices (to increase the productivity of land that still remains at the household's disposal) and providing loans on more favourable terms than on the local informal capital market. Direct material assistance might also be coupled with non-material measures of a less direct nature, such as an awareness-promoting campaign and building local organisations of similarly deprived people in order to help them address their common problems through collaboration.

We shall now compare more directly the problem structure that was presented in Figure 5.3, converging on the core problem of preventable diseases among a group of children, with a means–ends structure of a project that would aim at ameliorating that core problem. For easy comparison, the structure in Figure 5.3 has been reproduced in Figure 6.1, while the means–ends structure of the corresponding project is shown in Figure 6.2. We see that the negative statements at the highest levels have been directly (or almost directly) converted into statements of objectives in the means–ends structure, while we have deleted, adjusted and added categories further down in the structure.

This pattern tends to be typical in planning that follows a formalised problem analysis. Assuming that the analysis relates to a general matter that may be addressed in a corresponding programme or project (which should have been generally ascertained, at least, before embarking on the analysis), the overriding problem and directly connected problems may usually be converted into objectives almost by implication. Further down in the means–ends structure there tend to be more and bigger differences. Main reasons for this have already been mentioned. Moreover, we need to specify implementation tasks and inputs, categories for which there are, normally, no corresponding entries in the problem structure.

In line with our definition in Chapter 4 and a clarification earlier in the present chapter, the presented *outputs* (Figure 6.2) are the direct results of implementation. Also in line with earlier argumentation, the statements at

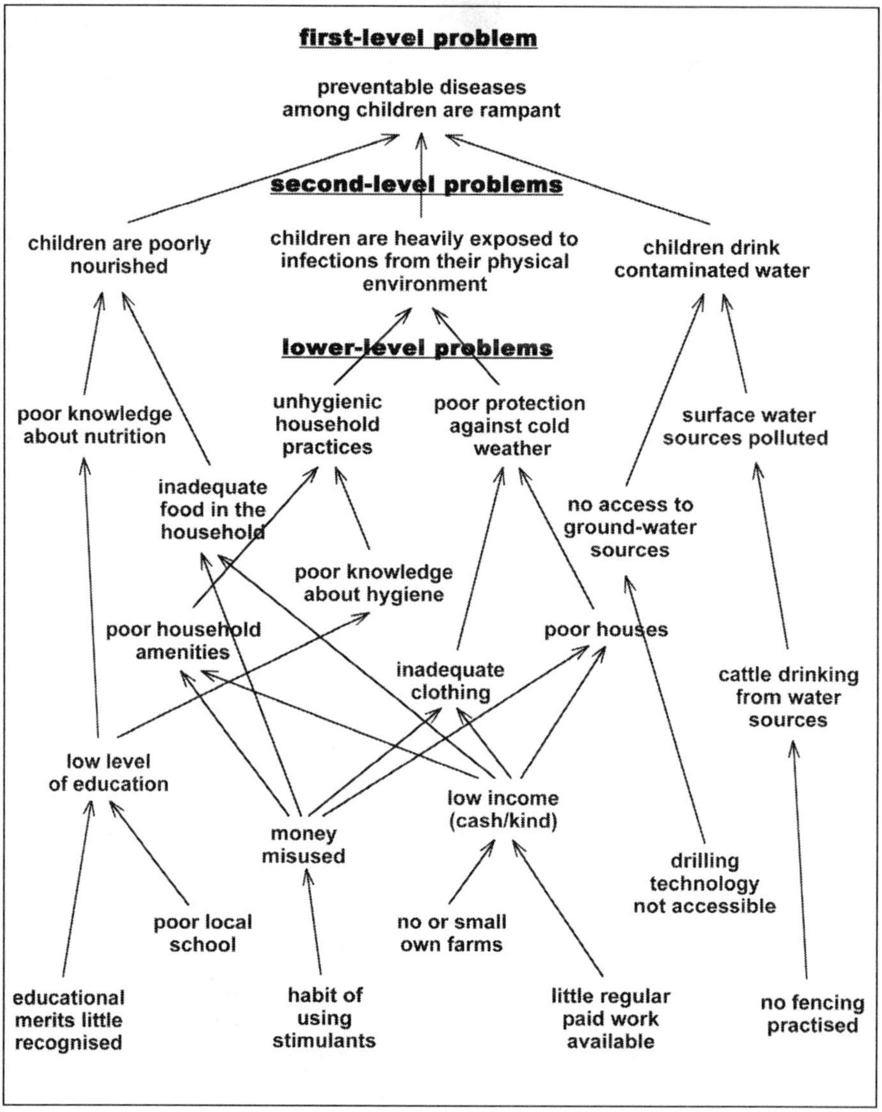

Figure 6.1 Children's Health: Problem Structure

the top levels of the structure express, in explicit terms, intended benefits for people – in this case, the children who are the target group of this project. By our standard terminology, these will be the *development objective* and the *effect objectives* of our project. Between the outputs and these categories of objectives are the *immediate objectives* (referred to as 'immediate achievements' in the figure), serving the role of linking the

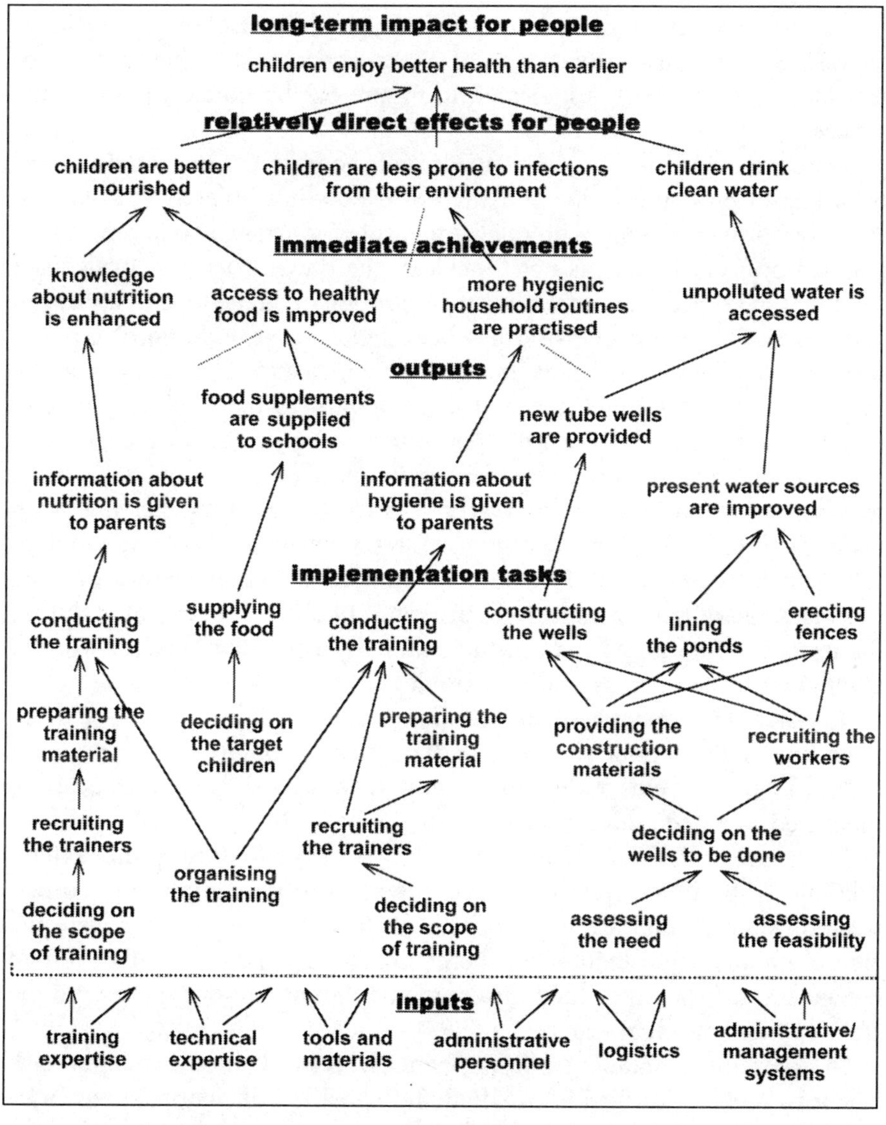

Figure 6.2 Children's Health: Means–Ends Structure

statements of outputs to the explicit statements of intended improvements in the quality of life.

Not all the specified subproblems (Figure 6.1) are intended to be addressed. Consequently, there are no corresponding entries for them in the project chart (Figure 6.2). This applies to 'poor protection against cold weather' (contributing to children's exposure to infections) and to 'poor household amenities' (contributing to unhygienic household practices) – as well as, obviously, to causes of these phenomena. The absence of measures against them is indicated in Figure 6.2 by dotted lines to open spaces.

Moreover, relations between 'inadequate food in the household' (contributing to poor nutrition) and the corresponding objective 'access to food is improved', along with related measures, warrant a comment. In the planned project, the aim is not to address the direct causes of inadequate food that have been identified during the problem analysis (and appear in Table 6.1). Instead, a decision has been taken to provide nutrition supplements to schoolchildren as an alternative measure. The reason may be that this activity is much more straightforward to plan and implement, while also thought to have sufficient effect to be justified. In a problem analysis, one may not normally identify things such as 'absence of school feeding' as a problem, particularly if such an activity has not been undertaken in the past or is not known to the participants of the problem analysis in other ways.[4] This reflects another common feature of such exercises: innovative perspectives are more likely to be generated during the process of planning than in the course of a problem analysis (to the extent that these processes are separable).

Another deviation from the problem structure is the plan to address poor knowledge about nutrition and hygiene through specific training efforts in those fields rather than through improved general education, identified as a need during the problem analysis.

In Figure 6.2, implementation tasks are specified to some extent, relating to the objectives it has been decided to pursue and the corresponding outputs that are to be produced. In order not to complicate the figure unduly, the inputs are here simply grouped into five broad categories, all shown to feed into implementation without specifying the links to the individual tasks.

In operational planning, the implementation tasks and the input–task relations need to be further clarified and specified. It may sometimes be helpful to illustrate more detailed connections in one or more supplementary flowcharts.

Specifying Means–Ends Relations in the Logical Framework

We shall now, to the extent possible, incorporate the elaborated means–ends structure into the logical framework (Table 6.1).[5] To do this we need to fill in the cells of the first column and the last cell of the second column.

Table 6.1 Improving Children's Health: Logical Framework (1)

DEVELOPMENT OBJECTIVE	INDICATORS	ASSUMPTIONS
Children (of estate labourers in district X) enjoy better health than earlier		
EFFECT OBJECTIVES	**INDICATORS**	**ASSUMPTIONS**
Children are better nourished Children are less prone to infections from their physical environment Children drink clean water		
IMMEDIATE OBJECTIVES	**INDICATORS**	**ASSUMPTIONS**
More healthy food is accessed More hygenic household routines are practised Unpolluted water is accessed		
OUTPUTS	**INDICATORS**	**ASSUMPTIONS**
Information about nutrition and hygiene given to parents Food supplements supplied to schools New tube wells provided Present water sources improved		
IMPLEMENTATION TASKS	**INPUTS**	**ASSUMPTIONS**
For the nutrition/hygiene training Conduct the training Organise the training classes Prepare the training material Recruit the trainers Decide on the scope of training	Training expertise Technical expertise Administrative personnel Management systems Tools and materials Logistics	

In principle, this is a straightforward exercise. However, if the framework is confined to one sheet of paper of normal size, the available space is so limited that we may have to be selective with what we incorporate, and we may also have to express some components more briefly than in a corresponding flowchart.

At the levels of objectives, lack of space may not be much of a problem, as we should have only one development objective and only a few objectives at lower levels. While we are at the level of objectives, we should also note the statement in parenthesis – '(of estate labourers in district X)' – in the development objective. This statement has been inserted to indicate that we may specify our objectives more than we have done in this case – in terms of location, beneficiaries and even details such as the percentage of a population that is expected to benefit. Of course, such specifications will be made in the underlying programme or project document; the question here is just how much we may put into this limited schema. Also note that 'knowledge about nutrition' has been omitted. In the full framework this is treated as an assumption (see Chapter 8).

To round up the argumentation on the structure of objectives – in Chapter 4 and earlier in this chapter – I invite the reader to try to replace the present set of statements under 'effect objectives' and 'immediate objectives' with *one* corresponding statement, as is recommended or required in the presently conventional logical framework (under the heading of 'purpose'). Whatever statement one may decide on would be a poor substitute indeed for the present structure, conveying much less information.

At the levels of 'implementation tasks' and 'inputs', the space limitation of the framework may become a real constraint. In the present case, we have 'solved' this problem by entering tasks relating to only two outputs of similar nature (provision of information, about nutrition and hygiene respectively) and by formulating the inputs in highly general terms only (which was done in the preceding figure as well). These variables, in any case, must be further elaborated and specified in a more comprehensive plan document.

The outputs, on the other hand, we have managed to incorporate as presented in Figure 6.2, with only small adjustments of formulations. These, too, will have to be operationalised further elsewhere.

Means–Ends Relations in Organisation-Building Programmes

We shall now address another kind of endeavour, namely, programmes of *organisation building* for development. That is, an organisation helps create or strengthen other organisations to undertake work for the benefit of people, rather than doing such work itself. Sometimes, the programme may be a collaborative venture between more than one organisation. New organisations may be formed or the capability of existing organisations may be augmented. Depending on the perspective applied, we may, alternatively, refer to such efforts as *institution building*. Here, it suffices to say that 'organisation building' may be the most appropriate term for relatively specific efforts to strengthen organisations, while 'institution building' may be most appropriate when referring to wider pursuits, including organisational policy, features of organisational culture and possibly contextual (environmental) factors influencing organisational performance. For further elaboration and discussion, see Chapter 10. Here, we also view organisation building in the perspective of means–ends relations, the topic of the present chapter.

The new organisations or the augmented capability of existing organisations are most appropriately referred to as the *outputs* of the programme; we are still not at the level of benefits for people. Developmental achievements – *effects* and *impacts* – of such organisation-building programmes should then be viewed as the benefits that are generated through the work that the new or strengthened organisations undertake.

To generate such effects and impacts, the organisations that have been built will conduct *their* planning, implement *their* tasks and produce *their* outputs. Consequently, to analyse such achievements we must shift our attention from the organisation-building programme (the support programme) to the new or strengthened organisations. This idea of *dual focus* is visualised in Figure 6.3. The figure builds on Figure 4.1 and also summarises other main features of development work that were addressed in Chapter 4.

The direct affairs of the organisation-building programme are shown as ending at the level of the built or strengthened organisations. These organisations will then undertake further work, as mentioned. Often, however, this may be a somewhat simplified notion. The organisation in charge of the support programme may also help the built organisations in their planning and implementation, at least over some period. Moreover, it will want to know that these organisations do useful work. This concern may be instituted as part of the monitoring system of the support organisation, as indicated in the figure.

Still, for effective capacity building, the basic distinction that we have made between the concerns of the support programme and those of the built organisations will generally apply. In order to avoid confusion about roles and responsibilities, it is essential that those in charge of the support

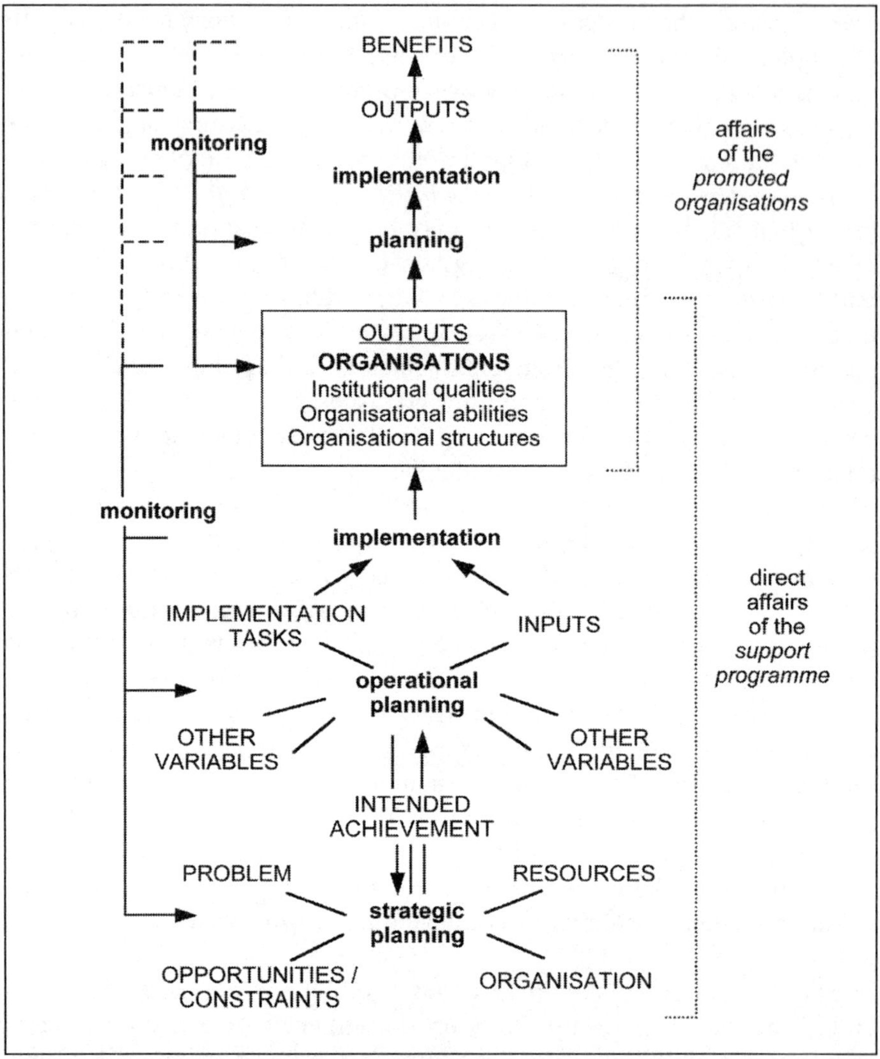

Figure 6.3 An Organisation-Building Programme

programme recognise and abide by this principle of clear separation of purpose and responsibilities.

An additional crucial feature is close interrelations between strategic planning, operational planning, implementation and monitoring, shown by two-way links between the two main categories of planning and the feedback link from monitoring to both of them. This signifies the *generative (process) nature* of virtually any institution- or organisation-building programme. Institutional and organisational abilities are almost invariably built gradually, through some interplay between support from outside and learning from experience. This learning process involves both the supporting and the supported organisations. Consequently, the former may, in most instances, formulate only indicative support measures initially and will normally need to modify its support over the programme period, considering effectiveness at any point in time and the long-term sustainability of the promoted organisations and the work that they do. Commonly, this also involves gradual expansion and then reduction of the support. Process planning was discussed in Chapter 3 and will be explored further in Chapter 10 in the context of organisation building.

In Table 6.2, an example is given of the means–ends structure of an institution-building (including organisation-building) programme, in logical framework format. The example reflects main features of an actual programme, on which I have done some research.[6] Briefly described, it is a local community-based programme with the following core activities: broad-focus social mobilisation (including conscientisation, motivation and training in a range of skills); building of people's organisations; and assistance to those organisations for generating financial resources for use by the organisations' members and for undertaking other activities. (Note that one of the implementation tasks and one of the outputs have been italicised. This indicates that they are considered to be the most central components in their respective cells.)

We see that, for this programme, we end up with a quite different means–ends structure than for more conventional development projects such as the health promotion project examined above. In this example, the *development objective* is very general. This is appropriate, in recognition of the number and variety of *effect objectives* and *immediate objectives* to which it is linked. These objectives encompass economic, social and person-specific dimensions. The broad development objective also reflects the flexibility that is promoted regarding the work of the people's organisations. These organisations are encouraged to analyse the problems and needs of their members in the specific local context, and to address those problems and needs, considering local opportunities and constraints.

With earlier arguments in mind, particular attention should be given to the *outputs* cell. It is here that we have the most substantial and obvious deviations from the conventional project perspective. Well-functioning people's organisations are here the core output, closely connected to and conditioned by the structure of these organisations and the attitudes and skills of people who form and become members of them. Moreover, 'functioning organisations' are at a higher level of the means–ends

Table 6.2 Community Institution Building: Logical Framework (1)

DEVELOPMENT OBJECTIVE	INDICATORS	ASSUMPTIONS
The organisations' members and their families enjoy higher quality of life, physically and mentally		
EFFECT OBJECTIVES	INDICATORS	ASSUMPTIONS
People feel more secure economically Children are more healthy People enjoy better housing People enjoy more harmonious interrelations		
IMMEDIATE OBJECTIVES	INDICATORS	ASSUMPTIONS
Common funds are available and used for emergencies Income is increased Informal loan taking is reduced Better collaboration among members/households		
OUTPUTS	INDICATORS	ASSUMPTIONS
People's organisations are functioning People's organisations formed People's skills improved People's motivation and understanding enhanced		
IMPLEMENTATION TASKS	INPUTS	ASSUMPTIONS
Regularly review progress *Help sensitise and train people* Train social mobilisers Recruit social mobilisers Continuously assess needs, opportunities and constraints	Policy/planning expertise Training personnel Administrative personnel Management systems Logistics	

structure than the other entries in the cell. Many planners may find it difficult to accept organisational qualities as an output of development work. They may also find it problematic that the mentioned core output is not directly created by the work that is done by the programme, but through a transformation process that also involves other outputs. Still, within the present set of categories of the logical framework and our definition of these categories, 'functioning organisations' are unquestionably an output. The statement says nothing about benefits for people.

I shall also draw attention to the categories of the *implementation tasks* cell. As we have seen, this programme involves process planning. An essential aspect of this is continuous assessment of needs, opportunities and constraints. This may be in communities where the programme is already active, in communities where it is about to be introduced, and in communities where it is not yet involved. Based on such continuous assessment, social mobilisers may be recruited and trained, after which the core activity of social mobilisation may be started in the respective communities. Progress review meetings are a further important component of the process, conducted in parallel and closely intertwined with the other activities. In other words, we have several interdependent and even interphased activities. Such circular and cumulative interdependence of activities is and has to be a core feature of successful institution-building programmes.

In this section I hope that I have (1) further demonstrated the importance of process planning in much development work; and (2) shown that complex and process-oriented development thrusts may also be structured within a logical framework, if one is ready to modify certain conventions of planning relating to relatively technical projects. Further analysis of the same programme in the next two chapters should substantiate the second point.

Notes

1 'Purpose' is by promoters of this terminology intended to express the direct concern of the programme or project, while 'goal' is meant to signify a more general sphere of desirable achievements, to which the programme or project is intended to contribute (see, for example, NORAD, 1992). In development planning, such a distinction is an obvious matter, providing no justification for this particular pair of terms.

2 Clearly, in this case, the shortcomings in means–ends formulation were also related to inadequate planning competence of the facilitators of the workshop. With the present emphasis on (even obsession with) the logical framework – in many donor agencies, in particular – this is probably a more general problem. Persons who may have a basic command of the tool itself are engaged to teach or facilitate, even though they may lack

the ability to apply the logical framework properly in the context of complex real-world development work. Thereby, they will also be unable to reflect properly on strengths and weaknesses of the tool and to address alternative approaches and techniques of analysis in the respective contexts.

3 At the same time, in Chapter 5 we emphasised the importance of carefully exploring any feedback links within problem structures and, if appropriate, constructing problem diagrams of more circular form. However, even in such cases, it may be clearest to construct corresponding means–ends structures of a more linear kind, possibly incorporating feedback links between variables within them.

4 Trainers in logical framework analysis may argue that this is no proper problem statement, anyway. A common recommendation by them is that one should avoid statements that express the absence of a solution.

5 Some readers may now want to read over again the section on the logical framework in Chapter 4. It is necessary here to be familiar with the general structure of the framework, to be sensitised to particular problems related to this tool, and to be well informed about the modifications we have made to conventional versions of it.

6 The research is documented in Dale, 2002a.

Chapter 7

Formulating Indicators of Achievements

The Concept of 'Indicator'

The issue to be addressed in this chapter is how to embed the achievements of development work – what is created, and what benefits follow – in clear and credible statements. Such statements may range from brief quantitative measures (as succinct as a single number) to elaborate verbal descriptions. Here we shall emphasise brief statements in quantitative, semi-quantitative and concise qualitative form. Yet we shall also draw attention to the limitations of such shorthand statements, and to the need to supplement them with additional information that has to be presented in more elaborate and lengthy form.

Brief and concise statements about certain phenomena are frequently referred to as 'indicators'. A further delimiting criterion of 'indicator' is that the statement is an approximation of the phenomenon that is examined. In other words, it is a simplified expression of reality.[1]

Indicators, as defined here, may be used for three main purposes: to evaluate something that has been done or changes that have taken place; to assess a future state; and to guide decisions to be taken. Thus, in the first instance, the concept is used retrospectively, while in the two other instances it relates to the future.

In our daily lives, we use indicators for all these purposes. For instance, we may indicate the benefit of an upgrade of our computer by the change of operating speed; develop an opinion about the amount of fruit we may expect on our fruit trees in the autumn by the amount of blossoms on them in the spring; or use outside temperature and wind strength to help us decide what clothes to wear.

In science, indicators may be used similarly. For instance, in the development field, we may indicate the benefit of an investment made in a road by the change of traffic on the road; predict the amount of erosion in a drainage area five years later by changes that are presently occurring in the vegetative cover of the area; or use population projections as an input for a decision about schools to be built (that is, as an indicator of what may be needed).

In this chapter, we shall focus on indicators for assessing the achievements of development work. Moreover, we shall explore indicators in the context of planning; that is, we are concerned with the specification of indicators as one aspect of a planning thrust. The specified indicators will then be used for later assessment of changes caused by the planned programme or project, exploring what has been created during implementation or what benefits are being or have been obtained. In other words, the indicators are used retrospectively.[2]

Normally, indicators are most comprehensively used at the highest levels of means–ends structures of development programmes and projects – in other words, as approximations of benefits for people, frequently expressed as effects and impacts. Sometimes, they may also be useful or even necessary at the level of outputs. In addition, one may use indicators for exploring phenomena in the scheme's environment.

Numerous kinds of effect and impact indicators may be conceptualised, applicable to different types of development work. For initial conceptualisation, let us illustrate the span by the following examples:

- a teacher's brief written statement (say, a couple of lines per child) of changes in the children's learning capability, as an indicator of the effectiveness of a pilot project on innovative learning methods;
- residents' answers to standard questions about their degree of satisfaction with noise prevention measures in a residential area, as an indicator of the adequacy of those measures;
- the composition of meals, as an indicator of mothers' knowledge about nutrition, promoted by a nutrition project.

At lower levels of means–ends structures, we may exemplify by indicators of organisational performance. For instance, stakeholders could be asked questions about how they perceive leadership and decision making in a project. The distribution of answers to these questions could be used as an approximation of the effectiveness of the project in these respects. A more specific indicator might be the adequacy and accuracy of accounts, as judged by a competent person, as an approximation of the quality of financial management.

An example relating to an external variable might be any change in the number of annual logging concessions awarded by the relevant government agency, as an indicator of change in environmental awareness in the government (which might be an important assumption for a reforestation project, for instance).

On several occasions we have drawn attention to the core question in development science of *qualitative versus quantitative* statements. This is a highly important dimension of indicators as well. In the natural sciences, only quantitative measures are normally considered to qualify as indicators. Some advocate this limitation for indicators when used in the social sciences also. However, if this restriction is imposed in fields where qualitative analysis is important or even predominant, the usual consequence is that the indicators fail to provide much information.

This is a very important question in development planning. Normally, indicators of achievements are regarded as an important component of programme and project plans, for use in monitoring and evaluation. If only quantitative statements are accepted, one may end up with a poor set of measures for assessing achievements, in view of the limitations of quantitative analysis in most development work. Expressing achievements in brief, concise terms has merit in many respects, and I want to encourage development planners to search for the best indicators to be found in the programmes and projects that they plan. But these will usually include expressions of a qualitative nature as indicators alongside quantitative expressions.

Consequently, in this book we shall include statements in verbal form in our repertoire of indicators of achievements of development programmes and projects. Among the examples given above, the teacher's verbal summary of children's performance and the finance expert's judgement of the quality of accounts are qualitative indicators. Yet we must also emphasise that only brief and concise verbal statements may be considered as indicators. How brief and concise a statement has to be to qualify will then be a matter of sometimes fine judgement. This injects a degree of ambiguity into the concept that we may have to live with. Generally speaking, a couple of hundred words would probably not qualify as an indicator, while a couple of succinct sentences – or, indeed, a single such sentence – might definitely fit the bill.

Sometimes, qualitative information may also be transformed into numerical form. This may be referred to as category-level measurement. For instance, people's answers to an open question in a survey may afterwards be grouped into a set of suitable categories, such as 'very poor', 'poor', 'just adequate', 'good' and 'very good'. The distribution of answers across these categories may then be used as an expression of performance on the variable that is examined.

Achievements need to be studied through one or more conscientiously selected *methods of analysis*. Quantitative measures are normally considered to be objectively verifiable; that is, by following a clearly prescribed procedure, any person should arrive at exactly the same result. The more qualitative the indicators are, the more difficult and even unrealistic this becomes. Consequently, in the development field, objective verification will be the exception rather than the rule.

In such instances, then, we will need to substantiate our findings as well as possible through methods that involve greater or lesser amounts of subjective judgement. If we want to address core matters and obtain a reasonably good understanding of them, there is frequently no alternative. All normal rules of good qualitative analysis will then apply. Compressing findings into indicators will be a related challenge. Normally, this will be much facilitated by relatively clear and unambiguous findings. Beyond that, one will need skills in synthesising information and in verbal formulation – requirements for good qualitative analysis more generally.

Characteristics of Good Indicators

For indicators to serve their intended purpose, they should meet certain quality criteria to a reasonable extent. The primary criteria are relevance, significance, reliability and convenience.

The *relevance* of an indicator denotes whether or to what extent the indicator reflects (is an expression of) the phenomenon that it is intended to substantiate. Embedded in this may be how direct an expression it is of the phenomenon and whether it covers the whole phenomenon or only some part of it.

An indicator's *significance* means how important an expression the indicator is of the phenomenon it aims at substantiating. Core questions are whether it needs or ought to be supplemented with other indicators of the same phenomenon, and whether it says more or less about the phenomenon than other indicators that may be used.

An indicator's *reliability* expresses the trustworthiness of the information that is generated on it. High reliability normally means that the same information may be acquired by different competent persons, independently of each other, and often also that comparable information may be collected at different points in time (for instance, immediately after the completion of a project and during subsequent years). Moreover, the information that is generated must be unambiguous, and it should be possible to present the information in terms so clear that it means the same thing to all who use it.

The *convenience* of an indicator denotes how easy or difficult it is to use. In other words, it expresses the effort that goes into generating the intended information. The effort may be measured in monetary terms (by the cost involved), or it may constitute some combination of the financial resources, expertise and time that are required.

Reliability and convenience relate to the means by which information on the respective indicators is generated; that is, they are directly interfaced with aspects of methodology. Some indicators are tied to one method of study, while others may be studied using one among alternative methods or a combination of methods. The feasibility of generating adequate information on specific indicators may differ greatly with the method or methods used. The quality of the information may also depend on or be influenced by a range of other factors, such as the amount of resources deployed in the analysis and the qualifications, interest and sincerity of the analysts. It may also vary substantially between societies and cultural settings.

We shall discuss these issues further through some examples of proposed indicators (among many more that could have been put forward), relating to three intended achievements. These are presented in Table 7.1. The respective indicators' appropriateness or adequacy is then assessed on each of the quality criteria we have specified. A simple four-level rating scale is used, where 3 signifies the highest score and 0 no score at all (meaning entirely inappropriate or inadequate). Note that the scores under 'relevance' and 'significance' are given under the assumption that reasonably reliable information is provided.

Upper arm circumference is a scientifically well-recognised measure of the nutrition status of young children. The indicator is therefore highly *relevant*. On *significance*, the score 2 (rather than 3) is given because the indicator still ought to be supplemented with other measures (such as weight and height by age and, if possible, changes in nutrition-related illnesses), for fuller information. The circumference is arrived at through simple direct quantitative measurement, and this may be repeated endlessly by persons who know how to measure. Therefore, under normal circumstances, we would consider the information on this indicator to be highly *reliable*. Assuming that the children may be reached relatively easily and that the work is well organised, the information may also be acquired fairly quickly and at low cost for large numbers of children. Consequently, this will normally be a highly *convenient* indicator as well.

Table 7.1 Indicated Quality of Selected Indicators

Intended achievement *Indicator*	Relevance	Significance	Reliability	Convenience
The nutrition level of children below 6 years is improved				
Upper arm circumference	3	2	3	3
Number of meals per day	1-2	1-2	2	2-3
Women's awareness about gender relations in their society is enhanced				
Analyst's judgement from group discussion	3	2	1-2	1-2
Women's answers to pre-specified questions	3	2	2	2-3
People's organisations are functioning well				
Analyst's judgement of observed practice	3	3	1-3	2
Attendance in member meetings	0-3	0-2	3	3

The **number of meals per day** is normally of some *relevance* and *significance* for assessing changes in nutrition level, since eating is necessary for consuming nutrients. However, the relation between eating habits and nutrition may vary substantially, between societies and even between households in the same society, for a range of reasons. The relevance and the significance will then vary accordingly. In most contexts, this measure may at best be used as a supplement to other indicators. The *convenience* of the indicator may vary with the methods used for generating information on it. With a questionnaire survey, the information may be collected relatively quickly and easily; if one in addition includes observation (which may be highly appropriate in this case), more time will normally be needed. The *reliability* of the information may normally be acceptable, but in most cases hardly very high, due to factors such as different perceptions of what constitutes a meal or, sometimes, reluctance among people to give correct answers.

For women's awareness about gender relations, an **analyst's judgement from group discussions**[3] must be considered as highly *relevant*, under the assumptions that the judgement is made by a competent person and that it is based on a substantial discussion in the groups about the issue to be analysed. The information will then also be *significant*. However, when using such highly qualitative indicators, information ought to be generated by more than one method, and if possible also by more than one person, for the matter to be considered as well explored.[4] For that reason, we have indicated a score of 2 (rather than 3) on the 'significance' criterion. If only one group discussion is conducted, the *reliability* of the information on such a complex matter may be rather low; if several discussions are arranged, it may increase substantially. The reliability also tends to depend substantially on aspects of design and implementation, such as the composition of participants and the facilitation of the discussion. If applied on a large scale, this method of information generation may be rather inconvenient (its *convenience* may be low): usually, it is time-consuming to organise such exercises and to generate substantial information from them. Often, therefore, the method may be most suitable as a supplement to other methods, for exploring relatively specific issues more deeply.

Changes in women's awareness may also be traced through preformulated questions to the women, in a questionnaire survey. These **answers to prespecified questions** may then be presented as a frequency distribution on an ordinal measurement scale (see earlier). If the questionnaire is well focused and the survey is properly conducted, the women's answers will be highly *relevant*. While *significant*, the information from a survey may not be considered to be sufficient: although the questions may address relevant matters, the information may be relatively shallow, since issues tend not to be explored comprehensively in such surveys. Question-based information may be more *reliable* than that from a group discussion, since it is, normally, more representative for various groups and often also more clearly expressed. Moreover, questionnaire surveys are usually a more *convenient* method than group discussions. However, the intricacy of the issue under scrutiny may complicate the survey substantially, compared with a survey of more overt and clearly delimited variables.

For assessing the functioning of people's organisations, one indicator may be professional **judgement of observed practice**. Well-planned and conducted observations by competent persons are often an effective method for generating both highly *relevant* and *significant* information about organisational performance. Consequently, we have given this indicator the top score on both these criteria. The *reliability*, though, may vary substantially. As with other qualitative indicators (such as 'analyst's judgement from group discussions', above), the trustworthiness of the generated information will be highly sensitive to aspects of design and implementation. The *convenience* of the indicator may be intermediate, considering alternative methods that may be used.

Attendance in meetings by the membership is a frequently used indicator of the performance of member organisations. This is largely because one may quantify meeting attendance easily, quickly and in unambiguous terms. Consequently, under normal circumstances, this indicator scores high on *reliability* and *convenience*.[5] When participation in the meetings is entirely or primarily driven by a genuine sense of purpose and high interest in the organisation's affairs, this indicator is also highly *relevant* and in addition clearly *significant*. However, it may hardly ever be significant enough to be given the highest score on this criterion, since there will always be numerous aspects of performance that attendance in meetings may not reflect, at all or adequately. Moreover, if the attendance is entirely or primarily driven by other motives than those just mentioned (for instance, to receive some short-term personal benefit, such as a loan), this indicator may even convey distorted or misleading information regarding an organisation's performance. That would affect both its relevance and its significance.

Specifying Indicators in the Logical Framework

We shall now enter indicators into the logical framework, using the two cases from Chapter 6 as examples. Subsequently, we shall briefly examine the means by which we may substantiate achievements – that is, the methods we may use for generating information on the indicators. Table 7.2 shows suggested indicators and means of substantiation for our first case, the *health improvement* project.

For *outputs*, the need for indicators is in this case limited, and may not even exist. In such relatively specific, technical projects one should usually be able to verify, through monitoring, the generated outputs in direct relation to the planned outputs specified in the project document. For example, before starting to teach the mothers nutrition and hygiene, one should be clear about, and specify in writing, what information to give and how to get the information across. In the course of implementation, one should then record what is taught and how.

However, in any ex-post evaluation (an evaluation done after the project's completion), indicators will be applied, since the evaluator will not have the opportunity of current follow-up and recording. Apart from drawing on monitoring records of activities, items or facilities, the evaluator may seek information by asking people who are supposed to be

Table 7.2 Improving Children's Health: Logical Framework (2)

DEVELOPMENT OBJECTIVE	INDICATORS	MEANS OF SUBSTANTIATION
Children (of estate labourers in district X) enjoy better health than earlier	Frequency of treatment of relevant diseases Health personnel's statements Mothers' statements	Examining clinic records Examining other health-monitoring reports Asking health personnel Asking mothers
EFFECT OBJECTIVES	**INDICATORS**	**MEANS OF SUBSTANTIATION**
Children are better nourished Children are less prone to infections from their physical environment Children drink clean water	Height, weight/age Frequency of diarrhoea Health personnel's statements Mothers' statements Observed practice	Direct measurement Examining clinic records Asking mothers Asking health personnel Evaluator's observation
IMMEDIATE OBJECTIVES	**INDICATORS**	**MEANS OF SUBSTANTIATION**
More healthy food is accessed More hygienic household routines are practised Unpolluted water is accessed	Mothers' statements Money spending pattern Use of water-sealed toilets Quality of water at the source Water storage practices in the households	Asking mothers Asking other household members Asking health personnel Direct measurement Evaluator's observation
OUTPUTS	**INDICATORS**	**MEANS OF SUBSTANTIATION**
Information about nutrition and hygiene given to parents Food supplements supplied to schools New tube wells provided Present water sources improved	Recorded activities/items/facilities Stakeholders' statements Observed activities/items/facilities	Checking food supply records Checking other progress reports Asking trainees Asking teachers Evaluator's observation
IMPLEMENTATION TASKS	**INPUTS**	
For the nutrition/hygiene training: Conduct the training Organise the training classes Prepare the training material Recruit the trainers Decide on the scope of training	Training expertise Technical expertise Administrative personnel Management systems Tools and materials Logistics	

knowledgeable on the matter or through observation. Questioning is, generally, a less than satisfactory approach for verification of outputs of such a specific nature, but may be needed if the monitoring has been inadequate or unreliable. Observation may also be used to remedy the same shortcomings in documentation, and may then often be similarly deficient. However, for facilities of a relatively standardised nature (for instance, a specific kind of tube wells), a skilled evaluator may be able to draw satisfactory conclusions entirely or primarily through personal observation.

In this project, the most important indicators are those relating to the *effect objectives*. Provided that poor nutrition, infections due to unhygienic practices and drinking of unclean water have been rightly identified as the main causes of poor health, attainment of the effect objectives will virtually automatically lead to attainment of the development objective, at least in the short term.

Yet the changes that are formulated at the level of *immediate objectives* are important, too: they express necessary links between the relatively controllable outputs and the benefits that these are intended to generate for people. Moreover, substantiation of attainments at this level may be easier than at higher levels. This is because the more specifically intended achievements are formulated, the easier it will be to provide indicators that are similarly more specific – and, usually, more informative and operational as well. Consequently, in many evaluations, one may choose to seek the most detailed and firm information of relatively immediate changes and supplement that with less specific information about effects and impacts.

The greater significance of effect and immediate objectives in this case also carries the implication that indicators for the *development objective* are of less significance. To take the present discussion further, let us then have a brief look at the indicators that have been formulated in relation to effect objectives and immediate objectives.

For the nutritional status of small children, directly quantifiable indicators exist, being also convenient to use and scoring high on other quality criteria (see above). We have specified 'height, weight/age'. 'Upper arm circumference', discussed earlier, might have been another. 'Frequency of diarrhoea' is commonly a good indicator of aspects of children's health. However, its usefulness may be reduced by the fact that it may have many possible causes and may, in this case, relate to any or all of the effect objectives. 'Use of water-sealed toilets' is an indicator of hygienic practices that may assume particular importance if such toilets are promoted as part of the hygiene training. 'Quality of water at the source' may be only a highly indirect indicator of the quality of the water that the children drink; that is, there is no obvious or certain relation between the two. An advantage is that the quality can be easily and reliably measured. 'Water storage practices' may be a main factor influencing the quality of the water when it enters the children's mouth.

'Mothers' statements' will mostly be of a highly qualitative nature. Still, they may be very important or even the main indicator of some of the intended achievements (for example, whether the children eat the provided food supplements, in the event that they are supposed to do so at home). In other instances (for example, whether children are better nourished), they may be used to supplement information that is generated in other ways. The same may apply to statements by others (in this case, health personnel) and to observations by the evaluator. In this example, 'observed practice' may relate to the objective of drinking clean water, but observations might also be made of other features expressed by other objectives.

In addition, we should consider how 'mothers' statements', and similar indicators in this and the next case, may relate directly to one or more of the objectives. Thus, if we get the mothers' opinion about any changes in household routines, the structure will be, when also stating the means of substantiation:

More hygienic household routines practised? ←
Mothers' statements ← Asking mothers

Alternatively, this indicator may be perceived to be linked to another indicator of the particular objective. That is, information on that other indicator is obtained through verbal statements, in this case by mothers. For the same objective and one such other direct indicator, the structure will then be:

More hygienic household routines practised ? ←
Use of water-sealed toilets ? ←
(Mothers' statements) ← Asking mothers

'Mothers' statements' is here placed in brackets, because it may be omitted without any loss of clarity. In this case (Table 7.2) and the next one (Table 7.3), this and similar judgement indicators are to be understood as referring directly to one or more objectives (that is, in the first-mentioned sense).

At the level of impact (corresponding to the development objective) we may have to rely entirely or largely on views of assumedly knowledgeable

Table 7.3 Community Institution Building: Logical Framework (2)

DEVELOPMENT OBJECTIVE	INDICATORS	MEANS OF SUBSTANTIATION
The organisations' members and their families enjoy higher quality of life, physically and mentally	Members' statements Other household persons' statements	Asking members Asking other household persons
EFFECT OBJECTIVES	INDICATORS	MEANS OF SUBSTANTIATION
People feel more secure economically Children are more healthy People enjoy better housing People enjoy more harmonious interrelations	Members' statements Health personnel's statements Clinic records of treatments Type of house roofing material Members' mode of communication in meetings	Asking members Asking health personnel Examining clinic records Evaluator's observation
IMMEDIATE OBJECTIVES	INDICATORS	MEANS OF SUBSTANTIATION
Common funds are available and used for emergencies Income is increased Informal loan taking is reduced Better collaboration among members/households	Credit disbursements, by member and purpose Members' statements Labour exchange Common contributions in community functions	Examining credit disbursement records Asking members Asking the social mobiliser Evaluator's observation
OUTPUTS	INDICATORS	MEANS OF SUBSTANTIATION
People's organisations are functioning People's organisations formed People's skills improved People's motivation and understanding enhanced	Rate of meeting attendance Adherence to procedures Adherence to other rules of member behaviour Social mobiliser's statements Members' statements	Examining meeting records Asking members Asking the social mobiliser Evaluator's observation
IMPLEMENTATION TASKS	INPUTS	
Regularly review progress *Help sensitise and train people* Train social mobilisers Recruit social mobilisers Continuously assess needs, opportunities and constraints	Policy/planning expertise Training personnel Administrative personnel Management systems Logistics	

persons such as intended beneficiaries. Sometimes, quantifiable data on relevant and significant indicators may be collected, normally by institutions that are mandated to do so. In this case, examples may be clinic records of relevant diseases and data on nutritional status. These may also be gathered beyond the project period.

Our second case, on *community institution building*, is shown in Table 7.3. This poses, on the whole, greater challenges of specifying meaningful and operational indicators. The institution-focused and generative nature of this development thrust makes it very difficult or impossible to identify specific, quantifiable measures of most intended achievements at any level. Thus, one needs to apply mainly qualitative indicators.

Unlike for the health improvement project, we here need indicators even for monitoring the generation of *outputs*. 'Motivation', 'understanding' and 'skills' of people may not be expressed in highly specific terms in a plan document, and may therefore not be subjected to direct verification in monitoring. Of course, this has direct implications for indicators and methods of monitoring. One will primarily have to judge changes on these phenomena through some kind of communication with the persons whose abilities the programme intends to augment, possibly supplemented with observation of their behaviour in relevant respects. This will normally be done frequently by field staff employed by the programme, here called social mobilisers. Additional monitoring may be done by persons who are in more overall charge, and any evaluation may be done by them and/or outsiders. These last-mentioned persons may get information from the people, from the mobilisers, or from both.

Likewise, 'functioning organisations' is not a clear-cut, unambiguous category that may be objectively specified and operationalised for monitoring. I have formulated one directly quantifiable measure, 'rate of meeting attendance'. Another could be 'regularity of meetings'. However, as clarified in the previous section, their relevance and significance may vary substantially. Usually, therefore, such simple measures need to be supplemented with more qualitative measures, as exemplified in the table.

Among the stated indicators relating to the *immediate objectives*, only one – 'credit disbursements' – is directly quantifiable. In addition, we might get figures for indebtedness and income. Usually, these would have to be obtained by asking the people, since written records are seldom kept. In addition, questions about finance may be regarded as sensitive. For both reasons, the information may be less reliable.

At the level of *effect objectives,* I have also suggested a couple of quantitative indicators. Let us reflect a little on one of them, 'type of house roofing material'. This belongs to a common category of indicators, namely, material assets that are thought to be highly valued in a particular society. Such indicators are often easy to resort to (highly convenient), and information that we get on them may be quite reliable. Often, however, their relevance may be low and sometimes highly questionable. Being, at best, indirect measures, it may be very difficult to substantiate to what extent any changes in them are caused by the evaluated programme or project or by other factors. Consequently, they normally have to be used within a wider context of more qualitative exploration of changes for the intended beneficiaries.

For the highly general *development objective* that we have formulated for this comprehensive development thrust, the only reasonably relevant and significant indicators may be expressions by people who are supposed to have their quality of life improved.

Generating Information on Indicators

Indicators are relevant and significant only in so far as we can generate information on them. How we may do that is the question addressed under 'means of substantiation', in our version of the logical framework. Conventionally in logical frameworks, the terms for ascertaining achievements and connected methods are 'verification' and 'means of verification'. I have replaced 'verification' with 'substantiation' because the notion of objectivity (proclamation of *the* truth), contained in the former, is untenable in much development work, as we have seen.

Let us start by looking back briefly at the set of methods presented for problem analysis in Chapter 5. Some of these methods are too casual to be applied for the present purpose. While they may throw up issues and ideas of value in a problem analysis, they will normally not enable proper assessment of achievements, at any level. Informal observation, casual conversation, lobbying and some techniques under rapid and participatory assessment belong in this category. The most applicable methods in the present context are: checking existing sources of data (such as written records), direct measurement, formal observation, formalised group discussions, questionnaire surveys and (more occasionally) in-depth interviews. In addition, individual and group stories may be recorded for analysing long-term impact.

The means of exploration stated in the third columns of tables 7.2 and 7.3 fit under these broader methods. They should be largely self-explanatory at this level of generality, though there may be highly intricate questions relating to their use. Such questions fall beyond the scope of this book, and may be studied in literature on research methodology.

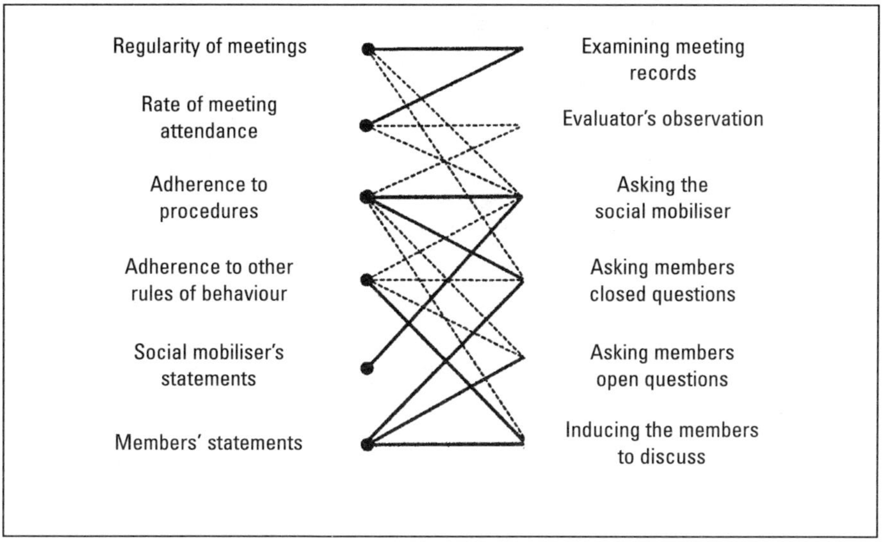

Figure 7.1 Relations between Indicators and Means of Substantiation

Let us then explore somewhat further the main relations between indicators and means of substantiating them. We shall do so by looking more closely at relations at one level of one of the presented frameworks. I have chosen the level of outputs in Table 7.3, as this should illustrate the main issues rather well. In Figure 7.1, the selected indicators have been listed and linked to the respective means of substantiation by connecting lines. Note that in this figure I have added 'regularity of meetings' (also mentioned earlier in the chapter) to the set of indicators.

The reader will quickly see that the category 'asking' has been broken down into three subcategories when referring to members (the context in which such a breakdown is most significant in this case). In fact, this substantially amplifies the repertoire of means of substantiation shown in the previous tables. Moreover, the three subcategories relate to different more general methods, listed on the previous page: 'asking open questions' is normally done in checklist questionnaire surveys, emphasising qualitative information; 'asking closed questions' is done in more quantification-oriented questionnaire surveys; and 'inducing to discuss' is primarily done in formalised group discussions.[6]

In the figure, I have indicated what commonly are the most important means relating to the respective indicators by full lines and supplementary and/or alternative means by dotted lines. However, the most important or even the possible means may vary substantially, for many reasons.

For substantiating the *regularity of meetings* and the *rate of meeting attendance*, examination of meeting records may normally be the easiest and most reliable method. If the records are sufficiently detailed and trustworthy, this may be all that is needed. If not, this source of information may have to be supplemented with or even replaced by orally conveyed information. The evaluator may also get an impression of meeting attendance directly, if he or she attends or visits many such meetings, preferably unannounced.

Information about *adherence to procedures* (mainly in meetings, in this case) may most readily and reliably be got from the social mobiliser, if there is such a person, as he or she would normally be sufficiently involved and informed. Supplementarily or alternatively, members may be asked, usually or mainly through well-specified (closed) questions. Other means of getting this information may also exist, as indicated.

Adherence to other rules of (member) behaviour may be a more multifaceted and less clearly delimited indicator, and may be open to more subjective judgement. This calls for exploration through many methods. Formalised group discussions (in which members will be induced to discuss) may be highly useful: they may bring up more issues and clarify perspectives and opinions better than other methods.

On *social mobiliser's statements* and *members' statements* no further comments should be needed.

A Conclusion on Indicators and a Reflection Beyond Them

I want to end this chapter by summing up the main messages on indicators from previous pages and then emphasising a point that has been alluded to a couple of times: while indicators may be important, they are normally not sufficient for generating the knowledge we should have about the performance and achievements of development programmes and projects.

If well designed and sensibly used, indicators are important in two respects: (1) they induce planners to focus and operationalise the development scheme and help monitoring and evaluating personnel to maintain focus in their pursuits; and (2) the information provided on the indicators constitutes a concise summary of main achievements.

To the extent that quantitative indicators meet the basic criteria of relevance and significance, reliable information on them will be informative. That is because, in such cases, the studied phenomena lend themselves to expression in a concise and unambiguous form.

With more qualitative indicators, the matter is more complex. Even in cases where the indicators are relevant and significant, the indicator statements may be more or less informative, largely depending on the extent to which the information may be expressed briefly enough, without losing an unreasonably high proportion of its content. Obviously, the power of qualitative indicators may then also depend on how brief we require the expressions to be if they are to serve as indicators.

Certain information of basically qualitative nature may be presented in ranked form. For instance, we may structure the opinions of members of an organisation about organisational matters into judgement categories such as 'highly satisfied', 'satisfied', 'somewhat unsatisfied' and 'highly unsatisfied'. With a closed question format, these categories may be specified in the questionnaire itself, and people's answers may be entered directly in the applicable categories, after which they are summed up, by category, for all the respondents. The indicator of performance will then be a simple frequency distribution across these pre-specified categories. If the analyst uses more open questions, he or she may sometimes be able to group the gist of the answers into similar categories, constructed in the aftermath. Since this involves much subjective judgement, the reliability may often be questioned.

Alternatively, the analyst may try to summarise the general messages emerging from answers to open questions, from group discussions or from observations into one or a few sentences. For instance, I would consider the following summary statement from a group discussion to be an indicator statement, in this case of benefits obtained from a project:

> The majority of the participants reported increased catches of [a fish species], by which their household's annual net income had increased, in some cases up to 50 per cent. Many fishermen who had only small boats said that their catches had not increased, because they had to fish close to the shore.

Although it is highly general and brief, the statement is informative. While no ranking is attempted here, we also note that a very rough grouping of benefits is indicated by the size of the fishermen's boats.

Irrespective of how well the indicators have been constructed and used, in most cases the scanty information that is contained in indicator statements needs to be supplemented with additional, more comprehensive information. Besides the strictly limited amount of information contained in most indicator statements, and the poverty of detail provided, the main constraint of indicators is that they provide no (or, at best, very limited) explanation of the phenomena that are addressed. Quantitative indicators contain, in themselves, no explanation, while any explanatory part of a qualitative indicator may have to be highly general or strictly limited, as in our indicator statement above: 'because they had to fish close to the shore'.

Seeking explanations for documented changes invariably means to explore cause–effect relations. We have comprehensively explored such relations and how we may present them, in the context of planning. The argument may now be extended to the exploration of achievements through monitoring and evaluation.

If we do not explore well beyond indicators, we may easily fall into the trap of assuming that any changes we may find are caused by the programme or project under study. This is a vulnerable feature of much evaluation, particularly at higher levels of means–ends structures where assessments of changes in aspects of people's life situation come into play. We should keep this argument in mind when, in the next chapter, we explore the context of development programmes and projects, and the environment of the organisations that plan and implement them.

Notes

1 For efforts to clarify 'indicator' in the development field, see Kuik and Verbruggen, 1991; Pratt and Loizos, 1992; Mikkelsen, 1995; Rubin, 1995; and NORAD, 1990; 1992; 1996. In this chapter, I shall discuss theoretical and practical aspects of indicators more comprehensively and in a more coherent manner than has been done in any of these publications. While I draw on their contributions, the presentation and discussion is more influenced by my own scientific exploration, along with experiences from practical development work.

2 Indicators for assessing a future state and for guiding decisions are utilised elsewhere in the book, and in planning practice. Problem analysis (see Chapter 5) often involves examination of features and processes based on which we conceptualise a future scenario. Prioritisation of development work (see Chapter 9) invariably uses guiding indicators of various kinds, which we may refer to as prioritisation criteria (whether explicitly stated or not).

3 To be termed an indicator, we assume that the judgement is presented in a summarised form (see preceding discussion).

4 Such multi-method approaches are often referred to as 'triangulation'.

5 Occasionally, existing records prepared by someone in the organisation may not be reliable. Another cause of unreliable data of such readily quantifiable kind may be that the evaluator may entrust data collection to assistants who may want to finish the work quickly, resorting to shortcuts in data recording.

6 An example of a *closed question* might be: 'In your judgement, how many per cent of the members adhere to [one specified rule of behaviour]?' A corresponding *open question* might be: 'In your opinion, how do members adhere to rules of behaviour that you have agreed on for your organisation?' In the present context, when *induced to discuss*, the participants are guided on the topic and broadly on how to address it, but beyond that encouraged to reason and exchange views as freely as possible.

Chapter 8

Assessing and Interacting with the Environment

Contextual Analysis: a Hallmark of Development Planning

We have emphasised that development planning is a normative pursuit, explicitly aiming at improving aspects of the quality of life. Any meaningful analysis of people's quality of life and how it may be augmented involves assessment of people's living environment and complex, changing and often less than predictable interrelations and interactions between people and a range of environmental factors. Such factors may be grouped under broad headings such as political, economic, social, cultural, organisational, built physical (infrastructural), natural environmental and so on. Many of them (notably political and administrative as well as other organisational, cultural and certain social factors) may be viewed as sub-entities of a broader category of 'institutional'.

Moreover, development programmes and projects are organised thrusts. From the point of view of a responsible organisation, strategic development thinking is about creating benefits for people through interaction between the organisation and aspects of the organisation's environment. This was emphasised initially in Chapter 2 by our general definition of organisational strategy as 'the mediating force between the organisation and its environment'. The intended beneficiaries may then belong to the organisation or be outsiders (in the organisation's environment) and may be involved in that interaction to various extents and in various ways.

We have further emphasised the high degree of uniqueness of programme and project environments. The implication of this recognition, already drawn in Chapter 1, is that development planning is a basically inductive thrust. Thus, theory building in its conventional sense, rooted in the natural sciences and parts of economics, is virtually impossible.

This high degree of uniqueness can be observed at all levels. At the national level, just consider the largely different opportunities, constraints and threats facing non-governmental development organisations (NGDOs) in countries such as Myanmar, Vietnam and Cambodia, located within the same region of Asia. In Myanmar, any work that is seen as posing the slightest challenge to the country's repressive government is prohibited. This leaves NGDOs with basically two options: supporting the government in the little development work it does for its population, on the government's terms, or limiting themselves to work of a basically charitable kind. In Vietnam, the freedom of work of NGDOs has been restricted as well. Still, such organisations have been able to collaborate with far more legitimate, democratic and accountable government bodies and, not least, a range of well-instituted 'people's unions' (one example being the Women's Union, with a hierarchical set-up from the national to the local level). Besides, the government's policy regarding NGDOs is now being liberalised. In Cambodia, in the wake of the country's extremely tumultuous and traumatic history of governance, a 'free-for-all' situation has prevailed over many years, even to the extent that a multitude of NGDOs have virtually monopolised the limited personnel pool, on which government agencies must also draw, for work that the NGDOs largely decide on and manage.

At regional and local levels, opportunities and constraints are similarly diverse. There are differences in many aspects of the natural environment, and there are differences in man-made physical environments, depending on the level of economic development, government policy and many other factors. For development planning, the institutional context (broadly understood) is invariably crucial.

In Chapter 3, I argued that much planning that has gone under the name of 'regional planning' has been less than effective. There may have been many reasons for that, but a main one has usually been a poor and often unclear political and wider institutional foundation for such planning. This has tended to insulate the planning operation from the main societal forces and processes and to exclude substantial participation by important external stakeholders. Thereby, regional planning efforts have tended to become the rather narrow technical pursuit of planning 'specialists', normally with its main emphasis on 'designing' future spatial patterns of settlement, physical infrastructure, industries and services, natural conservation areas and so on. In most instances, the ensuing plans have turned out to be poor instruments for guiding societal change, beyond legitimising certain investments by government line agencies, many of which might have been made anyway. This has tended to be the situation in both economically highly developed and less developed countries.

In most highly developed countries, in contrast to this 'social engineering' approach, one finds planning that has been instituted in strong local government bodies under pressure of accountability to the electorate. The planning that such bodies have done has usually been 'strategic' in a more substantial and varied sense. This has made it more untidy, but at the same time much more effective. Unfortunately, in most less-developed countries, local governments have been both weak and less than accountable to the population they have been intended to serve. In Chapter 3 I also argued that various 'participatory' approaches devised by NGDOs in such countries may be seen as efforts to compensate for the lack of democratic institutions and the related ineffectiveness of development work at the local community level.[1]

This brief scan of complex, largely unique and frequently changing societal settings should have further underlined earlier arguments about the centrality of contextual analysis in development planning. Problems to be addressed and people afflicted by them exist in complex societal contexts. The organisations that aim at addressing the problems are similarly situated, and have to relate to external stakeholders and numerous non-animate environmental factors.

In following up our initial framework for development planning, we have already, in Chapter 5, delved into problem analysis, one main dimension of contextual analysis in any kind of development thrust. We emphasised perspectives on problems, general approaches to exploring problems and more specific techniques for clarifying and understanding problems. In the present chapter, we shall delve more into the second broad field of contextual analysis, namely, exploration of opportunities, constraints and threats relating to work that one wants to undertake, and how to translate environmental conditions into assumptions connected to intended achievements.

Opportunities, Constraints and Threats

The concepts in the context of planning

In Chapter 2, we introduced the concepts of opportunity, constraint and threat, and we have briefly referred to them in some other contexts. They are features in the society of great significance for development programmes and projects, in the sense that they will influence their design, implementation and achievements, positively or negatively. There may be present and future opportunities and constraints. The future ones may be more or less uncertain. For that reason, we tend to call potential future negative influences threats rather than constraints. In the same vein, relating to the future, we often ought to talk of potential opportunities rather than just opportunities.

In the context of development work, there are two different *perspectives* on opportunities, constraints and threats that one must distinguish clearly between:

1 they may be concerns of planning, that is, variables that planners may actively relate to in various ways, depending on the intended scope of the scheme, the perspectives and competence of the planning agency, capabilities during implementation, and a range of organisation-contextual factors;

2 following the stage or stages of planning, they are programme- or project-external factors that may influence the performance or the achievements of the development scheme, in various ways and to different extents.

Thus, external factors to a programme or project (or any part of it) that has been planned (point 2) are actual or potential influencing forces that are outside the scope of action of the scheme. Thereby, they are opportunities, constraints and/or threats on which the responsible organisation or organisations exert no direct influence (or, at least, cannot be expected to exert influence), once the scheme has been planned.

Analysing environmental aspects is, we have stressed, a crucial part of *strategic planning* (point 1). In this context, 'environment' means features external to the planning and implementing organisation or organisations and other direct stakeholders (primarily, intended beneficiaries). At the stage or stages of planning, one may relate to relevant aspects in the environment of these bodies in basically two ways:

a one may give them direct attention in the respective programme or project, that is, internalise them;

b one may seek to harmonise as well as possible what one decides to do with what will remain outside the programme's or project's scope of action.

By such measures, one should, in strategic planning, seek to exploit opportunities maximally and to minimise constraints and threats.

In Chapter 3, we distinguished between different conceptions of planning basically by the *time horizon* applied, being related to the scope, specificity and degree of connectedness of the plans or plan components that are worked out. We used 'long-range planning', 'issue-focused planning', 'strategic management' and 'environmental scanning' to express categories on this uneven continuum of time horizons and related aspects of planning and plans.

The basic rationale for this categorisation is differences in perceptions about the context (environment) in which the planning is done. Long-range planning is based on an image of relatively high certainty about relevant aspects of the environment, even in a relatively distant future. For this to be realistic, the planning normally has to be confined to general matters and should avoid conflict-ridden issues. At the other end of the continuum is environmental scanning, based on an image of an ever-changing and unpredictable environment, to which one may need to relate virtually continuously, in a highly flexible manner. Issue-focused planning and strategic management are the most comprehensive planning concepts of the four, addressing environmental aspects substantially and systematically in the context of a broad-based strategy analysis.

Moreover, in Chapter 3, we connected these notions to the more operational concepts of *process* and *blueprint* planning. We clarified that process planning is at least primarily applied in order to cope better with uncertainties of various kinds. This also involves a need for continuous learning in the specific programme context. Commonly, therefore, a closely connected purpose of process planning is gradual augmentation of the capacity of involved organisations and individuals, through learning from work they have done or are doing.

Related notions and perspectives

There are some additional, more specific, features of and perspectives on environmental variables that we should consider. We have already alluded to a distinction between *animate* and *inanimate* opportunities, constraints and threats. The former are external human beings (individuals or groups) or organisations that exert influence on the development programme or project, or may do so, normally through purposive action. They are, in other words, actual or potential stakeholders (see also Chapter 2). In sensible development planning, one will, normally, interrelate with them rather than just influence, command or avoid them. Inanimate factors, on the other hand, may not respond (for instance, the hours of sunlight) or may do so only mechanistically (soil quality, in reaction to some treatment).

Linked to this, an obviously crucial question in planning is whether or to what extent opportunities, constraints and threats are *amenable to change*. This may decide whether, to what extent and how one may or should address them. For instance, in a watershed reforestation project, the amount of rainfall (on which survival and growth of the tree seedlings may depend) may not be influenced. On the other hand, it may be possible to address a problem of incompatible activities of people in the watershed, such as cultivation – for instance, through voluntary resettlement of the people who cultivate there.

Finally, it may often be difficult or even impossible to distinguish clearly between internal and external phenomena, that is, to establish a clear *boundary* between them; or there may be different perceptions of what is internal and external. This may be the case primarily in programmes with broad participation and in programmes and projects that are collaborative efforts between two or more organisations.

For instance, in community development programmes, local people may be involved in numerous activities in various ways, ranging from well-formalised participation to involvement of an entirely informal nature. Thereby, the boundary between the programme and its environment becomes blurred, and different involved persons may sometimes view their own and other actors' roles differently.

In cases of collaborating organisations, the matter of internal versus external may be particularly complex and sometimes also ambiguous. Let us illustrate this by a community-based pre-school programme – a collaborative venture between an NGO, a community-based organisation (in each of the many programme communities) and a government department. The NGO provides most of the support from outside the local communities, including motivation, training, provision of teaching materials, advice in various fields and overall monitoring over a certain period. The exception is a modest salary to the pre-school teachers that is to be paid by the government department. The community-based organisations are supposed to do all that is possible with local resources and capabilities, such as recruiting local persons as teachers, erecting a simple building, and operating and maintaining the pre-school over the longer term.

In this case, we may distinguish between three main categories of variables on the internal–external dimension: variables internal to the organisations individually; other variables internal to the programme as a whole (whether considered as internal or external to the individual organisations); and variables external to the entire programme.

Success of this programme will depend on the extent to which all the collaborating partners fulfil their obligations. At the same time, each organisation will have different degrees of control of or influence on different activities. For example, although the NGO has an overall co-ordinating and monitoring role, it cannot ensure the quality of the other organisations' work in the same direct way as the quality of its own work. Thus, although it may provide comprehensive support to all the community organisations, some of the latter may perform poorly for reasons beyond its ability to influence. Likewise, the NGO may not be able to stop any general policy change by the government regarding payment of pre-school teachers.

Moving Boundaries between the Internal and the External

It should already be quite clear that the boundary between internal and external variables of a development programme or project is a strategic issue, explored and decided on in the course of planning. We have also emphasised that the feasibility of addressing aspects of relevance varies along an axis that stretches from the readily feasible to the absolutely impossible.

The issue has more facets, of course. Here we shall reflect further on relations between this dimension of internal–external and other dimensions of planning and management. For the sake of clarity and consistency of the argument, our perspective will be *expansion of the scope* of a development scheme – normally, this is also the most challenging scenario. We shall seek to clarify reasons for expanding the scope and the major consequences of doing so for programme or project design and implementation.

There may be at least four main arguments for expanding the scope of a development thrust. For a particular scheme, one or more of them may apply. One argument for expanded scope may be to *reach more people*. For instance, a regional development programme may be gradually broadened through additional and more diverse projects to address the needs of more and more diverse groups among the region's population.

A second argument for expanding a programme or project may be to make it *more normative*. As we have seen, this means, basically, to move the main focus higher up in a conceivable means–ends structure. For instance, a recognition may have emerged from a nutrition project that emphasis solely on nutrition interventions has had a limited effect on the overall health of the target population. Consequently, it may have been decided to shift the emphasis of the project more to the latter, which would require incorporation of other health-promoting activities as well. In other words, more direct emphasis on people's quality of life would lead one to design a more comprehensive project. This is a typical scenario and, in fact, discloses the reason for the hierarchical form that means–ends structures tend to get.

A third argument for expanding the scope may be to make the scheme *more robust* against future threats. For instance, one may increase the sustainability of an irrigation-based land settlement scheme by broadening it from mere construction of irrigation facilities and land allocation to also include promotion of community-based institutions of various kinds, development of other physical and social infrastructure, training in cultivation techniques, etcetera.

The two last-mentioned justifications, in particular, may be closely related with the *increased effectiveness* of the scheme. More direct concern with critical aspects of people's living situations may help augment the benefits of a development thrust, while greater robustness may promote the sustainability of attained benefits.

Sometimes, just doing more of the same thing – that is, increasing the scale of a programme or project – may have the above-mentioned effects. For instance, producing more of a new product in an area may promote a more effective and sustainable marketing system for that product from the area, and training more people in a specific vocation may indirectly help promote an industry that needs persons with that particular skill.

Normally, however, we include more in the idea of expanded scope than an increase of scale. The scope may even be augmented without any change of scale or despite a reduced scale. What we primarily have in mind is greater diversity of components and activities. The latter, in particular, may have substantial implications for planning and implementation, largely depending on the type of development work and the degree of expansion of the programme or project. Greater diversity normally means that the work will be done by a larger number of organisations, organisational units and/or individuals. Moreover, for the sake of efficiency and often also effectiveness, different components and activities commonly need to be interrelated, often both operationally and in terms of complementarity of outputs and benefits.

All this creates additional challenges of management. Using common terminology of management science, we may broadly summarise the most important ones as challenges of leadership and coordination. *Leadership* is sometimes used with a relatively narrow meaning, including motivation, inspiration and informal guidance. More frequently, it is used in a broader sense, also including formal guidance in policy and strategy formulation, clarification of role structures, and outward promotion of the organisation and its work. *Coordination* may be an even more obviously important concept in relation to challenges from increased diversity. Unfortunately, in the development field, the concept has tended to be used rather vaguely for a rather narrow set of collaborative arrangements in planning and, particularly, implementation. I have in another context (Dale, 2000a) formulated a typology of mechanisms of coordination, which planners and managers may choose from for promoting effective and efficient management of complex development programmes and projects. The mechanisms and related tasks were briefly summarised in Chapter 4.

In some instances, expanding the scope of a development thrust may involve a more substantial *change of approach.* This may include major aspects of organisation, composition of components and mode of work. A good example is programmes for making financial services available to poor people.

For decades, issuing credit in the form of standardised packages from state or state-controlled banks has been a main measure to promote production and alleviate poverty – particularly among farmers, but also for others. Over the years, it has become increasingly recognised that such schemes have been less than effective, for a range of reasons that have gradually become better understood.[2]

These experiences have led to searches for alternative approaches to augment financial services for poor people. A main lesson from conventional credit disbursement schemes has been that they have been too narrow and rigid, besides alienating the people they have been intended to benefit. Consequently, in many programmes, more participatory approaches have been explored, normally coupled with a broader array of financial services and the incorporation of these services in more comprehensive development thrusts, including non-financial components. Moreover, many development agencies now promote systems of financial services that are anchored in people's own organisations. To this end, social mobilisation and various organisation-building measures are normally essential.

Thus, a recognised need for more comprehensive and flexible systems of financial services, often along with ideas of people's empowerment, has led to the promotion of new organisational structures and modes of operation. Through these, the financial services have become embedded in more elaborate systems of decision making and operation relating to a broader set of people's concerns.

In other words, increasing the programme scope – from mere delivery and recovery of credit to a broader range of services linked to a broader set of concerns and a more comprehensive involvement by the beneficiaries – has required a fundamental change of approach in virtually all senses.[3]

Incorporating Assumptions into the Logical Framework

The third column of the logical framework is reserved for specification of assumptions relating to the development work that is being or has been planned. If we use two columns for 'indicators' and 'means of substantiation' (as we did in Chapter 7), we will need a fourth column for specifying the assumptions.

As we saw in Chapter 4, assumptions are normally considered to be external factors (opportunities, constraints and threats) on which the performance of a planned development programme or project depends, to larger or lesser extent. Yet, as we have also seen, in many instances the distinction between a development scheme and what is external to the scheme may be a porous boundary rather than a clear-cut dividing line. This should become even clearer in the course of discussion later in this chapter, particularly in the last section.

Moreover, in incrementally planned programmes, only rather general assumptions may be stated with any long-term applicability. This applies to the second of the two cases that will now be presented. More specific assumptions will have to be clarified and formulated incrementally – that is, as and when activities are planned.

In Tables 8.1 and 8.2, I have incorporated assumptions pertaining to the two cases that we know from Chapters 6 and 7, in logical framework format. In order to save space, 'means of substantiation' has been omitted, enabling us to use the third column for assumptions. The statements in this column of the framework are direct responses to the question: 'under what conditions may the intended outputs be produced/may the intended benefits be generated?'. This basically equals: 'what are the requirements in the programme or project's environment that need to be fulfilled for the intended outputs/intended benefits to materialise?'.

Note that the specified assumptions in any row relate to fulfilment of the outputs or objectives (as the case may be) in the row above. That is, they are conditions under which tasks/outputs/objectives in the same row are expected to be converted into related outputs/objectives in the next row. For example, in Table 8.1, they are factors wholly or largely outside the scope of the project that will determine or influence the conversion of the output 'information about nutrition given to parents' into the intended achievement 'more healthy food is accessed'. Thereby, of course, they also become conditions for the intended effect 'children are better nourished'.

In the case of the project for improving children's health, shown in Table 8.1, I have not specified any assumptions for conversion of the

Table 8.1 Improving Children's Health: Logical Framework (3)

DEVELOPMENT OBJECTIVE	INDICATORS	ASSUMPTIONS
Children (of estate labourers in district X) enjoy better health than earlier	Frequency of treatment of relevant diseases Health personnel's statements Mothers' statements	No offsetting negative changes in related fields The improved practices are continued The wells are maintained
EFFECT OBJECTIVES	INDICATORS	ASSUMPTIONS
Children are better nourished Children are less prone to infections from their physical environment Children drink clean water	Height, weight/age Frequency of diarrhoea Health personnel's statements Mothers' statements Observed practice	*None* (If the main causes of diseases have been addressed, improved health is virtually guaranteed in the short term)
IMMEDIATE OBJECTIVES	INDICATORS	ASSUMPTIONS
More healthy food is accessed More hygienic household routines are practised Unpolluted water is accessed	Mothers' statements Money spending pattern Use of water-sealed toilets Quality of water at the source Water storage practices in the households	Children's total consumption of more nutritious food is increased Children drink unpolluted water Children drink no other water
OUTPUTS	INDICATORS	ASSUMPTIONS
Information about nutrition and hygiene given to parents Food supplements supplied to schools New tube wells provided Present water sources improved	Recorded activities/items/ facilities Stakeholders' statements Observed activities/items/ facilities	The trainees are motivated The households can afford additional food items Household members accept changed composition of meals Household members accept to spend time on new practices
IMPLEMENTATION TASKS	INPUTS	ASSUMPTIONS
For the nutrition/hygiene training Conduct the training Organise the training classes Prepare the training material Recruit the trainers Decide on the scope of training	Training expertise Technical expertise Administrative personnel Management systems Tools and materials Logistics	*None* (Under normal circumstances and if well planned and implemented)

planned tasks into the planned outputs. That is due to the clearly delimited and specific (technical) nature of the outputs in this case. This should enable the planners to design the outputs, as well as the tasks and processes for producing them, in sufficient detail and with sufficient firmness for them to be implemented in a highly controlled manner. The feasibility, in this case, of highly controlled implementation may be better substantiated in the means–ends chart for this project, which was presented in Chapter 6 (Figure 6.2). Even for the provision of information (which may be the least technical output among those presented), we see that the tasks involved are clearly delimited and specific pieces of work, which one should be able to undertake without much uncertainty or deviation from the plans.

In this case, by far the most critical conversion links are between the outputs and the immediate objectives and between the immediate objectives and the effect objectives. It is here that the means–ends relations of the project will be most exposed to influencing factors from the project's environment. In other words, in this project, the dominant concern is the likelihood of generating the intended benefits for people from the created outputs. For relatively technical projects, at least, this tends to be the situation more generally.

Of course, the stated assumptions are just examples of conditions that are considered to be relevant and important for such a project. The assumptions should be fairly self-explanatory. Let us mention two examples of sets of them. The conversion of the information provided about nutrition into better nourished children is stated to depend on (1) whether the trainees are motivated for learning, whether the households can afford additional food items, and whether the household members accept changed composition of meals; and then (2) whether the children's total consumption of more nutritious food is increased. The conversion of the provision of unpolluted water into the children drinking clean water is stated to depend on (1) whether household members consent to spend the required time collecting the water, and then (2) whether the children drink the unpolluted water and no other water.

In this project, attainment of the development objective should be a virtually automatic consequence of attainment of the effect objectives. Of course, this will hold only if the problem structure to which the means–ends structure relates – that poor nourishment, poor hygiene and contaminated water are the major causes of preventable diseases – is a good reflection of the reality.

This argument is also limited to the relatively short term. In the longer term, numerous things may change or occur – in fields directly related to

Table 8.2 Community Institution Building: Logical Framework (3)

DEVELOPMENT OBJECTIVE	INDICATORS	ASSUMPTIONS
The organisations' members and their families enjoy higher quality of life, physically and mentally	Members' statements Other household persons' statements	No offsetting negative changes in other spheres Benefits are perceived to outweigh additional effort in the long term
EFFECT OBJECTIVES	**INDICATORS**	**ASSUMPTIONS**
People feel more secure economically Children are more healthy People enjoy better housing People enjoy more harmonious interrelations	Members' statements Health personnel's statements Clinic records of treatments Type of house roofing material Members' mode of communication in meetings	No strong negative influences in other spheres on individuals/households No strong programme-related strains on individuals /households
IMMEDIATE OBJECTIVES	**INDICATORS**	**ASSUMPTIONS**
Common funds are available and used for emergencies Income is increased Informal loan taking is reduced Better collaboration among members/households	Credit disbursements, by member and purpose Members' statements Labour exchange Common contributions in community functions	The additional financial resources are used wisely No strong negative influences in other spheres on individuals/households
OUTPUTS	**INDICATORS**	**ASSUMPTIONS**
People's organisations are functioning People's organisations formed People's skills improved People's motivation and understanding enhanced	Rate of meeting attendance Adherence to procedures Adherence to other rules of member behaviour Social mobiliser's statements Members' statements	Exploitable local resources for production Cooperation of other household members Permissive wider social environment
IMPLEMENTATION TASKS	**INPUTS**	**ASSUMPTIONS**
Regularly review progress *Help sensitise and train people* Train social mobilisers Recruit social mobilisers Continuously assess needs, opportunities and constraints	Policy/planning expertise Training personnel Administrative personnel Management systems Logistics	No strongly repressive social structures No blocking religious tenets/ cultural traditions Permissive family environment

the project and in other fields – that may influence the prevalence of diseases among children. This is the issue of concern in the top cell of the 'assumptions' column. Here, then, are stated conditions that the planners think will need to be fulfilled for the benefits of the project to be maintained (or augmented) in the future.

Here, once again, we can discern different degrees of firmness or clarity of the boundary between parts of the project and its environment. Some assumptions may not be expressions of exclusively external factors. For example, the participants' motivation to learn may depend mainly on aspects of their living situation that the project does not address, but it may also be influenced by the mode of teaching. On the other hand, the economic ability of the households to buy additional food items will not be effected at all by this project.

For the institution-building programme, shown in Table 8.2, assumptions have been specified between implementation tasks and outputs. In other words, although the work may be done well, there may still be forces in the programme's environment that may influence the relatively direct results – the outputs – of that work. That is because the individual- and organisation-related qualities that we consider to be the outputs in this case are less specific and controllable than, for instance, the outputs of our health promotion project (see also Chapter 6).

An exception may be 'people's organisations formed'. 'Organisation' here means a physical entity with a set of formal characteristics (which may also be more or less standardised for all the organisations created under the programme). These entities are then more similar to the outputs of the health promotion project, and their formation should be more controllable than the other outputs of the institution-building programme.

The elaboration in the preceding pages should have provided a sufficient basis for understanding the specified (and, in the present case, selective) assumptions at the different levels of this programme without further clarification.

A Further Reflection about Assumptions

We shall examine somewhat further relations between (1) statements of the means–ends structure and (2) corresponding assumptions that we may formulate. The examination largely builds on arguments we have already made. It should sensitise us even more to what we address in planning, the level of specificity at which we operate, and the implications of our focus and scope for constraints and threats – and, therewith, the degree of certainty or uncertainty in our work.

To illustrate, we shall start by repeating a nexus of statements from Table 8.1, connecting (1) the provision of nutrition-related information to the parents of the target children to (2) the intended achievement of better nourished children. The nexus is reproduced for our present purposes in Figure 8.1.[4]

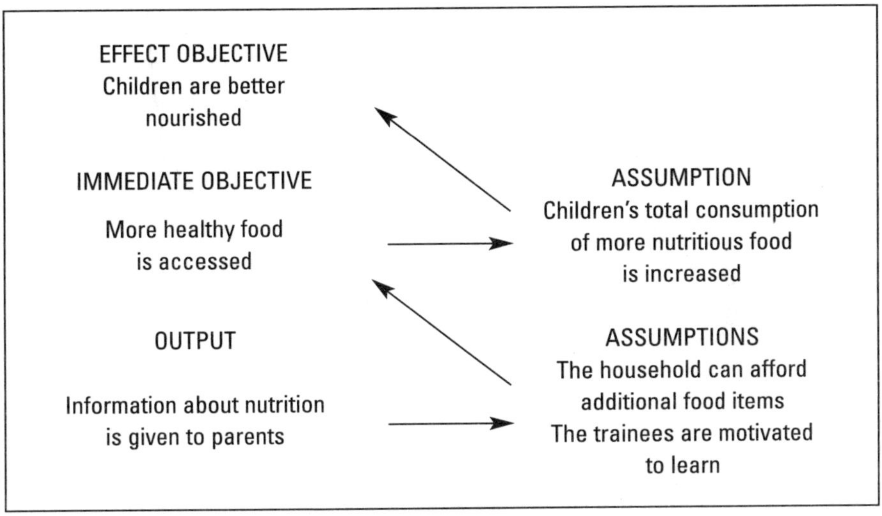

Figure 8.1 Relations between Means–Ends Categories and Assumptions (A)

We shall now contract and expand the above means–ends structure, and consider implications for assumptions. First we shall formulate a means–ends structure that is at present more common in logical frameworks. We have already mentioned this structure, in Chapters 4 and 6. At the levels of objectives, it consists of one (only one) 'purpose' and one 'goal'. Moreover, we have mentioned that 'purpose' is meant to express the general intended achievement for people of the particular development scheme, while 'goal' is meant to signify a more general sphere of improvements, to which the scheme is intended to contribute. By this logic, it would be appropriate to retain our development objective as the 'purpose', and formulate a broader statement of quality of life as the 'goal'. A credible formulation of the latter might be 'children enjoy better lives than earlier'.[5]

Figure 8.2 shows consequences for a simplified outputs–objectives structure (here, 'outputs–purpose') for formulation of assumptions. For direct comparability, we have maintained the categories in our logical framework (that is, we have not added or deleted anything).

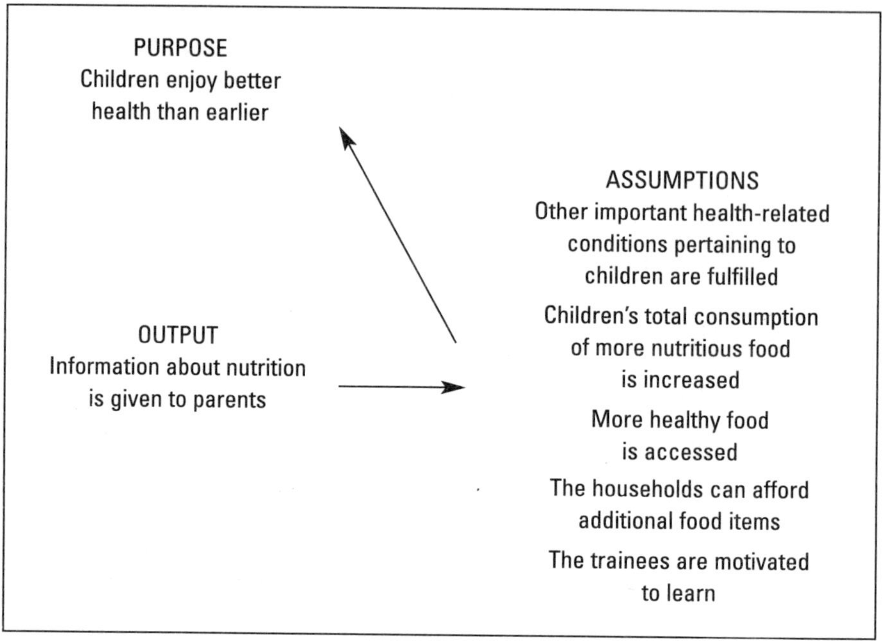

Figure 8.2 Relations between Means–Ends Categories and Assumptions (B)

We see that we have now substituted categories of our original means–ends structure with a long list of assumptions between the output and the general intended achievement (purpose). This list would have been even longer had we also specified the immediate objectives and effect objectives for the other fields of intervention (in general terms: food supplements, hygiene and water supply) along with the assumptions relating to those objectives. In the figure, we have simply grouped all such other aspects into the broad category 'other important health-related conditions pertaining to children are fulfilled'. Moreover, we see that some assumptions are related to one another, just as with components of the means–ends structure that they partly substitute.

Thus, by this restriction to only one 'purpose', achievements and related assumptions will be presented in the same list, if they are to be stated at all. This gives an untidy and unclear picture of components of the project. And, by thus mixing intended achievements with assumptions relating to them, differences between internal and external variables will be confused. In practice, in logical frameworks, one will not specify such long lists of assumptions – for lack of space, if no other reason. Thereby, a semblance of tidiness is created, at the expense of hiding important pieces of

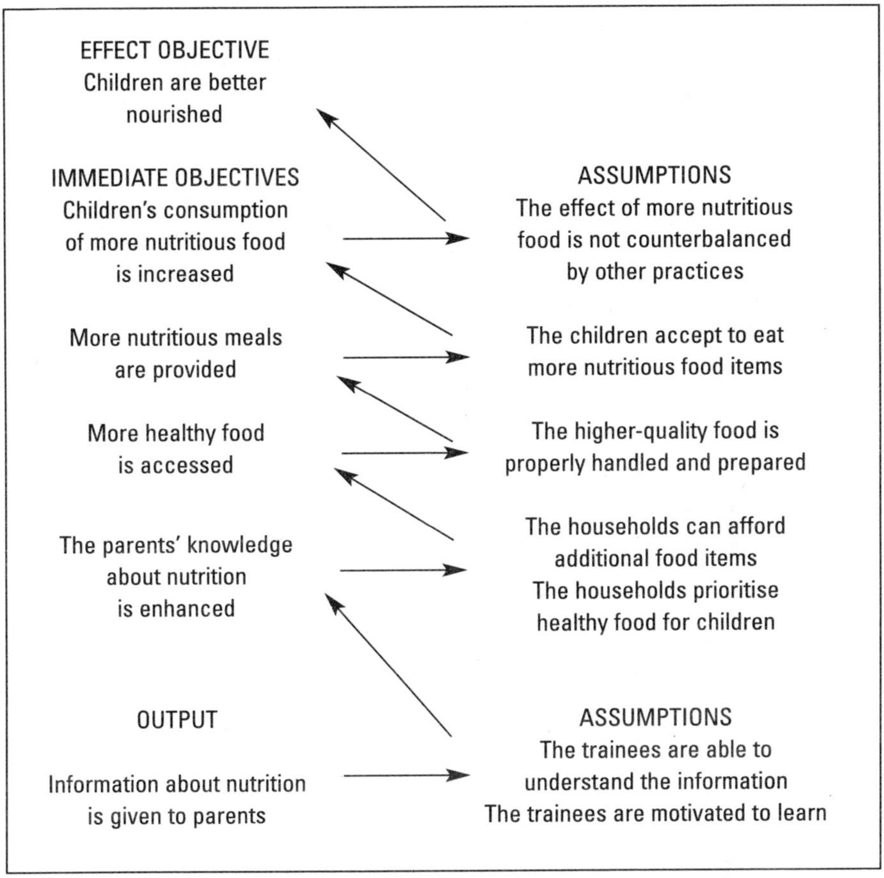

Figure 8.3 Relations between Means–Ends Categories and Assumptions (C)

information. To conclude, then, our manipulation should have amplified earlier arguments about the extent to which the logical framework is impoverished through the simplistic 'goal–purpose' constellation.

Yet, while clarifying categories and relations much better than the just-addressed version, even our more elaborate structure is a simplification of means–ends relations that will exist in reality. In Figure 8.3, therefore, we have moved in the opposite direction – elaborating a part of our original means–ends structure somewhat further. This, too, has implications for the formulation of assumptions.

We have here specified a means–ends chain from the same output upward in greater detail. All the new entries have been categorised as 'immediate objectives'. The appropriateness of this has been substantiated earlier in the book (in Chapters 4 and 6). With this more specific set of means – ends categories, we are also able to specify a more elaborate and specific set of assumptions.[6] In particular, this helps clarify in greater detail variables that one should explore in monitoring and evaluation of this project component. Finally, note that we have drawn one original assumption into the means–ends structure: 'children's consumption of more nutritious food is increased'. This is obviously appropriate here. It underlines, once more, the porous nature of many relations between internal and external variables.

In practice, then, when formulating means–ends structures and assumptions relating to them, one needs to strike a reasonable balance between (1) the possible scope of details, considering the nature of the development scheme, the underlying analysis, etcetera; and (2) the amount of information that may be appropriate for the purpose at hand. Normally, one needs to explore and formulate structures in greater detail in the operational planning of a development scheme than what is presented in a logical framework for the scheme. Simultaneously, one should not simplify so much in the logical framework that one loses sight of essential means–ends relations and assumptions pertaining to them. This, I have argued, is the case with the presently conventional version of the framework. The version I have formulated in this book provides substantially more information while being, I think, equally easy to use and understand.

Notes

1 For further elaboration and discussion of the argument about regional planning, see Dale, 2000b. On local government, see, for example, Chandler, 1996; Shotton, 1999; Kammeier and Demaine, 2000; and Aziz and Arnold, 1996. The two last books focus on decentralised administration and local government in Asian countries.

2 For a brief and instructive overview of the main issues and experiences, I recommend Birgegaard, 1994.

3 A case of local institution building with micro-finance is elaborated in Chapter 10, in the perspective of modes of planning. The reader will get a better understanding of the scope and mode of work of such programmes by reading the more detailed description of that case. For further elaboration and discussion of the issues involved, reference is made to much recent literature on community organisation and micro-finance. I have done some research on this myself (Dale, 2001; 2002a).

4 Some statements in this and in the following figures are slightly modified from those in the logical framework, since we are less constrained by space.

5 The goal statement hardly contributes much of value to our means–ends structure, and we shall not discuss further relations between these statements of purpose and goal.

6 One of these additional assumptions, 'the trainees are able to understand the information', could have been stated in the original framework as well.

Chapter 9

Tools of Prioritisation

Introduction

Development wants are normally huge, while resources and abilities for development work are limited. A major challenge, therefore, is to obtain the largest possible benefits for people as efficiently as possible. Of course, the magnitude of this challenge varies vastly, reflecting the different and often changing wants among people, uneven distribution of resources and abilities at any given time, and different possibilities for augmenting resources and abilities. Moreover, all these variables are interrelated with numerous others.

Development work is not undertaken in a market economy setting, in which a general price mechanism matches (or is thought to match) supply and demand, whereby resources get allocated in specific quantities for specific uses. Consequently, the very concepts of 'supply' and 'demand', if utilised at all, will have different meanings than in conventional economics. Supply is purposively managed and mediated, and needs to be clarified by the kinds of resources and abilities that are at one's disposal or may be generated – such as money, voluntary labour, land, equipment, individual competence and organisational capacity. Demand is, normally, more appropriately expressed as 'priorities', the topic of exploration in the present chapter.

The matter is further complicated by the focus on, involvement by and interests of the different groups of people, now referred to by the widely used term 'stakeholders'. The core question to be posed in this connection is: whose resources are utilised by whom, and for whose benefit? This question and more specific related questions may be decided on in many ways by various numbers and combinations of stakeholders. Normally, the degree and mode of involvement by different categories of stakeholders tend to vary primarily with (1) the type of programme or project and (2) the attitudes and interactive abilities of core actors, mostly those at top levels. The intended beneficiaries themselves may be involved to larger or lesser extents in planning and implementation, or they may be left out of these processes.

Generally, processes of prioritisation become the more complex the more stakeholders are involved and the more diverse the stakeholders are in terms of background, needs, interests and power. From this point of view, decision making primarily from above, by top managers with the required authority, has merit. This tends to make such processes more straightforward and efficient.

There may be other arguments too for top-down planning. In particular, such planning may be appropriate for schemes where certain professional standards need to be ensured. In the development sphere, this primarily applies to many kinds of physical infrastructure and to the provision of standardised services based on specified criteria such as quantity, quality and accessibility. Examples from these two categories might be a technically advanced bridge or the location of primary and secondary schools under a national system of education. In many such instances, the final decision taker (who may not always be technically competent) will rely heavily on advice from specialists, whether these are staff within the same organisation or outsiders. While this may improve the information basis on which decisions are taken, it hardly makes the planning process more participatory, in the sense of involving a much wider array of stakeholders.

On the other hand, there are many and strong arguments for involving a wider range of stakeholders – including intended beneficiaries – in decision making, whenever and to the extent possible. Main arguments for broader participation may be to get additional or more reliable information for decision making or to obtain certain contributions from certain people (for instance, beneficiaries). Even more significantly, the participants may be expected to influence the type and magnitude of benefits and even to become empowered through these processes of decision making and action. This is most obviously the case in some kinds of capacity-building programmes, in which part of the intention is to empower the people, and often organisations to which they belong, through learning from their own work. For further discussion, see Chapter 10.

We need to realise that all prioritisation is based on numerous assumptions, which often tend to be implicit rather than explicit. They may be implicit because they reflect personal values or organisational cultures that are too complex to grapple with, but they may also remain unexposed because planners may not make much effort to analyse values and norms.

Negotiation

All prioritisation is done through some kind of reasoning. Most often, this is a process of wholly or primarily qualitative nature, in the mind or minds of one or more persons. When a decision on a matter has consequences for more than an individual, there may be good reason or even a need for those persons to share each others' thoughts, get feedback on them and jointly explore various aspect of the matter, with a view to arriving at a decision that takes into account various interests and views. We shall refer to such a process of interactive communication among individuals or groups towards decision taking as 'negotiation'.

Negotiation, in some form, is the most common means of arriving at decisions on matters that involve more than one person, in the development sphere and elsewhere. In the context of development work, negotiations mostly relate to intended benefits. They may focus on a range of questions, such as the magnitude or nature of the benefits, who are intended to receive them or how they are to be shared, efforts that are needed for generating them, and a range of more specific matters. Frequently, the negotiators also address any connected disadvantages, and ways and means of reducing the latter.

Commonly, one may also have to consider more or less formalised criteria of choice. These criteria may have been established by the negotiating persons themselves or by some external body, normally an organisation with a general authority in that field. In some instances, negotiations are not part of a regularised decision-making process, but are resorted to as a contingency measure – to solve an unexpected problem, for instance. An example of this might be an *ad hoc* discussion of new terms of repayment of a loan, which the borrower is not able to pay back according to the stipulated schedule.

Even in cases of strongly conflicting views, negotiations should aim at reaching the widest possible consensus among those involved. Still, some stakeholders will usually be more satisfied with an eventual decision than others. In some instances, decisions are even taken (and may have to be taken) against the will of one or more individuals or groups.

Various approaches, concerns and processes of negotiation are structured and elaborated further below, under four main headings.

Informal mutual adjustment

What we call informal mutual adjustment is defined as the coordination of work through non-formalised communication between involved bodies

(Mintzberg, 1983; Dale, 2000a).[1] The adjustment may be a one-time effort in relation to a single decision, or it may be an ongoing process, relating to decisions that are to be taken frequently or incrementally.

In our daily lives, most prioritisation involving more than one person is made through informal mutual adjustment. This mechanism is common in organised development work too. Thus it tends to be a main or even the dominant mode of prioritisation in organisations that are founded on principles of collective action, such as community-based groups of various kinds. Generally, informal mutual adjustment is the more applied the less rule-bound the organisations are and the greater flexibility they have in deciding what to do and how to work, but it tends to be important in other kinds of organisations too, in many situations.[2]

Overall, negotiation in this form is a more important mechanism of prioritisation than we tend to think. Its importance may often be underestimated because the processes are usually less overt than more formalised mechanisms of prioritisation.

Meetings

More formally structured processes of prioritisation may also differ widely. A distinction has been made between 'discussion' and 'dialogue' (for example, Innes and Booher, 1999). Formalised discussions with the explicit aim of arriving at one or more decisions (or, at least, preparing the ground for them) are normally referred to as 'meetings' (see also Chapter 5).

Meetings are chaired events with an agenda and normally also a time frame and general structure of the planned discussion. Within this formalised framework, individuals or groups will present their views and ideas, which will be critiqued by others, often in many rounds of interaction. In the process of discussion, the meeting chair tries to distil main ideas or clusters of ideas and normally seeks to guide the participants towards a conclusion that all or most may agree on or somehow accept. Frequently, however, consensus is not achieved, and decisions may have to be undertaken by voting among the participants (see later); or they will be taken by others, using the discussion in the meeting (or several meetings) as input.

Meetings may often be effective, alone or as part of a process, for generating decisions in a reasonably democratic manner. They are the most recognised and widely used mechanism of negotiation in government agencies and other relatively highly formalised organisations, for debating matters on which decisions are to be arrived at within certain time limits and often also other constraints. A common negative feature of meetings is that they tend to become more or less dominated by certain individuals or groups of stakeholders, for a variety of reasons.

Facilitated group communication

A structured group communication event tends to distinguish itself from a meeting in three main senses: (1) it is intended to be a forum of relative equals, in terms of their willingness and ability to contribute in the communication, and frequently also in terms of basic relevant interests; (2) the participants are intended to engage in a freer dialogue than is usually the case in a meeting; and (3) the event is facilitated, rather than chaired. Facilitation normally means that one person helps promote a common understanding of the purpose of the event, provides any basic initial information that all the participants should share, helps ensure a reasonable degree of focus and structure of the dialogue, and services the participants in other ways, largely on the latter's initiative.

Ideally, this is a highly democratic mode of problem analysis and decision making, in the sense of providing relatively equal opportunities for the participants to influence the course of events and the outcome of the process. For this to happen in practice, this ideological foundation should be recognised and well understood by all the participants.

In a deeper sense, the idea of facilitated communication on equal terms is linked to a major current in the thought of Jürgen Habermas (1975; 1984). A main concern in his writings is to bring to light distortions in communication in societies, a process requiring free communal self-reflection, referred to as 'discursive communication' and 'discourse'. Thereby, the participants will be able to challenge the prevailing norm structures and states of affairs, which typically have been created by and in the interests of the powerful. In other words, Habermas seeks a re-construction of the public realm, enabling members of societies to pursue public discussion and organise public affairs without being dominated by élite groups. For this to be fully attained, an 'ideal speech situation' must exist, in which everybody is equally free to speak, and in which all other motives are put out of play than a willingness to come to an understanding in accordance with basic shared norms. Of course, such an ideal situation will never exist. However, given a reasonably secure setting and a basic amount of mutual recognition and respect, Habermas thinks that most people – in their capacity as speakers and listeners – have the ability required to understand each other, rationally evaluate the process of communication and engage in mutual learning.

Habermas connects this argument to a broader theory of societal change, having substantial similarities with the idea of 'structuration' developed by Antony Giddens (1984). Most such processes are best managed in relatively small groups. A common problem is to strike a reasonable balance between, on the one hand, a high degree of similarity of perspectives and interests (promoting free communication) and, on the other hand, broad participation by those who may have a stake in the matter that is discussed (which may impede free communication, owing to the power relations and conflicts of interest that may be involved).

A strategy for reducing this problem may be to begin by organising communication within groups of relative equals, and subsequently to juxtapose the priorities of the different groups in a bigger and more diverse forum (which may resemble a meeting). Alternatively, or in addition, the outcome of group discussions may constitute inputs into a further process of planning by another body such as a group of professional planners.

Role playing and bricolage

Innes and Booher (1999), drawing on previous work by themselves and others, sketch a theory of collaborative planning with role playing and bricolage[3] as core elements. The process is usually formally introduced by some public organisation, to try to deal with what are seen as intractable problems or with frustrations that have developed over years of conflict or stalemate (see also Ostrom, 1990). Consensus building, then, is viewed as a highly challenging process in which the dialogue partners may need to become more open-minded, suspending their assumptions or subjecting them to examination – all in an atmosphere of the greatest possible collegiality and high freedom of association.

Of course, these ideas are akin to Habermas's 'ideal speech situation', and largely incorporate the features of facilitated group communication that were outlined above. There are, however, some specific notions involved. First, a main idea in role playing and bricolage is that the participants are induced to unlock fixed positions by moving to more abstract levels of association. They may then 'allow themselves' to question earlier held assumptions, and they may become more open to any innovative idea that may be brought up. Commonly, to this end, participants may play different roles in different dialogue situations, through which their perspectives may be broadened.

Second, the process of communication is considered as justified in itself. There may even be no clear idea about alternative outcomes of the negotiation process, in the sense of having to establish priorities. In exceptional instances, the participants may, during the process, reach agreement on the entire problem complex; in other instances, agreement may be reached on some specific matters; and in yet other instances, it may be hard to document any accomplishment whatsoever (Innes and Booher, 1999). However, even when that is the case, the participants are expected to have undergone a process of learning, which may also promote their ability to address similar matters later.

Third, the above features have implications for the time that the participants may have to spend in negotiation. Consensus building in this mode will virtually always be a drawn-out process. Since normally, the outcome will be highly uncertain as well, the participants need to find the process itself engaging (like the players of a game).

In the context of development planning – including prioritisation – two particularly important questions emerge from these specific features and the connected deliberations. They are (1) the kinds of development problems that may best be addressed through this approach, and (2) the kinds of persons who may participate in such processes. Efforts of this magnitude and uncertainty may only be justified for complex and big schemes. The cases presented by Innes and Booher (1999) underline the question of scale. All the mentioned exercises relate to very large and complex thrusts, namely, metropolitan transport planning, a water management strategy for a whole river and principles of state governance (all in the USA).

A related very important question is the extent to which people's time is considered to have an opportunity cost, and if so, whether the participants may get some material remuneration for their involvement in the exercises. In most cases, it may be difficult, and even unfortunate, to pay people substantially for the time they spend. This raises the question of the kinds of people who may be involved in such long-lasting, even open-ended, processes. Highly deprived persons who struggle to meet their households' most basic needs from day to day cannot usually be expected to participate, being normally short of time and energy (Chambers, 1983; 1995; Dale, 2000a). Innes and Booher's statement that the 'players typically are young people conscious of growing up in the postmodern context' (1999: 9), with related freedom of action and choice, underscores this concern.

It is hard to escape the conclusion that deprived people may easily be excluded from lengthy processes that require a very considerable investment of time with highly uncertain returns. Arguably, it may even be immoral to induce them to get involved in such processes.

Voting

In many instances, negotiation may not be feasible or sufficient, either because decisions must or should be based on more formalised criteria or because it may not be possible to reach agreement through negotiation or through negotiation only. One may then resort to a range of other techniques of prioritisation. The simplest such technique is voting, or direct choice by individuals among clearly specified alternatives (two or more). The votes are then summed up, resulting in a frequency distribution of the number of votes for each alternative.

Voting is widely applicable. A few examples in the development field might be: a national referendum on a new social security system; voting within a political body on any development question; voting through a survey among people in a local community to establish their preference among stated design options for a communal facility; and voting among cultivators of a collective farm to choose the crop combination for the next season.

Table 9.1 shows the outcome of voting on the allocation of money that a community-based member organisation had earned from some activity. Prior to the voting, the members had decided on five alternatives, which they were to choose among. They were: (1) all the money would be saved in a bank in the organisation's name; (2–4) specified proportions (as stated in the table) would be saved and distributed respectively; and (5) all the money would be distributed to the members.

Table 9.1 Voting on Allocation Alternatives of Earned Money

Alternatives	Number of votes	% of votes
100% saved	12	25
75% saved, 25% distributed	14	29
50% saved, 50% distributed	12	25
25% saved, 75% distributed	3	6
100% distributed	7	15

The members had also agreed to implement the alternative that got most votes, irrespective of the distribution of votes. This illustrates an important general principle of voting, namely, clarity about subsequent action or direct consequences. The largest number of votes was received for the second alternative (75 per cent saved, 25 per cent distributed). In compliance with the established rules for the voting, the money would be allocated accordingly.

Techniques of Ranking

Needs or preferences of people can also be clarified by asking individuals to prioritise between items and then summing up the statements by all the information providers. This may be done by a researcher or planner. Alternatively, such prioritisation may be done by some group of people, normally facilitated by one person, and usually prioritising items relating to themselves.

There are several variants of generating people's views, namely:

- asking people to state their priorities freely within a specified field of inquiry (in this context, normally done by an external analyst);
- having people rank an entire list of stated items (normally given to the participants in writing or displayed on a board in the case of a group exercise);
- making people choose a specified number of prioritised items out of a pre-prepared list of items (either given to them in writing or read out to them individually, or displayed to all of them);
- asking the participants to give a value within a given range – such as 0, 1, 2 or 3 – to every item on a list or to a certain number of prioritised items on the list (either given to them in writing, read out to them, or displayed in front of them).

With the first variant, after all the people have been asked, the answers to the open questions must be sorted and arranged into a set of analytical categories that are standardised enough for reasonably informative and reliable comparison. For ranking people's priorities (our concern here), the statements – normally expressed in purely qualitative terms – may even be converted into numerical statements, in the form of a frequency distribution across categories that are specified by the analyst in the aftermath (see also Chapter 5). Since exploration through open questions is often important and therefore also common in the development field, such subsequent sorting and structuring is an exercise that development planners and managers ought to be familiar with.

With the other variants mentioned above, the analytical categories have already been specified. In all quantitative ranking, the pattern of priorities is then established by calculating the numbers under each category and possibly manipulating those numbers through some specific technique.

Weighted direct ranking

In weighted direct ranking, the pattern of priorities is arrived at by calculating the total number of entries (scores) and then applying some weighting system that reflects the priority or priorities of each information provider. In most instances, the information-providing units are households or individuals. The information is most frequently gathered through a survey of a sample of such units. But it may also be collected on forms distributed at a meeting or another similar event.

We shall illustrate this method through a survey of perceived development priorities among households in a slum area of a city, based on a pre-specified set of options. Such a survey may be undertaken by a researcher, the city administration or some development organisation. In this case, each of a total of 80 household representatives (respondents) has been asked to state the three options that he or she considers to be of highest priority, in ranked order. The order of priority is specified by the numbers 3, 2 and 1 for the first, second and third priority option respectively. The aggregated result is shown in Table 9.2.

The first three columns show the distribution of the answers for the listed development options, by the priority given to them by the respective respondents. The fourth column shows the total number of scores for each option (item). The scores have then been weighted by the weight numbers (3 for the first, 2 for the second and 1 for the third priority option), based on which an index of aggregated priorities, referred to as a 'priority index', has been calculated. The mathematical formula of the index is:

$$\text{Priority index} = [(f_{ONE} \times 3) + (f_{TWO} \times 2) + (f_{THREE} \times 1) / r$$

where: f_{ONE} = frequency of first priority
f_{TWO} = frequency of second priority
f_{THREE} = frequency of third priority
r = total number of respondents

For example, the table shows that altogether 42 of the 80 respondents mentioned 'housing' as one among their three priorities, 20 of whom had it as their first priority, 12 as their second priority and 10 as their third priority choice. The total scores are shown unweighted; we could, in addition, have had a column for weighted scores.

Table 9.2 Weighted Ranking of Development Options

Development options	Scores				Priority index	Rank
	Weight			Total		
	3	2	1			
Housing	20	12	10	42	1.18	***1***
Sanitary facilities	14	12	15	41	1.01	***2***
Renovation	2	6	7	15	0.31	*7*
Water supply	2	4	6	12	0.30	*8*
Internal streets/paths	0	2	3	5	0.09	
Shops	0	0	2	2	0.03	
Children's education	12	14	6	32	0.88	***3***
Adult education	2	1	1	4	0.11	
Health services	12	10	4	26	0.75	***4***
Cultural centre	0	0	4	4	0.05	
Premises for industries	6	2	2	10	0.30	*8*
Recreational park	4	7	4	15	0.38	*6*
Sportsground	6	10	16	32	0.68	***5***
Total	80	80	80	240		

The priority indexes range from 1.18 to 0.03, which by any reasonable standard is a wide distribution. A closer look reveals that the options fall into three broad clusters, by the priority they have been given by the respondents: those in the range 1.18–0.68, those in the range 0.38–0.30, and the rest (all of which have an index value below 0.12). For quick information about the general priorities, a 'rank' column has been added. The development options that fall into the first cluster are here displayed in bold italics, those falling into the second cluster in ordinary italics, and the others have not been ranked. This indicates that the last ones may not be considered in subsequent planning.

Pair-wise ranking

Pair-wise ranking is a tabular technique for clarifying, among a group of persons, the order of priority of alternatives, by comparing all listed options two by two. If there are differences of opinion (normally the case, to larger or lesser extent), the majority view prevails. Thus, the method is not sensitive to social differentiation in whatever sense, unless the ranking is done by different groups (see later).

Pair-wise ranking is mainly used in the context of community development work. The ranking is normally done in an organised session, usually for one of three purposes: generating general information to outsiders (such as a researcher, government administrators or a development organisation), initial planning of a development programme in the community, or choosing between already identified options in a programme. It is the equivalent of pair-wise problem analysis (addressed in Chapter 5) and may be used in combination with that.

Pair-wise ranking is illustrated here by choices among possible training programmes in a range of fields (Table 9.3). Such an exercise would usually be done as part of the planning process of a community development programme. Depending on the focus, scope and other aspects of the programme, the participants of the exercise may be representatives of the whole community or a section of it, for instance, the members of a community-based organisation. The categories that are subjected to ranking (the potential training programmes) may have been arrived at through some preceding exercise, such as a household survey, or decided at the joint session itself, for instance, through an initial round of brainstorming among the participants.

Table 9.3 Pair-Wise Ranking of Alternative Training Programmes

Training programmes	1	2	3	4	5	6	7	8	9	10	11	Score	Rank
1. Literacy		2	3	1	1	6	7	1	9	1	1	5	*6*
2. Accounting			3	2	2	6	7	2	9	2	2	6	*5*
3. Primary health care				3	3	3	3	3	3	3	3	10	*1*
4. Cooking and nutrition					5	6	7	8	9	10	11	0	*11*
5. Blacksmithry						6	7	5	9	5	5	4	*7*
6. Flower binding							7	6	9	6	6	7	*4*
7. Crop cultivation								7	9	7	7	8	*3*
8. Chicken rearing									9	10	8	2	*9*
9. Weaving										9	9	9	*2*
10. Hand-tractor repair											10	3	*8*
11. Traditional music												1	*10*

The categories to be ranked are listed both vertically and horizontally in the table, and each category is compared with every other category. The number in each table cell signifies the prioritised category between the two that are juxtaposed. For instance, when comparing the importance of literacy training and training in primary health care (1 and 3), the latter is prioritised. Since the categories are compared with each other only once, only half of the diagram space will be utilised. The pattern of priorities is arrived at simply by counting the number of entries in the respective cells. In this case, the participants consider training in primary health care to have the highest priority among the listed options, while they give training in cooking and nutrition the lowest priority.

Multi-Dimensional Ranking

Multi-dimensional ranking means ranked prioritisation between directly comparable entities across a number of dimensions. A few examples of relevance in a development context might be fish species, designs of fishing boats, types of traditional medicines, or the genetic properties of two or more varieties of a crop. The ranking may be done by some or all stakeholders, together or in subgroups. Examples of stakeholders might be local community inhabitants, farmers of a cooperative society, or elected representatives in an organisation.

The technique is exemplified here through the ranking of tree species by their perceived usefulness for a range of purposes (Table 9.4).[4] The scores in each cell may be calculated in different ways. In this case, each

Table 9.4 Multi-Dimensional Ranking of Tree Species by Their Perceived Usefulness

	Tree Species												
Uses	a	b	c	d	e	f	g	h	I	j	k	l	m
Firewood	10	2	1		1	2		7	4		3	2	2
Poles for housing	5				7	7		9	2		5		
Fencing fields	6				6	3			2				
Fencing wells		5										9	
Fencing cattle	2				8			9					
Fibre making	5									10			
Grinding seeds			9										
Squeezing beer							5						
Eating	5		8	6									3
Medicines			4		8	1							7
Animal fodder	4	2					1						6
Shade	4		8	8		2				5		6	

10 <—> 1: Degree of usefulness (highest <—> lowest)

entry expresses the average value of the values given by the participants separately, for the respective species/uses. For example, the table shows that species *a* is considered to have outstanding firewood value among a large number of species that are perceived to be useable for that purpose, while species *c* is viewed as the only useful one for grinding seeds.

Note that the ranking scale is freely relative: any value from 1 to 10 may be allocated to any species for any specified purpose. Blank cells denote no perceived use value of the respective species for the particular purpose. An alternative approach might have been to rank the species for each usage category on a fixed directly comparable scale (which might have been 1–10 as well). That is, the best species for any purpose would have got the top score and the others would be compared with that.

Stratified ranking

All the methods of direct choice and ranking that we have addressed in previous pages may be used by different groups among the participants of a prioritisation exercise. Such stratified ranking may, and commonly should, be done whenever one is concerned with the needs or interests of specific sections of a population, and one simultaneously believes or suspects that those needs or interests vary in some systematic way within the population. Any differences in priorities may then be taken into account in subsequent planning and decision taking.

The participants may be stratified, or may stratify themselves, for this purpose by any relevant criteria in the particular context. A few examples of criteria may be gender, occupation or main source of livelihood, size of land holding, place of residence, or formal position in an organisation.

Stratified ranking is here illustrated by the case (presented earlier) of ranking of training programmes, now done separately by women and men (Table 9.5). In other words, the participants are stratified by gender, after which the results for the two groups (women and men) are compared. In the table, the direction of ranking is from top to bottom. The highest prioritised programmes are shown in bold type, for the sake of easier comparison. In this case, there are relatively small differences between women and men's priority of two among the three programmes ranked highest overall (primary health care and crop cultivation), while there are relatively large differences regarding other programmes that either gender has given high priority.

Moreover, by comparing the distributions for each gender with the overall distribution, we see that there is greater similarity between the priority list of the women and the aggregated list than between the list of

Table 9.5 Ranking of Alternative Training Programmes by Gender

TRAINING PROGRAMMES		
Women's priorities	Men's priorities	Overall priorities
Primary health care	Accounting	**Primary health care**
Weaving	**Crop cultivation**	**Weaving**
Flower binding	**Primary health care**	**Crop cultivation**
Crop cultivation	Blacksmithry	Flower binding
Literacy	Hand-tractor repair	Accounting
Accounting	Literacy	Literacy
Chicken rearing	**Weaving**	Blacksmithry
Blacksmithry	Flower binding	Hand-tractor repair
Hand-tractor repair	Traditional music	Chicken rearing
Cooking and nutrition		Traditional music
		Cooking and nutrition

the men and the latter list. A likely explanation is that more women than men participated in the ranking exercise. In such instances, if one wants to ensure equal importance to the views of the two groups, one would have to weigh the frequencies by the number of participants in each of the groups. Generally, then, when comparing priorities of different groups, one needs to be sensitive both to the criteria by which the groups are composed and to the proportion of participants in each group.

Criteria-Based Prioritisation

Development planners often have to take into account criteria of choice specified by some legitimate body (authority). Normally, such criteria have been formulated in advance of or at the start of the planning process. They may be absolute – that is, they must be adhered to – or they may express various degrees of preference. Approaches to criteria-based prioritisation will be illustrated by an example – a modified version of a real-world case – that needs to be elaborated through some text to be understandable.

The government of a country gives high priority to supplying good water to the population of one of its most water-deprived provinces, which we shall call Dry Province. The people of the province live in highly scattered villages over an area of 200,000 square kilometres.

The approximate distribution of the population by villages is:

Village size category	No. of villages	No. of inhabitants
< 100 persons	500	40,000
100–200 persons	500	80,000
200–500 persons	600	200,000
> 500 persons	100	80,000

The spatial distribution of villages is such that one water supply facility may normally serve only one village.

Most of the smallest villages are located in peripheral areas where access to water is particularly difficult. A shortage of surface water and a low groundwater table mean that only tube wells can solve the water problem for the people in these villages. Most of the villages with more than 200–300 inhabitants are situated in river plains with a high groundwater table and have enough water from their traditional hand-dug shallow wells. However, over time most of these sources have become polluted, some severely so.

The estimated costs of the alternative types of water supply facilities are (in US$):

	Investment	Annual maintenance
Tube well (with pump)	30,000	300
Dug well (with pump)	15,000	200
Upgraded traditional source	3,000	25

The government has had insufficient money to maintain such facilities elsewhere in the country. It has therefore been decided that the villagers themselves will have to bear all the maintenance costs.

The willingness of people to pay for water has not been substantiated. However, most people have been used to considering water a cost-free good. A rule of thumb used by the water supply authorities is that people may be willing to spend at most 1 per cent of their cash income for this purpose. The annual median *per capita* cash income is roughly estimated as US$120. No information is available about the distribution of that income within the province.

Now, money has been allocated for a household water supply programme in Dry Province. The investments can meet only a small proportion of the need. The programme will be planned and implemented by the national and provincial water supply authorities, using the cost estimates and other information presented above. The main priority criteria of the programme are:

- highest weight to the areas with the greatest need;
- high cost-effectiveness (adequate facilities for as many people as possible for the money allocated);
- financial ability of the villagers to maintain the facilities.

Based on these criteria and the additional information given above, how should the investments be prioritised, in terms of categories of villages and types of facilities? This poses a bigger challenge than our previous prioritisation examples. Unlike most of those examples, a case such as this may hardly be addressed through a collective participatory exercise. Moreover, the prioritisation is of facilities within a whole province, requiring action at the provincial level, at least.

Again, we shall analyse the priorities with the help of a table. In Table 9.6, the three main decision-making variables – the three prioritisation criteria, the type of well and the known categories of villages – are specified on the two axes. Note that we have information about only two main types of villages: small villages with the poorest access to water, and relatively large villages with a polluted water source.

Table 9.6 Criteria-Based Prioritisation of Water Supply Facilities

Criteria	Need of villages			Cost-effectiveness			Maintenance ability		
Villages / Type of well	Type One	Type Two	Others	Type One	Type Two	Others	Type One	Type Two	Others
Tube well	1	:	0	3	:	[2] ↑	N	:	[Y]
Hand-dug well	–	:	0		:	2	–	:	[Y]
Upgraded well	–	2	0	–	1	2	–	Y	Y

Type One: The small villages with the poorest access
Type Two: The big villages with polluted traditional source
1, 2, 3 General level of priority (highest–lowest)
Y Yes
N No
→ Decreasing priority within category
[ ] Possibly
– Not applicable
: *A priori* not prioritised
0 No information available

Based on the information that we do have, we end up with a mixture of clear-cut entries and entries that rely more on judgement. Still, if we are to abide fully by the criteria that have been specified, we arrive at a clear conclusion. While the need seems to be greatest in the group of small villages, a combination of the most expensive type of wells and the fewest people to be served by a facility means that the supply of water to those villages would be the least cost-effective. And, decisive in itself, we would not expect the small villages to be able to finance the maintenance of the wells. In fact, based on the information we have about cost, income and willingness to pay for water, only upgraded traditional sources may be maintained through payment by the villagers. Since there are relatively big villages with polluted traditional facilities that may be upgraded, all the money will be spent there.

A major weakness is the scanty information we have about the local communities. Information is only available about certain types of villages; even the information we have is general and vague; and our judgement of the ability to maintain the facilities is based on rudimentary income data and probably speculative assumptions about people's willingness to spend money on water. Unfortunately, a weak and less than reliable informational basis for prioritisation is a common deficiency in much development work. In this case, the only way to reduce this deficiency substantially would be the generation of additional information by the programme itself at the community level.

Economic Tools of Prioritisation

Benefit–cost analysis

Benefit–cost analysis, as conventionally understood and normally used by economists, is a quantitative methodology for estimating the financial or economic soundness of investments and/or current economic operations. Both the benefits and the costs need to be expressed by comparable monetary values. In the development field, such analysis may occasionally be undertaken of effects (hardly ever impacts) of projects or parts of projects (hardly ever programmes). Sometimes, alternative investments or economic operations are compared.

Let us start with an example of how the method, in its most simple form, may be used for comparison in the development sphere. We shall here compare the profitability of cultivating alternative crops. The profitability may be viewed as the immediate financial benefit (effect) of cultivating the respective crops. For instance, such an exercise may be undertaken for providing information to agricultural extension personnel, to help them guide the farmers in their crop selection, in a relatively homogeneous environment (such as a new settlement area).

The calculations are presented in Table 9.7. The table shows income and costs for a specific period (say, a season) for a specific unit of land (say, an acre).

Table 9.7 Income per Household from and Benefit–Cost Ratio of Alternative Crops

	Crop 1	Crop 2	Crop 3
		Gross income[1]	
Market value[2]	*1000*	*1400*	*850*
		Costs[1]	
Hired labour	200	200	250
Machinery[3]	250	600	100
Fertiliser	150	150	100
Pesticides	100	200	100
Other	50	50	0
Total costs	*750*	*1200*	*550*
		Net income	
	250	200	300
		Benefit–cost ratio	
	1.34	1.17	1.55

[1] in a given currency, per season and per specified land unit

[2] based on estimated yield and market price

[3] based on estimated working hours, by type of machinery

This is a case in which benefits and costs can be quantified relatively easily. Still, upon closer examination, we find that even this simple case reveals limitations of quantitative benefit–cost analysis in the context of development work. The method requires simplifications that may be more or less acceptable or unacceptable and assumptions that may be more or less realistic or unrealistic.

Thus, the benefits are considered to be equal to the income derived from the cultivation, measured in market prices. In the present example, that may be acceptable. However, besides any uncertainty attached to estimates of future market prices, there may be other aspects of benefit that reduce the appropriateness of this measure. For instance, the households may assign an additional food security value to one or more of the crops, or one of them may have a valued soil-enriching property. Conversely, any soil-depleting effect of cultivating a crop may be considered as a disadvantage (which may be viewed as a cost in a wider sense than an immediate financial one). Moreover, work that goes into the cultivation by household members is not considered. This might have been done, but estimates of the economic value of own labour might be indicative only, as they would need to be based on an assessed opportunity cost of labour that might be highly uncertain.

Of course, the reliability of the calculations also depends on an assessment of technical and economic factors relating to the cultivation. Examples might be: the quality of the land, the amount and distribution of rain, the availability of irrigation and aspects of marketing. More or less comprehensive feasibility studies may be needed to provide reliable information on such variables.

An even more problematic issue may be that the calculations assume specific attitudes and a specific pattern of behaviour on the part of the farmers, which may not conform to the reality. This may relate to aspects such as the priority given to sale versus home consumption and the use of various kinds of inputs. Such assumptions about attitudes and behaviour represent a major hindrance to the use of benefit–cost analysis in much development work, since such work addresses different kinds of intended beneficiaries, who normally take their own decisions under the influence of their own priorities and aspects of complex and diverse environments.

In the example presented, only costs involved in the actual cultivation process are included, normally referred to as operating costs. The costs of any initial investment are not considered. Commonly, in development schemes, such investments are involved, posing additional challenges for benefit–cost analysis. Moreover, development projects aim at generating long-lasting benefits. For this to happen, facilities normally have to be maintained and most physical facilities will at some stage have to be replaced, involving additional expenses. There may also be other current or recurrent expenses such as taxes and insurance payments.

Additionally, in our example, the analysis of economic performance is limited to one season only. Frequently, one year may not be representative for the performance over a longer period of time, since both costs and income may change or fluctuate. For instance, planting of fruit trees will involve an initial investment cost, while the trees will only start to generate income after some years.

A further important point is that we need to convert the values of future costs and monetary benefits into a common base of present values. Future costs and earnings are worth less at the present time than present costs and earnings (a point which will be readily understood by considering interest received on a deposit in a bank). This process is referred to as discounting and the rate at which the value is reduced is called the discount rate. The basic principles are illustrated in Table 9.8.[5]

Table 9.8 Earnings and Costs of an Income-Generating Project

(1) Year	(2) Gross income	(3) Costs	(4) Net income (2) – (3)	(5) Discount factors[x]	(6) Present value of net income (4) x (5)
1	0	22145	–22145	0.893	–19775
2	8500	4915	3585	0.797	2857
3	10500	4915	5585	0.712	3977
⋮	⋮	⋮	⋮	⋮	⋮
9	10500	4915	5585	0.361	2016
10	10500	4915	5585	0.322	1798
Total of positive values					24979
Total of negative values					–19775

[x] at 12 per cent discount rate

The estimated lifetime (the conventional economic term) of this project is ten years. This commonly means that production is expected to be possible over this period without any new investments, or that this is the period for which plans can be prepared without much uncertainty (even though the facilities provided or parts of them may last longer). In this case, then, the expenses for the first year are for investments (for instance, in buildings, machinery and/or other equipment), while the expenses for the subsequent years are recurrent costs. We see that identical estimated net annual incomes over years 3–10 (at fixed prices) are calculated to have decreasing present value, based on a discount rate of 12 per cent.

The numbers in such a table may be used to calculate alternative measures of profitability. The three common ones are: the net present value (NPV), the benefit–cost ratio (B/C) and the internal rate of return (IRR). The NPV is the difference between the total present positive and negative net values. For this project, it is 24979–19775 = 5204. A related concept is the break-even point, being the point of time at which the accumulated earnings equal the accumulated costs. In this case, the break-even point is estimated to be reached in the eighth year.The B/C is obtained by dividing the total present value of benefits (in this case, gross income) by the total present value of costs. In our example, these values are 48367 and 43161 respectively (not shown in the figure). Of course, the difference between these values equals the difference between the shown total net positive and net negative values (except for a minor rounding-off difference). In this case, then, the B/C is 1.12 over the ten-year period. The IRR is an expression of the financial return on an investment, similar to the return one may get as interest on a bank deposit, for example. It is calculated from the net income figures and may be compared with returns on alternative usages of the invested capital.[6]

After this brief presentation of the method, let us now return to the theme of this chapter by considering Table 9.9, which makes a comparison between the profitability of cultivating three alternative crops, for which initial investment costs and other costs differ. We may well consider these crops to be the same as those in Table 9.7, over a cultivation period of four–five years.

Table 9.9 Comparing the Profitability of Three Crops

	Present value of: Initial investment	Other costs	Gross income	NPV	B/C
Crop 1	900	3300	4100	–100	0.98
Crop 2	1000	4800	6000	200	1.04
Crop 3	400	2400	3500	700	1.25

NPV = Net present value
B/C = Benefit–cost ratio

For the given period of cultivation, the profitability differs much. For Crop 1, the NPV is negative and the B/C is below 1. Thus, the investor would earn less from this pursuit than from some alternative use of the money – assuming, of course, that the discount rate (not stated here) is realistic. Crop 3 is by far the most profitable one.

Assumptions and uncertainties of the kinds that we mentioned in relation to Table 9.7 apply here as well. Still, if good information about aspects of feasibility has been acquired, financial benefit–cost analysis may be useful or even necessary for projects that aim directly at generating income. Commonly, the reliability of the analysis may increase substantially if one can draw on some relevant prior experience, not least because such experience will have incorporated in it aspects of behaviour which may otherwise be very difficult to assess.

By and large, however, the applicability for development planning of benefit–cost analysis, in its rigorous quantitative sense, stops here. Even for income-generating projects, where financial profitability may be the core issue, financial return usually needs to be viewed in a broader context. This may include assessment of and choices between intended beneficiary groups, any expected wider economic or social multiplier effects, and a range of other social, institutional, cultural and/or ecological variables.

In some instances, one may try to quantify wider economic benefits (beyond financial ones). One example might be envisaged economic multiplier effects in a local community of a planned increase in income from some agricultural project. Generally, however, more qualitative methods are needed to analyse broader economic changes and, even more obviously, changes of a social, cultural, institutional or ecological nature. Intended benefits of development work such as increased consciousness and understanding, greater gender equality, increased organisational ability or improved quality of a natural habitat cannot sensibly be assigned a token monetary value.

Cost-effectiveness analysis

The concept of 'cost-effectiveness' denotes the efficiency of resource use; that is, it expresses the relationship between the outcome of a thrust – in this case some development work – and the total effort by which the outcome has been generated. In the development field, the outcome may be specified as outputs, effects or impacts, and the total effort may be expressed as the sum of the costs of creating those outputs or benefits. Thus far, cost-effectiveness analysis resembles benefit–cost analysis.

However, the specific question addressed in cost-effectiveness analysis is how (by what approach) one may obtain a given output or benefit (or, a set of outputs or benefits). In other words, we assume that what one creates, through such alternative approaches, are identical facilities or qualities.

Widely understood, considerations of cost-effectiveness are crucial in development work (as in other resource-expending efforts). In any rationally conceived development thrust, one wants to achieve as much as possible with the least possible use of resources, of whatever kind. By implication, we should always carefully examine and compare the efficiency of alternative approaches, to the extent that such alternatives may exist or be created. The approaches encompass the magnitude and composition of various kinds of inputs as well as a range of activity variables – that is, by what arrangements and processes the inputs are converted into outputs and may generate benefits.

As normally defined by economists and commonly understood, cost-effectiveness analysis is a more specific and narrow pursuit, restricted to the technology by which an output (or set of outputs) of a highly specified, unambiguous and standardised nature is produced. An example, mentioned by Cracknell (2000), is an analysis that was undertaken of alternative technologies of bagging fertilisers at a donor-assisted fertiliser plant, basically to quantify cost differences between labour-intensive and more capital-intensive methods.

In cost-effectiveness analysis, there is no need to specify a monetary value of outputs or benefits. This is often assumed to make cost-effectiveness analysis more widely applicable and more useful in much development work than benefit–cost analysis. This is a highly questionable proposition. Used conventionally (as just mentioned), cost-effectiveness analysis has very limited applicability in development work, for two main reasons.

First, although the monetary value of the outputs or benefits do not have to be estimated, what is achieved will normally have to be specified by some other quantitative measure (examples of which might be number of items, weight or physical extent). This is needed for any assumption of identical outcomes to be made; that is, quantification is the only way in which standards of this nature may be established and objectively verified. This limits such analysis to, at most, only small parts of the benefits that development programmes and projects normally aim at creating.

Second, irrespective of whether such quantitative measures may be used or not, the benefits generated through different approaches may only rarely be identical or even close to that. This may be a serious constraint even for clear-cut technical projects. Take, for example, alternative technologies for constructing a road. Would we expect the quality of the road to be identical when (1) it is constructed by a large number of labourers using hand tools and (2) it is built with the use of bulldozers, scrapers and compacting machines? If not, conventional cost-effectiveness analysis would only make sense to the extent that differences in quality could also be quantified, that is, to the extent that the costs incurred with each technology could be related to comparable monetary values of the benefits. One would then be back to benefit–cost analysis.

For more normative and broader development programmes and projects, assumptions of identical benefits would be yet much more problematic than in the case mentioned – irrespective of whether or not we would be able to identify clearly distinguishable alternative approaches.

We may, then, draw three main conclusions from our analysis in this section. First, effectiveness and efficiency of development work will virtually always have to be assessed much more broadly than is possible through conventional economic analysis of costs and benefits. Second, financial benefit–cost analysis may be important for specific interventions, and may in such instances be appropriate if its strict limitations and underlying assumptions are well clarified and recognised. Third, financial cost-effectiveness analysis tends to be a particularly poor tool for assessing efficiency, except in very specific and rare contexts.

Notes

1 See Chapter 4 for an overview of the main mechanisms of coordination.
2 For further discussion, see Dale, 2000a; 2002a.
3 Bricolage is broadly defined as a highly creative process, in which participants 'play with heterogeneous concepts, strategies and actions with which various individuals in the group have experience, and try combining them until they create a new scenario that they collectively believe will work' (Innes and Booher, 1999: 12).
4 The idea is borrowed from a case of Participatory Rural Appraisal (PRA) in Botswana, presented in Mukherjee, 1993. The tree species, identified by their local names in the book, are here named by aliases (single letters).
5 The numbers in the table are borrowed from Wickramanayake (1994: 56).
6 The technique of calculation will not be shown here. See Wickramanayake, 1994 for a simple and clear step-by-step presentation and Nas, 1996 for a more elaborate analysis. The former considers Actual Rate of Return (ARR) to be a more informative alternative term.

Chapter 10

Community Institution Building and Participatory Planning

Participatory Development: Justification, Principles and Implications

Participation in development work is normally taken to mean involvement by ordinary people – non-professionals – in a particular field or fields. Frequently, these people are intended beneficiaries of the work that is done. One then often talks of 'people's participation'. But 'participation' may also denote involvement by a range of other stakeholders with various interests and abilities.

Much recent development discourse emphasises active involvement by groups of people. Two main reasons for this may be (1) greater stress among development agencies on 'good governance', in a broad sense; and (2) widespread disappointment with the long-term impacts of much development work, which has often been partly attributed to a delivery (top-down) attitude in such work.

We have addressed aspects of participatory development work in all the preceding chapters, to various extents and in various ways. For instance, in Chapter 1 we indicated differences of rationality between planning professionals and non-professionals and reflected generally on the implications of such differences for development planning; in Chapter 2 we connected the concept of stakeholder to participation, and reflected on the role and mode of strategy analysis in participatory programmes with process planning; in chapters 5 and 9 we explored participatory techniques of problem analysis and prioritisation; and in chapters 6, 7 and 8 we analysed one participation-promoting programme in the context of the logical framework. In the present chapter, we shall explore further various aspects of participatory planning, mainly in the context of institution-building programmes.

Any planned participatory development process should be founded on some clearly perceived justification and related principles of behaviour and work. Most fundamentally, as stated by Keough (1998: 194), participatory development should be considered as 'at heart a philosophy', embedding the belief that 'it is the right way to conduct oneself with other human beings'. An essential feature of this philosophy is profound *respect* for other people. This is closely connected to *humility* regarding individual persons' perceptions of factors that contribute to shape their own lives, regarding development priorities that different people may have, and regarding knowledge and skills that participants may possess. Underlying these principles is also the practical consideration that people may be reluctant to share their ideas and knowledge and to contribute comprehensively and constructively if they do not sense such respect and humility from planners, facilitators, managers and other persons in key positions.

Development planners and managers should be sensitive to the significance and potential of *local knowledge* for development thrusts in the respective local environments. Standardised knowledge that tends to be carried by professional development workers may be superior in many respects and adequate in many local contexts. Still, the additional and more specific knowledge that local residents have about their own environment, and related ideas about development work, may often enhance the effects and sustainability of such work.

Sometimes, the perceptions and ideas of local residents may conflict with those of development agencies, and may be seen to pose obstacles to the methods and techniques of planning and implementing development work of trained professionals. In such instances, the development problems and any related development work should be thoroughly discussed among the persons and agencies involved, and choices of action should be arrived at in which the local people believe.

On a more theoretical note, this connects to conceptions of rationality addressed in Chapter 1. The participatory perspective embeds recognition of *lifeworld rationality* as an important complement to instrumental rationality. A main justification may be to combat tendencies of 'colonisation of the lifeworld' by the modernising state and the industrialising economy (Servaes, 1996), through which the influence of ordinary people may be reduced or even marginalised. Of course, the relative importance of the two notions of rationality depends much on the nature and the context of development programmes and projects, as already mentioned in relevant contexts.

One of the most difficult lessons to learn for development agencies that want to develop a commitment to participation is to *embrace and manage uncertainty*. Unquestionable and unambiguous answers are not common in development work. The reader will certainly remember that we have viewed strategic decision making as a process involving deliberations about uncertainties of many kinds, and that such uncertainties have been seen as constituting much of the rationale for process planning. In highly participatory processes, uncertainty is normally higher than in other development work, reflecting the variety of knowledge, perceptions and interests that the participants will usually have. Consequently, in participatory programmes, one needs to develop an ability to relate to and deal constructively with issues for which many interpretations and choices exist.

Modes and Means of Participation

Drawing on Oakley *et al.* (1991), fundamental **perspectives** on participation in development work may be captured by juxtaposing two notions, namely, participation as contribution and participation as empowering.

Participation as contribution

This is contribution to programmes and projects that are being or have been planned by others, on terms that those others have determined or at least framed. The contribution may be entirely voluntary, induced to various extents, or even enforced. It may be provided in the form of ideas, judgements, money, materials, or unpaid or lowly paid labour.

Participation as empowering

In a development context, empowerment means increased capacity for own decision making and involvement in other ways. To that end, capacity building might include influencing attitudes and perceptions, promoting people's own organisations, training in various skills or promoting a more appropriate legal or administrative environment. Much of this may be initiated and driven by those who are to be empowered. Most often, however, initiatives from, communication with and support from outsiders are important, even essential. Many options exist for such communication and support. Generally, external organisations and workers must emphasise information exchange, soft inducement and genuine response, rather than instruction and persuasion.

Another feature of empowering processes is that they tend to bring to the surface conflicts of perception and interest. Such conflicts need to be addressed conscientiously and systematically, but can hardly ever be resolved through any standard set of actions. Normally, therefore, empowering planning must proceed in a process mode.[1]

These contrasting perspectives link to a distinction between participation as a *means* and participation as an *end* in development. Or, more succinctly stated, participation may be seen as occurring at lower or higher levels of means–ends structures of development work. Generally speaking, participation as empowering is a high-level end.

Participation may occur in different **work categories** of development schemes: in problem analysis, plan formulation, implementation, monitoring, evaluation, operation and/or maintenance. Participation as *contribution* may be enlisted primarily in the implementation of programmes and projects or in the operation and maintenance of created facilities. But planners may also seek contributions by various people in the stage or stages of planning, in terms of their judgements, opinions and ideas for action. This is commonly referred to as consultation.

Usually, participation as *empowering* occurs primarily in strategic planning, since it is here that problems to be addressed are analysed and main courses of action are decided. In planning, empowerment may be achieved in one of two senses, or in a combination of the two. First, it may materialise through the influence that the participants may exert on the benefits for themselves of the planned development work. Second, it may materialise through the analytical skills that the participants may obtain from their involvement in the processes of analysis and decision making. Participation in monitoring and evaluation may also be empowering, especially when the information that is generated is fed back into planning – that is, when the information is utilised for re-examining and, possibly, modifying or supplementing work that has been done.[2]

Some kind of **organisation** may make participation more effective. For instance, planning committees may be established for problem analysis and proposal generation, implementation may be done by promoted enterprises, and maintenance may be undertaken by user groups created for that purpose. For organisation to become a means of empowerment, the created or strengthened organisations must be 'learning organisations' (Korten, 1980; Uphoff *et al.*, 1998). Normally, this means that they are self-critical (accepting, embracing and learning from errors), that they seek to match technology with organisational abilities, and that they start working on a small scale and expand their activities gradually, in line with increasing competence and capacity (Uphoff *et al.*, 1998).

There are several **additional dimensions** on which participation may be classified and analysed. Uphoff *et al.* (1979) presents a simple and widely known framework for analysing participation in rural development. It broadly distinguishes between three perspectives: participation *in what*, *who* participates and *how* the participants are involved.

The 'in what' perspective broadly complies with our presentation above of participation by work category (in planning, implementation, operation, monitoring or evaluation). 'Who' participates (or may do so) depends, of course, on the kind of development thrust and a range of other factors. In many community development programmes, for instance, a broad distinction may be made between residents, local leaders and government personnel. The 'how' perspective is the most challenging one and may invite specification of a range of subperspectives, depending on the type of organisation, programme or project and the emphasis and depth of the analysis. Uphoff *et al.* (1979) distinguish broadly between the basis of participation (in terms of impetus and incentives), forms of participation (basically the organisation of it) and extent of participation (the range of activities and the time used).

We have already emphasised that broad participation frequently makes development work more complex. In this perspective, the question of *direct versus indirect* participation is often crucial. Indirect participation is the principle of representative government. In relation to local-level development work, this is pursued by creating or improving formal systems of local governance through well-instituted local government bodies. Yet, as mentioned in Chapter 3, over large parts of the less developed world, local governments tend not to be perceived as genuinely representative of large sections of the population, and they tend to be riddled with other weaknesses as well. In fact, deficiencies in these respects have been a main reason for numerous efforts to involve people more directly in development work, mostly within NGO programmes and projects.[3]

Participation may be **constrained** by several factors. Some common ones are: the political environment, power structures in local communities, administrative obstacles, rigid professional attitudes among programme and project staff, conservative attitudes among people, little awareness among people of rights they may have or opportunities they may exploit, and little emphasis on qualitative achievements of participation (such as aspects of empowerment). Of course, constraints will be situation-specific, and need to be carefully analysed in particular contexts.

Participation may be promoted through many **methods**. In Chapter 5, we mentioned a range of tools under the broad concept of 'participatory assessment', and we gave examples of a couple of techniques of participatory problem analysis. In Chapter 9, we addressed several techniques of prioritisation, some of which are genuinely participatory.

Building Capacity, Organisations and Institutions: Some Definitions

In Chapter 6, we explored general means–ends relations in organisation-building programmes and visualised such relations in a figure (Figure 6.3). The main messages were that the outputs of such programmes are organisations with certain abilities, and that benefits for people will materialise through the work that these organisations do. Thus, we have two main organisational-cum-operational entities: (1) an organisation-promoting facility (a support programme) and (2) the built or strengthened organisations and their work.

We shall now clarify the concept of 'organisation building' and distinguish it from the related concepts of 'capacity building' and 'institution building'. The broadest concept is **capacity building**. This may relate to people directly (whether individuals or non-organised groups), to organisations and to institutional qualities of a non-organisational nature.

When this concept relates directly to *people*, we may distinguish between two main notions. First, capacity building may mean to augment people's resources and other abilities to improve their life situation through their own efforts. The resources and abilities to be augmented may be varied: from money, land and other production assets to health for working, vocational skills, understanding (of any issue relating to the person's living environment) or negotiating power.

In the development sphere, capacity building in this sense will normally apply to disadvantaged people, that is, people who do not have capacities that they need for ensuring reasonable welfare for themselves and their dependants. Thus we are talking of the empowerment of deprived people. In order to achieve empowerment, participation may be required, but certain resources or measures may have to be provided directly by others. Examples might be an allocation of land or the curing of a debilitating illness.

Second, development agents may seek to augment capacities of individuals not for their own benefit, or not primarily so, but for the benefit of others. One example might be the training of health personnel, for the purpose of improving the health of the people they are intended to serve. Another example might be the training of entrepreneurs, for the sake of increasing production and employment in an area, intended to benefit people who live there.

When the concept relates to *organisations*, capacity building may focus on a range of organisational dimensions and processes such as need and policy analysis; strategic and operational planning; aspects of technology; a management information system; individual skills of various kinds; and the organisation's form, culture and incentives.

In development fields, the capacity building of organisations is usually done by some other organisation. The promoting organisation may then augment capacity directly by measures such as formal staff training, supply of office equipment and improvement of work systems and routines. It may also provide financial and other kinds of support for development work that the new or strengthened organisations undertake. Under certain conditions, the latter type of support may also be capacity-promoting, more indirectly, by helping the planning or implementing organisations learn from work that they do.

We may, then, define **organisation building** for development simply as building the capacity of organisations for whatever development work they undertake or share.

An organisation may be said to be institutionalised – that is, to be an *institution* – when it is widely recognised by those for whom it is or may be of concern as a distinguishable unit with its own legitimate purpose and tasks (see, for example, Uphoff, 1986). Thus, organisations that are formed or strengthened to undertake development work should normally be institutions as well, or should be intended to become such.

Simultaneously, the concept of institution is considered to extend beyond that of organisation, and thus **institution building** is a broader concept than organisation building.

For instance, 'institution building for a more democratic society' may go beyond the formation or strengthening of organisations (if incorporating organisation building at all). It may encompass components such as formulating new national laws and regulations (for instance, regarding the permitted role of voluntary organisations); conducting training in democratic principles of governance; influencing attitudes of politicians; encouraging participation by a wider public in decision-making forums; and promoting freedom of the press.

Or, 'institution building for deprived people' in local communities may involve measures complementary to the building of any organisations of deprived people or organisations in which such people may participate. Two examples of wider measures might be: assisting local governments in formulating regulations to secure access by poor people to forests or other local natural resources; and promoting cooperation between people of different ethnicity or religions.

Institution Building as Process

All development work involves processes, in the sense that through their more or less complex actions sets of actors create outputs that may also be more or less complex. Additionally, outputs generate benefits through processes of change, in interplay with a range of external factors.

Institution building may involve processes in particularly diverse and profound senses. Most institution-building measures create outputs and benefits that tend to be uncertain and highly change-prone. As Mosse (1998) points out, effective institution building entails acceptance of unpredictable and idiosyncratic elements that are central to the success or failure of the respective programmes. These uncertainties result from fairly immediate and strong exposure to varied and, often, changing external forces that may interact with internal features and processes in less than predictable ways. In addition, abilities and qualities may be influenced by feedback from experience.

These dimensions of process are well illustrated in organisation-building programmes. The built organisations are constellations of individuals with a range of interests, abilities and attitudes, some of which may also change frequently and substantially; the organisations become exposed to a variety of forces in their immediate and wider environment that may substantially influence their structure, other features of organisation and modes of work; and the organisations are expected to undertake development work, from which they will be gaining experiences from the very beginning.

Institutional achievements of a non-organisational nature (such as laws, procedures and empowered groups) will normally be influenced by similar forces and subjected to similar feedback from practice.

These features of change and dynamism call for reassessment and even new ideas and actions by development agencies and workers, in the course of implementation of institution-building programmes. The relatively great *complexity* and the high level of *uncertainty* that are involved cannot be managed through conventional blueprint planning. Substantial *process planning* will be needed. Normally, this involves starting slowly and accelerating gradually (Uphoff *et al.*, 1998).

An essential part of the process will be identification and analysis of *external forces* that may influence the achievements of the programme, in the short and in the longer term, enabling the development organisation to relate to these forces as constructively as possible during its work. Usually, this requires relatively current assessment of the types of forces at work, their strength, the kind of influence they presently exert or may exert in the future, and how one may exploit opportunities they may represent or threats they may pose. We have earlier used terms such as 'strategic monitoring' and 'environmental scanning' to denote such frequent and flexible assessments. Moreover, the interests, perspectives and influence of various *stakeholders within the organisation* may be uncertainty-promoting factors in need of current assessment and negotiation.

This perspective of process has, of course, implications for information collection for planning and management. Mosse (1998) suggests that good *information management* for process planning and related modes of management (under the concept of 'process monitoring') should among other things be:

- continuous (providing current information for deciding on any expansion, contraction or adjustments);
- oriented to the present;
- directly linked to action (being therewith also directed to participants who have the authority to react, as warranted);
- inductive and open-ended (enabling exploration of any events, relationships, or outcomes – in contrast to conventional systems, which tend to be confined to examination of specified intended outputs or effects).

For the institution-building programmes that we emphasise here, we must add to this list the feature of being 'self-empowering'. By this is meant that the process of information collection and analysis promotes the understanding and skills of the participants, enabling them to influence aspects of their life situation more than they could before, directly or more indirectly. Commonly, as already stressed, the ability to influence and decide is further augmented by collective action, through organisations of the participants.

In conclusion, then, participatory development in this deep sense, involving empowerment through augmented organisational capacity and connected institutional qualities and abilities, may only materialise through basically iterative and generative processes of analysis, plan formulation, implementation and information feedback. That is, information generation, decision making and action are closely interrelated activities, rather than clearly separated 'stages' of development work. Normally, this also means that progress is achieved in small steps, through small but often cumulative entities of organised work, many of which may be referred to as small projects.

A main weakness in much recent development work has been a contradiction between, on the one hand, ambitions for institution building for participatory development and, on the other hand, continued emphasis on 'rational comprehensive' planning (see Chapter 3), constituting much of the scientific heritage of the planning profession. As shown in earlier chapters, this planning mode requires specialised analytical skills (making the exercises basically top-down), and it tends to lead to the formulation of comprehensive plans of a blueprint character.

Figure 10.1 summarises the main features of what we may refer to as an *organisation-building–participation–process planning nexus* in development work.

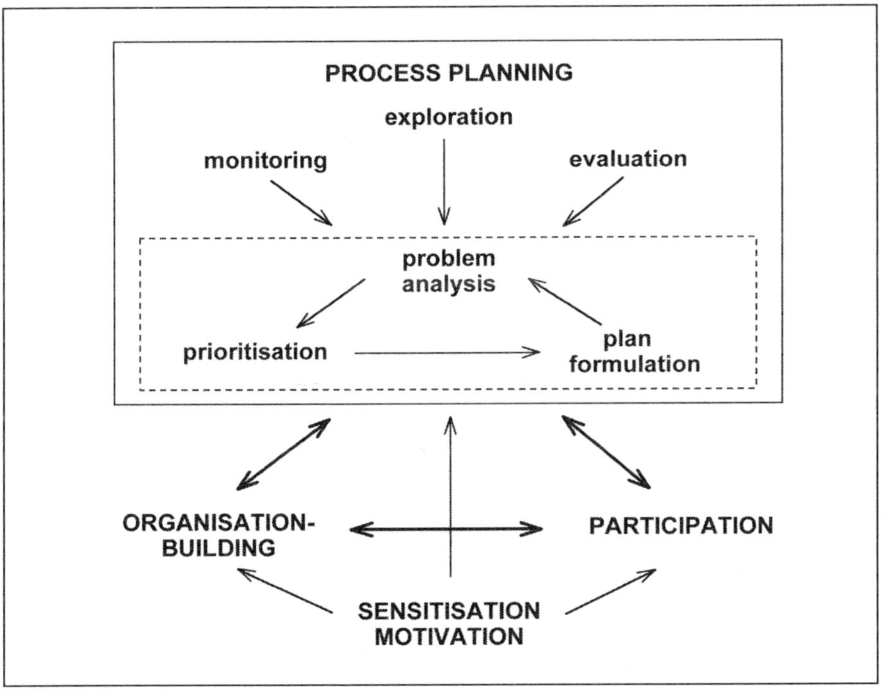

Figure 10.1 Institution Building for Participatory Development

Problem analysis, prioritisation and plan formulation are iterative processes, involving the use of information generated by the participants as an integral activity of these processes. The information is partly acquired through exploration of any issue that may emerge as relevant and important at any time, and partly through monitoring and evaluation of work that has been or is being undertaken. All the components of the basic nexus (organisation building, participation and process planning) are also shown to be supported by sensitisation and motivation, undertaken through what is often called 'social mobilisation' (see below).

For practical management reasons, formalised planning will normally have to be structured in cycles (for instance, in annual plan documents). This may still allow fairly continuous generation of information and learning.

Our emphasis above on process planning does not mean that each and every activity in a programme that is pursued in a process mode should be designed incrementally. While the general perspective is one of flexibility and corresponding process planning, certain programme components may, and often must, be planned in a blueprint mode. In other words, the typical desirable format of programmes of the kind we are addressing here is (1) an overall process planning perspective; and (2) a combination of process and blueprint perspectives, to varying degrees, for individual components.

Since this essential point is often not well understood, we shall explore the matter further later in this chapter, through exploration of two cases (one of which focuses exclusively on this issue).

Social Mobilisation

Before getting to these cases, we shall clarify the concept of social mobilisation briefly referred to above. This helps us understand features of Figure 10.1 better; the concept is central to the case that we shall discuss in the next section; and mobilisation tends to be important in empowering programmes more generally.

I shall define social mobilisation broadly as the engagement of a number of people in joint reflection and related action for achieving development goals through self-reliant effort (see also Cohen, 1996). Most often, the term is used for activities in local communities, although not necessarily confined to such communities.

The main purposes of social mobilisation and the general underlying ideology are well expressed by Stan Burkey in discussing the concept of conscientisation:

> Conscientisation ... means the stimulation of self-reflected critical awareness in people of their social reality and of their ability to transform that reality by their conscious collective action. A self-reflected critical awareness is achieved by 'looking into one's self' and using what one hears, sees and experiences to understand what is happening in one's own life ... [That is,] conscientisation is a process in which the people try to understand their present situation in terms of the prevailing social, economic and

> political relationships in which they find themselves … From this understanding arises an inner conviction that you yourself, together with like-minded others, can do something to change your lives – to transform reality ... [Thereby,] those who have been considered objects for development – poor men and women – become active subjects in their own development. (Burkey, 1993: 55)

Normally, social mobilisation does not occur spontaneously. It needs to be organised and undertaken in a reasonably systematic manner. Sometimes, local resource persons or community-based organisations try to sensitise and motivate people for various purposes in various ways. On a larger scale, social mobilisation is normally initiated and continued over a shorter or longer period by an external organisation. The organisation will then employ trained persons for working in the respective communities. Commonly used designations of these persons are social mobiliser, community mobiliser, facilitator, community worker, catalyst, change agent or animator.

In somewhat more specific terms, the common *aims* of social mobilisation tend to be, with varying emphasis:

- promoting *awareness* among community or group members about structures and processes that influence their life situation negatively, about opportunities for improvement that may be exploited, and, commonly, about the development programme to which the social mobilisation is affiliated;
- strengthening people's *ability to analyse* their problems and possible solutions, through facilitated discussions in groups about matters of concern to them;
- helping people who have little influence over processes that shape their lives to gain some decision-making *power* regarding such processes;
- promoting effective use of people's own and other unutilised or underutilised *resources*;
- in interaction with the above, seeking to augment people's *self-confidence* and inclination to take *initiatives*;
- to the above-mentioned ends, helping people to see the advantages of working together, and assisting them to *build their own organisations*, for mutual support and common action;
- establishing *links* between the promoted organisations and outside institutions, for various kinds of support or dealings;

- commonly, promoting links between the same kinds of organisations within the same local community or in different communities, often with the aim of creating *umbrella organisations* over the primary organisations.

Organisations that may thus be promoted through mobilisation may encompass the whole population of local communities or, more commonly, specific groups of intended beneficiaries.

In some cases, particularly when the programme includes generation and use of savings (being common), the social mobilisers may also be engaged in simple *enterprise development services*, either by providing such services directly or by helping the people's organisations and individual members to access them elsewhere. Some examples of services might be training in cultivation and other production techniques, creation of links with professional financial institutions, or assistance in testing the sale potential of new products.

Although normally the emphasis is on promoting people's own analysis and action, much social mobilisation incorporates elements of *advocacy:* that is, the mobilisers and the organisation that they represent want to promote some social values or development ideal. Work among disadvantaged people to help them improve their lot is usually grounded on an ideal of greater social equality, and the advocacy element may become particularly strong when this involves organisation and other measures against what is seen as oppression by others.

Development organisations and their social mobilisers need to be highly conscious about the mix of advocacy and people's own analysis in their mobilisation efforts. They should also clarify their attitudes and approaches in open discourse, both within their organisation and in their interaction with the people among whom they work.

Process versus Blueprint Planning for Local Institution Building

In Chapter 3 we examined the crucial planning dimension of process–blueprint and clarified it through one example, namely, a comprehensive programme with several projects. Some process–blueprint issues were analysed further in Chapter 6. Here we shall explore this planning dimension through yet another example, this time involving a case of community-based institution building. We can consider this as one additional scenario of operationalisation of the process–blueprint dimension.

The exploration will also be at a somewhat more detailed level than in Chapter 3, focusing on more specific work tasks.

Case: building community organisations with micro-financial services

The type of programme I have chosen belongs to a broad category of development thrusts that are frequently referred to as people-centred micro-finance programmes. From the outset, we need to recognise that financial services in these programmes are a core activity within a broader thrust. Dale (2001) refers to the set of interrelated activities of such programmes as a 'mobilisation–organisation–finance nexus'.

The deliberations relate to a real programme, in one district of Sri Lanka, called the Social Mobilisation Programme.[4] Close to 15 per cent of the households in the district are now represented in the member organisations that have been built. The structure and approach of the programme resemble those of many other programmes that aim at augmenting the capacities of deprived people. Our case should thus be viewed as one manifestation of a now common approach to community development with an empowerment agenda.

We have stressed earlier that in such programmes we need to distinguish clearly between the people's organisations and the support facility to those organisations.The **support facility** has involved planning and administrative personnel at the district and divisional level and social mobilisers at the field level. The latter have been the most important actors overall. It is they who have been directly in charge of building people's institutions, and they have been a much-needed stabilising element during periods of programme instability and uncertainty. We shall soon elaborate more on the specific activities of the support bodies.

The basic set of **people's organisations** is small Groups and above them Societies (named Self-Banking Societies). Most of the Groups have between four and seven members and the number of constituent Groups of a Society ranges from four to nine. Thus, the membership of the large majority of Societies is between 30 and 55. Recently, a third tier of organisation, named Union Banks, has been established. We shall disregard this tier here.

The membership of the people's organisations is mixed, but the large majority of members is women, mostly from among the poorest households in their communities.

Virtually all the *Groups* organise their meetings and pursue decision making and other deliberations in a genuinely collective manner. They are, therefore, appropriately referred to as 'collectives', in a typology of organisational forms (see also Dale, 2000a).

Most matters are discussed and agreed on and dealings transacted at the formalised meetings, normally held weekly. The Group meeting has a pre-specified agenda, including a simple opening ceremony, reading and approving the minutes of the previous meeting, and financial transactions (deposits, loan repayments and issues of new loans). In addition it has freer sessions in which the members may discuss any matters of importance and undertake other common activities of their choice. With a few exceptions, the collective activities do not encompass production supported by money from their organisations; income-generating activities are pursued overwhelmingly by the members individually. The Groups are also units for organising and undertaking a range of other common activities such as casual mutual help of basically any kind, formalised labour exchange, voluntary community works, and contributions to functions and ceremonies in the community.

The financial operations of the Groups are savings and the disbursement of short-term loans to and from the Group fund. Most of the fund is built up through two mechanisms: (1) regular compulsory contributions by the members; and (2) interest on the loans taken by the members and sometimes by others. Loans from the Group fund may be taken for any purpose.

At the *Society* level, the regular meetings are even more central events, in which virtually all decisions at that level are made and common dealings conducted. The Society meetings are held monthly. Most of the dealings are of a financial nature, primarily collection of savings, repayment of loans and issues of new loans. The Society fund is built up through an initial purchase of shares, compulsory monthly savings, additional voluntary savings, interest on loans, and occasionally other mechanisms. Loans are taken for investment or working capital in production, housing and, in some instances, even for consumption.

Modes of planning

In Chapter 6 and earlier in this chapter, we have emphasised a need for high flexibility in institution and organisation building programmes and a concomitant requirement in such programmes for an overall process mode of planning. Let us now look at planning modes for specific activities in greater detail.

Table 10.1 shows a combination of modes that is generally practised in our case programme, and which may be needed or at least advantageous in such programmes more generally. Reflecting the crucial distinction in

Table 10.1 Process versus Blueprint Planning in Community Institution Building Programmes

	PROCESS		BLUEPRINT	
	Strong	Moderate		Strong
The support facility				
Overall current exploration of priorities, fields of emphasis and feasibility	X			
Decision taking on programme communities				X
Employment of social mobilisers				X
Formulation of work programmes: long-term and annual	X		X	
Budgeting: long-term and annual	X		X	
Social mobilisation: general exploration		X		
Social mobilisation: sensitisation and motivation			X	
Social mobilisation: organisation building			X	X
Scheduling/organising regular review meetings				X
Conducting regular review meetings			X	
Deciding on *ad hoc* review meetings	X			
The people's organisations				
Scheduling of member meetings			X	X
Deciding on and following a meeting agenda				X
Deciding on loans to be granted				X
Financial transactions				X
Preparing/presenting financial accounts and other required records				X
Addressing other matters in the meetings	X	X	X	X
Other mutual/individual support for members	X	X	X	
Collective activities in the local community	X	X		

such programmes between (1) the support component and (2) the work of the promoted organisations, these activities are clearly separated in the table. Moreover, degrees of application of each mode are indicated by a simple framework of four categories: strong process, moderate process, moderate blueprint and strong blueprint.

The most outstanding general feature of the table is a mix of process and blueprint modes over the range of activities. This mix may even be said to constitute the most typical planning characteristic of institution-building programmes – and, indeed, programmes of a flexible, generative nature more generally. It is thus the feature that most clearly distinguishes such programmes from more conventional projects. In the latter, all the components are normally planned in blueprint mode.

In other words, good planning of programmes of an overall process nature is in reality some combination of process and blueprint planning of its various components. Even in highly flexible programmes, for effective work and efficient use of resources there is a need to take firm decisions about certain activities at certain points of time.

To elaborate further, we shall distinguish between activities of these two main components, starting with the *support facility*. The type, variety and strength of needs, opportunities, present constraints and future threats will differ between and within such programmes. These will also interact in complex ways with values, capacities and modes of work of the supporting organisation and individuals within this. Thus, the number of people's organisations that may and will be promoted, the speed of social mobilisation and organisation formation, certain features of the promoted organisations and numerous aspects of their operation are bound to be largely unique in each setting and may not be notably predetermined.

Consequently, a process approach will be needed for the general exploration of priorities, fields of emphasis and feasibility as well as for formulation of work programmes and budgets over any longer term. Normally, only highly general and indicative long-term plans are prepared. Yet relatively firm work programmes and budgets will be needed for a shorter period ahead (say, one year), in order to enable reasonably efficient use of resources, and possibly also to get a financial allocation. This is closely interrelated with decisions about the communities in which the support organisation will work during this period and the number of social mobilisers who will be employed.

In social mobilisation, we see a similar difference between planning perspectives. The general exploration that the mobiliser gets involved in when entering a community will be generative, while more firmly planned programmes will be needed for sensitisation and motivation, and even more for organisation building, including organisation-focused training. The justification for the latter lies in the aim of these activities of promoting a reasonably homogeneous foundation of perceptions, attitudes, organisational structures and modes of operation for large numbers of people and organisations under the programme.

As already emphasised, people involved in such programmes need frequent feedback of experiences from work that they do. Most of this is provided through direct communication in review meetings of some kind. These meetings need to be firmly instituted, normally at specific times and at specific places. The agenda and much of the proceedings may also have to be largely standardised, for the sake of good preparation, good coverage of topics and issues, and cumulative learning. In addition, there may be a need to organise more *ad hoc* meetings for discussing matters that may come up erratically or unexpectedly, and for taking timely decisions on those matters.[5]

A dominant feature of the *people's organisations* is the number of activities that are undertaken in a blueprint mode. In the present context, this also means that the activities are highly standardised; that is, they are executed (or, at least, intended to be executed) in the same manner in all the organisations. This observation runs contrary to a widespread perception of genuine people's organisations as bodies that work in a highly flexible mode, in response to largely unique needs, opportunities and constraints in their local settings.

In this case, standardisation is particularly strong for the financial operations. This is now widely considered as necessary to promote and maintain the needed financial discipline.[6] All or most of the financial dealings take place in meetings of the organisations, in order to ensure full transparency. Even finance-related activities that may be undertaken outside the meetings, such as preparing accounts and any other financial reports, need to be presented and endorsed in the meetings.

Other matters than financial services may also be addressed more or less regularly by individual Groups or Societies, and in a more or less standardised manner (see the right-side entries in the table for 'Addressing other matters in the meetings'). For example, the Groups may agree on regular reporting by members on any benefits they may be getting from the programme and any programme-related problems they may face.

Moreover, the crucial role of the formal meetings (in the present case, both Group and Society meetings) requires that they be scheduled at regular intervals. For orderly proceedings, there must also be a clear and agreed meeting agenda, which the participants must respect and adhere to in a disciplined manner.[7]

This standardisation of the basic common operations must be clearly distinguished from the variability and fluidity of the organisations' environment and a corresponding flexibility that the organisations have for addressing various problems confronting their members through various additional means. Such flexibility may even be allowed and also encouraged during the formal meetings – for instance, under a point on the agenda of raising and discussing any matters of concern, for one or more of the members (see the table's left-side entries for 'Addressing other matters in the meetings').

Even more importantly, the organisations may themselves engage in various kinds of practical work, for or involving all or some of their members. Such activities may range, for instance, from fairly regularised labour exchange among the membership to emergency assistance to a household in the case of an accident affecting a household member. The organisations' members may also participate jointly in local community works, and they may render various services to outsiders or to the local community at large. Most such activities tend to be irregular, and they will be decided on and planned as and when information or ideas about them come up.[8]

Creating Synergies between Planning and Institution Building

In this section, we shall supplement perspectives and views that have been presented so far by looking at efforts for building an institutional (including organisational) foundation for more general planning within contiguous local areas. Our more specific concern will be to explore inter-relations and synergies between (1) augmentation of capacities of the respective local organisations for planning and related work (including support from outside to this effect), and (2) the kind and quality of planning that the local organisations do.

We shall refer to the local areas as communes and the planning that is done as commune-level planning. A commune is usually understood as the geographical area of authority of a local government body. The latter is a formally authorised entity (an institution) for planning and managing development work, in addition to routine administration, within its area of authority. Thus, it is a public service organisation (not a mutual benefit organisation, addressed in the previous section). It is also supposed to be a democratic body, in the sense of representing and being directly accountable to the local population (see also Chapter 3). By this last-mentioned characteristic, it is distinguishable from any local administrative units of the central government.[9]

Systems of planning and decision making at local government level vary hugely, depending on the authority, capacity, resource base and other characteristics of these bodies. Being democratic institutions for promoting development, they should in any case apply a clearly normative perspective on what they do, and they should often consult and involve the population more directly in decision making than through the ballot.

Case: commune-level planning in Bhutan

Again, we shall use a case for illustrating issues, this time a programme for strengthening local governance in Bhutan. At present, we can only talk of embryonic local governments in that country. This case should thus illustrate quite well the basic requirements that may need to be fulfilled and the systems that may need to be developed for good commune-wide planning to be instituted.

For ages, local community institutions have existed for managing local resources and other common affairs in Bhutan. From the seventeenth century the *geog* has been recognised as the spatial unit of political representation and community-level decision making, and it is now officially endorsed as the unit of modernised local government. To play this role it needs to be strengthened through new legislation and other support. There are at present 196 geogs in the country, with an average population of about 2,500 in rural areas. Within a geog there are several villages (*chiwogs*).

The head of the geog is the *Gup*. Traditionally, the Gup was from a privileged family and the position was hereditary. From 1963, the Gup has been elected. The Gup and representatives from the villages and hamlets (smaller clusters of households) within the geog constitute the official local governance body in Bhutan, called the *Geog Yargay Thsogchung* (*GYT*). The GYT is supposed to have regular meetings, in which a few local staff of the central government (appointed by its regional district administration) also participate as observers.

So far, the GYT has had minimal financial resources at its disposal. Its main roles have been to propose projects in the geog for central government bodies, and to organise local works through the pooled labour of the inhabitants (either of the entire geog or of individual villages). Thus virtually all development work with financial implications has been undertaken by central government units, mostly bodies at the district level. The district (*dzongkhag*) constitutes the second and lowest tier of central government administration in Bhutan.

This, then, is the general setting within which institution building for local-level development work has been initiated, under the programme to be briefly addressed. The presentation that follows represents a combination of (1) actual changes, (2) plans for further changes and (3) recommendations by consultants working with the Bhutanese government.[10]

Institution building for commune-wide planning

Integrating facilitation and training with a realistic planning process

Initially in the programme, a national training institute undertook a comprehensive facilitation-cum-training effort for one geog as a pilot exercise, with the general purpose of initiating a participatory planning process. This consisted of a workshop at the dzongkhag level, for staff there who were intended to play support roles; a first round of training of the GYT, on the latter's intended development roles and related rules and regulations; a second stage of training of the GYT, on planning and management skills; and participatory workshops in the chiwogs, on problem analysis, prioritisation of development work and contributions by the local population. The last of these exercises has been referred to as 'participatory learning and action' (PLA).

This process led to a list of project proposals for each chiwog, some of which were channelled to district-level agencies for further prioritisation and feasibility studies. However, substantial problems were encountered, most notably:

- the staff of many district-level departments did not show the commitment that was expected of them for general coordination and facilitation of local-level planning, largely because they were already loaded with ordinary department work;
- the community-based workshops brought up project proposals that were too numerous and too costly without sufficient prioritisation;
- the process of training and initial facilitation of planning took up far too much time to be replicable over the whole country.

A more realistic mechanism of facilitation and training was required, which would take up less time and be better connected to the kind of development work that could be expected by the local authorities, at least during the first few years. The following modifications were then accepted:

- department staff of the dzongkhag would be involved primarily in accordance with their ordinary responsibilities;

- the PLA component would be scaled down to one four-day exercise per geog, with participation by the following: the elected members of the GYT (the Gup and the representatives from the chiwogs and hamlets), the observer members of the GYT (the school headmaster and other central government staff in the geog) and one or two additional representatives from each chiwog.

The first of these measures aimed at securing realistic long-term support for the local authorities from agencies of the central government. The second aimed at linking facilitation and training more unambiguously with the instituted (while still embryonic) local government body. At the same time, it aimed at promoting broader participation of citizens, including women, in that body (at least until a more democratic election system was in place). Through these measures, the time needed for initial facilitation and training would also be much reduced.

At this initial stage of geog-based development work, the trainers would also need to promote interaction between geog and dzongkhag authorities, on various matters in different phases of planning and implementation. This should become clearer when we now turn to the planning process.

The local planning process

The team of consultants mentioned above recommended the following general planning *process*.

After the participatory need-cum-problem analysis and project identification (briefly addressed above) comes a preliminary assessment of the feasibility and cost of the proposed projects. For simple projects, all or most of this may be done in the geog, by intended beneficiaries and/or local staff. Bigger and more complex projects may have to be assessed primarily or wholly by dzongkhag-level agencies.

This assessment will be followed by preliminary prioritisation of projects, either by the GYT in its present form or by an extended forum, including additional chiwog representatives (see above). For some projects, additional feasibility studies and cost estimation may be required, along with clarification and formalisation of implementation responsibility, before the final selection of projects can be made.

The list of selected projects, with basic information about each of them, is then to be forwarded to the dzongkhag for an administrative check. This check should be limited to the legality of the projects or parts of them: that is, whether what has been planned complies with the general policy and conforms to laws and regulations of local government in the country.

However, during the further examination and related communication between the bodies involved, one may find that some projects or parts of them are still unclear or have not been adequately planned: more work may then have to be done on them. In extreme cases, a project or certain of its components may be found, eventually, to be too costly or impossible to implement for other reasons, and may have to be substantially re-planned, postponed or even discarded.

After such clarifications have been made, a final annual plan document for geog-based development work (see below) will be compiled in the geog and approved by the GYT. In many cases, bodies that will be responsible for implementing components (projects) of the plan may also have to undertake some further (detailed) operational planning before implementation of the projects concerned may start. This may, for example, include contractual details if the project or some part of it is to be contracted out (for instance, from the GYT to a private contractor or to a central government line agency).

A range of variables needs to be considered in *project selection*. The main ones are, in the present context: the needs revealed through the participatory problem analysis and the project proposals that are generated from that; the financial resources available (initially, mainly a donor grant);[11] voluntary labour by the intended beneficiaries; the geographical spread of projects or project components; and, not least, the existence and capacity of organisations, besides the GYT, that may take on implementation responsibility.

Within the framework of prioritisation variables that may be applied, projects may be chosen using the techniques of prioritisation addressed in Chapter 9 (various forms of negotiation, pair-wise ranking, possibly other techniques of ranking, and voting). Conventional benefit–cost analysis would be unlikely, except, perhaps, occasionally for relatively big engineering or production-related projects, planned by central government line agencies or external consultants.

Finally, a few words are warranted about the direct outcome of planning – the *plan documents*. The annual planning process will result in two types of documents: project documents and an annual geog development plan. The latter relates to a third type that should be instituted over time: a longer-term indicative investment programme, to be reworked annually.

In the end, the projects need to be planned in sufficient detail for a final decision to be taken on them and for effective and efficient implementation. We shall not delve further into that here, but refer to Chapter 3 for a list of variables that may need to be addressed in operational planning. We shall only add that the large majority of projects that are expected to be generated through this mechanism will be small and simple, requiring only simple planning.

The annual plan should be simple, too. It may consist of no more than a compilation of main data on each project, one by one, in tabular form, with the project documents attached to this summary table. Some projects may extend over more than one year. For these, money for continuation will have to be allocated in the following year or years.

Analysing and using experiences

All planning bodies should make systematic use of experiences from previous and ongoing work, in order to improve planning and implementation of subsequent work of similar kind. In this case, the GYT and the other bodies involved should learn from work that they have already done, when planning the next annual programme (and, in future, the intended longer-term investment programme).

Part of the learning will occur through day-to-day monitoring of the implementation of projects. Additional systematic learning may be promoted through more comprehensive annual evaluations, primarily of the previous year's work. Such formative evaluations may be particularly important during the first years of the intended geog-based planning process.

The evaluations should be participatory exercises, involving the same set of actors as those involved in the need-cum-problem assessment and project generation (although some individuals may be different). Moreover, in order to connect planning, implementation and learning from experience, the trainers (see earlier) may be involved in facilitating these evaluations as well.[12]

Conclusion

In this section, we have provided some additional perspectives and insights regarding development planning, the institutional context within which it may take place, an organisational apparatus for undertaking it, and external measures for promoting an appropriate institutional foundation and the required organisational capacities. We have done so for a very important arena of development action: instituted local governments that are intended to be in charge of essential development functions within their spatial areas of authority. Our example took the case of a weak present local government structure that – this is the intention – will be able to play a more significant development role in the future. That is a typical present scenario in many parts of the less-developed world.

We have emphasised interrelations between (1) the types and quality of planning, (2) institutional qualities and organisational abilities for planning (and development work more broadly) and (3) mechanisms for building the capacity of organisations to take charge of the planning (and related work). An important mechanism for promoting sustainable capacity is well-tailored support by external bodies, including, in this case, agencies of the central government. The support encompasses provision of a conducive policy framework, facilitation of processes of planning, technical training and participation in (and even responsibility for) planning and implementing some kinds of projects. An equally important factor for augmenting the capacity of local governments is instituted systems of information feedback and learning from the organisations' own work.

Obtaining a good fit between these main elements is essential for building the capacity of local government bodies and for effective and efficient development work on their part. We emphasised similar factors and relations in our previous case as well, albeit largely through somewhat different specific mechanisms. We can safely say that this general set of factors and relations tends to be important, even essential, in building development organisations and related institutional qualities.

This case should also have provided additional understanding of the mechanisms of and requirements for process planning, the overall mode in programmes for institution building in development work. We have clarified time horizons in and the timing of planning events; implications of these aspects for the formulation and the format of plan documents; interrelations between problem analysis, plan formulation, monitoring and evaluation; and the need to combine an overall process approach with the formulation of firm plans (blueprints) for implementation.

Notes

1 For real-world examples, see the last sections of this chapter.

2 Evaluations that aim at providing information for further planning within the same organisation or development scheme or for planning a connected programme or project may be referred to as 'formative evaluations'. For further elaboration, see Dale, 1998. That book also contains a section on evaluation as a tool of empowerment.

3 As also mentioned in Chapter 3, even in countries with reasonably representative and effective local governments, indirect participation through these bodies may be combined with more direct forms of participation. The local governments themselves may even actively promote a range of interest groups and organisations, and such bodies commonly constitute an important part of a comprehensive and deep notion of local democracy.

4 The programme is documented in detail in Dale, 2002a.

5 In programmes of this nature, there may also be other support components than those we have mentioned. Two common ones are allocation of money to the Group/Society fund and training of members in vocational skills. Such activities have also been undertaken on a modest scale in the Social Mobilisation Programme.

6 This is a main message from the groundbreaking work of the Grameen Bank in Bangladesh. In its programme, the routines of financial management are specified in minute detail, and have been fully standardised across the hundreds of thousands of groups and societies that are now operational. For insightful analyses, see Fuglesang and Chandler, 1993, and Bornstein, 1996.

7 In extension of this argument about standardisation, reference may be made to an analysis by Jain (1994) of management practices of successful development organisations in several Asian countries more generally. The author concludes that routinisation and other forms of standardisation of most activities at the field level were a main reason for success.

8 In the presently analysed programme, Dale (2002a) identified several entirely voluntary common activities of the people's organisations. The main ones were:

- mutual help in cases of need of any kind in a member's household;
- labour exchange among the group members, particularly in various agricultural activities, house construction and digging of wells;
- voluntary community works *(shramadana)*, such as maintenance of village roads, renovation of the village temple, repair of the local school building, etcetera;
- common contributions, in the form of labour, food or gifts, for local ceremonies and other local functions;
- buying household commodities in bulk and selling them, to members and others, the profit from which being deposited in the Group fund.

9 For further clarification and discussion, I refer to literature on public administration and local government, such as Kammeier and Demaine, 2000; Aziz and Arnold, 1996; Chandler, 1996; and Shotton, 1999.

10 I was a member of this team of consultants.

11 Efforts should also be made to gradually mobilise money from other sources. In order to become a fully fledged local government body, the GYT will need to impose certain taxes and fees within its geographical area of authority. For this, new national legislation will be needed, as will staff qualified in local taxation.

12 See Dale, 1998 for elaboration of the concept of formative evaluation and an overview of modes and means of evaluation.

Bibliography

AIT NGDO Management Development Program (1998), *NGDO Management Development Training Manual*, Bangkok: Asian Institute of Technology (AIT).

Aziz, Abdul and **David D. Arnold** (eds.) (1996), *Decentralised Governance in Asian Countries*, New Delhi: Sage Publications.

Bernstein, Henry (1992), 'Poverty and the Poor', in Henry Bernstein, Ben Crow and Hazel Johnson (eds.), *Rural Livelihoods: Crises and Responses*, Oxford: Oxford University Press.

Birgegaard, Lars-Erik (1994), *Rural Finance: A Review of Issues and Experiences*, Uppsala: Swedish University of Agricultural Sciences.

Bornstein, David (1996), *The Price of a Dream: The Story of the Grameen Bank*, Chicago: The University of Chicago Press.

Brett, Teddy (2000), 'Understanding Organizations and Institutions', in Dorcas Robinson, Tom Hewitt and John Harriss (eds.), *Managing Development: Understanding Inter-Organizational Relationships*, London: Sage Publications.

Bryson, John M. and **Robert C. Einsweiler** (eds.) (1988), *Strategic Planning: Threats and Opportunities for Planners*, Chicago: Planners Press / American Planning Association.

Burkey, Stan (1993), *People First: A Guide to Self-Reliant, Participatory Rural Development*, London and New Jersey: Zed Books Ltd.

Carroll, A. B. (1989), *Business and Society: Ethics and Stakeholder Management*, Cincinnati, OH: Southwestern Publishing.

Chambers, Robert (1983), *Rural Development: Putting the Last First*, London: Longman.

—— (1993), *Challenging the Professions: Frontiers for Rural Development*, London: Intermediate Technology Publications.

—— (1995), 'Poverty and livelihoods: whose reality counts?', *Environment and Urbanization,* Vol. 7, No. 1, pp. 173–204.

Chandler, J. A. (1996), *Local government today*, Manchester and New York: Manchester University Press.

Cohen, Sylvie I. (1996), *Mobilizing Communities for Participation and Empowerment,* in Jan Servaes *et al*. (1996).

Cracknell, Basil Edward (2000), *Evaluating Development Aid: Issues, Problems and Solutions*, New Delhi: Sage Publications.

Creswell, John W. (1994), *Research Design: Qualitative and Quantitative Approaches*, Thousand Oaks: Sage Publications.

Crow, Michael and **Barry Bozeman** (1988), *Strategic Public Management*, in John M. Bryson and Robert C. Einsweiler (1988).

Cusworth, J.W. and **T.R. Franks** (eds.) (1993), *Managing Projects in Developing Countries*, Essex: Longman.

Dale, Reidar (1992), *Organization of Regional Development Work*, Ratmalana, Sri Lanka: Sarvodaya.

—— (1998), *Evaluation Frameworks for Development Programmes and Projects,* New Delhi: Sage Publications.

—— (2000a), *Organisations and Development: Strategies, Structures and Processes,* New Delhi: Sage Publications.

—— (2000b), 'Regional Development Programmes: From Prescriptive Planning to Flexible Facilitation?', *Public Management* Vol. 2, Issue 4, pp. 499–524.

—— (2001), 'People's Development with People's Money: The Mobilisation–Organisation–Finance Nexus', *Development in Practice*, Vol. 11, No 5, pp. 606–21.

—— (2002a), *People's Development through People's Institutions: The Social Mobilisation Programme in Hambantota, Sri Lanka*, Bangkok: Asian Institute of Technology and Kristiansand: Agder Research Foundation.

—— (2002b), *Modes of Action-centred Planning*, Bangkok: Asian Institute of Technology.

—— (2003), 'The Logical Framework: An Easy Escape, a Straightjacket, or a Useful Planning Tool?', *Development in Practice*, Vol. 13, No. 1, pp. 57–70.

Dale, Reidar and **Jan Hesselberg** (1979), 'Living Situation and Integration in a Rural Area in Southern Sri Lanka', *Norsk geogr. Tidsskr.*, Vol 33, pp. 7–21.

Dixon, Jane and **Sindall, Colin** (1994), 'Applying Logics of Change to the Evaluation of Community Development in Health Promotion', *Health Promotion International*, Vol. 9, No. 4, pp. 297–309.

Eggers, Hellmut W. (2000a), *Project Cycle Management 2000: An Integrated Approach to Improve Development Cooperation Projects, Programs and Policies*, Paper, Brussels.

—— (2000b), *Project Cycle Management (PCM), A Visit to the World of Practice*, Paper, Brussels.

—— (2002), 'Project Cycle Management: A Personal Reflection', *Evaluation,* Vol. 8 (4), pp. 496–504.

Faludi, Andreas (1973), *Planning Theory*, Oxford: Pergamon Press (Second edition 1984).

—— (1979), 'Towards a Combined Paradigm of Planning Theory?', in Chris Paris (1982), *Critical Readings in Planning Theory*, Oxford: Pergamon Press.

—— (1983), 'Critical Rationalism and Planning Methodology', *Urban Studies,* Vol. 20, pp. 241–56.

—— (1984), 'Foreword' to the second edition of Andreas Faludi: *Planning Theory.*

Friedmann, John (1992), *Empowerment: The Politics of Alternative Development*, Cambridge, Massachusetts: Blackwell.

Friend, J.K. and **W.N. Jessop** (1969), *Local Government and Strategic Choice: an Operational Research Approach to the Processes of Public Planning*, Oxford: Pergamon Press.

Friend, John and **Allen Hickling** (1997), *Planning Under Pressure: The Strategic Choice Approach*, Oxford: Butterworth-Heinemann.

Fuglesang, Andreas and **Dale Chandler** (1993), *Participation as Process – Process as Growth: what we can learn from Grameen Bank, Bangladesh*, Dhaka: Grameen Trust.

Giddens, Anthony (1984), *The Constitution of Society*, Cambridge: Polity Press.

Grimble, Robin and Man-Kwun Chan (1995), 'Stakeholder Analysis for Natural Resource Management in Developing Countries', *Natural Resources Forum,* Vol. 19, No. 2, pp. 113–24.

Habermas, Jurgen (1975), *Legitimation Crisis*, Boston: Beacon Press.

—— (1984), *The Theory of Communicative Action: Vol. 1: Reason and the Rationalisation of Society*, London: Polity Press.

Healey, Patsy (1997), *Collaborative Planning: Shaping Places in Fragmented Societies*, Vancouver: UBC Press.

Iddagoda, Kusum S. and **Reidar Dale** (1997), *Empowerment through Organization: The Social Mobilization Programme in Hambantota, Sri Lanka*, Pathumthani, Thailand: Asian Institute of Technology.

Innes, Judith E. and **David E. Booher** (1999), 'Consensus Building as Role Playing and Bricolage: Toward a Theory of Collaborative Planning', *Journal of the American Planning Association*, Vol. 65, Winter, pp. 9–26.

Jain, Pankaj S. (1994), 'Managing for Success: Lessons from Asian Development Programs', *World Development*, Vol. 22, No. 9, pp. 1363–77.

Kammeier, Hans Detlef and **Harvey Demaine** (eds.) (2000), *Decentralization, Local Governance and Rural Development – Proceedings of the International Workshop on Decentralized Planning and Financing of Rural Development in Asia*, Bangkok: Asian Institute of Technology.

Keough, Noel (1998), 'Participatory Development Principles and Practice: Reflections of a Western Development Worker', *Community Development Journal,* Vol. 33, No. 3, pp. 187–96.

Korten, David C. (1980), 'Community Organization and Rural Development: A Learning Process Approach', *Public Administration Review*, September/ October.

—— (1984), 'Rural Development Programming: The Learning Process Approach', in David C. Korten and Rudi Klauss (eds.) (1984).

Korten, David C. and **Rudi Klauss** (eds.) (1984), *People-Centered Development: Contributions toward Theory and Planning Frameworks*, West Hartford: Kumarian Press.

Kuik, Onno and **Harmen Verbruggen** (eds.) (1991), *In Search of Indicators of Sustainable Development*, Dordrecht: Kluwer Academic Publishers.

Lindblom, Charles E. and **David C. Cohen** (1979), *Usable Knowledge: Social Science and Social Problem Solving*, New Haven: Yale University Press.

Mackintosh, Maureen (1992), 'Questioning the State', in Marc Wuyts *et al.*, *Development Policy and Public Action* (1992).

Mikkelsen, Britha (1995), *Methods for Development Work and Research: A Guide for Practitioners,* New Delhi: Sage Publications.

Mintzberg, Henry (1983), *Structures in Fives: Designing Effective Organizations,* Englewood Cliffs: Prentice-Hall International (New edition 1993).

—— (1989), *Mintzberg on Management: Inside Our Strange World of Organizations*, The Free Press.

Moore Milroy, B. (1991), 'Into post-modern weightlessness', *Journal of Planning Education and Research*, Vol. 10, No. 3, pp. 181–7.

Moris, Jon and **James Copestake** (1993), *Qualitative Enquiry for Rural Development: A Review,* London: ODI.

Mosse, David (1998), 'Process-Oriented Approaches to Development Practice and Social Research', in David Mosse, John Farrington and Alan Rew (eds.), *Development as Process: Concepts and Methods for Working with Complexity*, London: ODI and Routledge.

Mukherjee, Neela (1993), *Participatory Rural Appraisal: Methodology and Applications*, New Delhi: Concept Publishing Company.

Narayan, Deepa with **Raj Patel, Kai Schafft, Anne Rademacher** and **Sarah Koch-Schulte** (2000), *Voices of the Poor: Can Anyone Hear Us?*, New York: Oxford University Press for the World Bank.

Nas, Tevfik F. (1996), *Cost–Benefit Analysis: Theory and Application*, Thousand Oaks: Sage Publications.

NORAD (the Norwegian Agency for Development Cooperation) (1990/1992/ 1996), *The Logical Framework Approach (LFA), Handbook for Objectives-oriented Planning*, Oslo.

Oakley, Peter *et al.* (1991), *Projects with People: The Practice of Participation in Rural Development*, Geneva: ILO.

Ostrom, Elinor (1990), *Governing the Commons: The Evolution of Institutions for Collective Action*, Cambridge, MA: Cambridge University Press.

Pratt, Brian and **Peter Loizos** (1992), *Choosing Research Methods: Data Collection for Development Workers*, Oxford: Oxfam.

Rubin, Frances (1995), *A Basic Guide to Evaluation for Development Workers*, Oxford: Oxfam.

Salamon, Lester M. and **Helmut K. Anheier** (1997), *Defining the Nonprofit Sector: A Cross-National Analysis,* Manchester: Manchester University Press.

Sapru, R. K. (1994), *Development Administration*, New Delhi: Sterling Publishers.

Scott, W. Richard (1987), *Organizations: Rational, Natural, and Open Systems,* Englewood Cliffs: Prentice-Hall International.

Servaes, Jan (1996), *Participatory Communication Research with New Social Movements: a Realistic Utopia,* in Jan Servaes *et al.*

Servaes, Jan, Thomas L. Jacobson and **Shirley A. White** (eds.) (1996), *Participatory Communication for Social Change*, New Delhi: Sage Publications.

Shotton, Roger (1999), 'Policy and Institutional Analysis and Programming Strategies for Local Development Funds', *Regional Development Dialogue,* Vol. 20, No. 2, Autumn 1999, pp. 160–72.

Taylor, Nigel (1998), *Urban Planning Theory since 1945*, London: Sage Publications.

Uphoff, Norman *et al.* (1979), *Feasibility and Application of Rural Development Participation: A State of the Art Paper,* Cornell University Ithaca: Rural Development Committee.

Uphoff, Norman (1986), *Local Institutional Development: An Analytical Sourcebook With Cases*, West Hartford, Connecticut: Kumarian Press.

—— (1996), 'Why NGOs Are Not a Third Sector: A Sectoral Analysis with Some Thoughts on Accountability, Sustainability, and Evaluation', in Michael Edwards and David Hulme (1996), *Beyond the Magic Bullet: NGO Performance and Accountability in the Post-Cold War World,* West Hartford, Connecticut: Kumarian Press.

Uphoff, Norman, Milton J. Esman and **Anirudh Krishna** (1998), *Reasons for Success: Learning from Instructive Experiences in Rural Development*, West Hartford, Connecticut: Kumarian Press.

Wickramanayake, Ebel (1994), *How to Check the Feasibility of Projects,* Bangkok: Asian Institute of Technology.

Wuyts, Marc, Maureen Mackintosh and **Tom Hewitt** (1992), *Development Policy and Public Action*, Oxford: Oxford University Press.

Index